WHITE MAN'S GAME

WHITE MAN'S GAME

SAVING ANIMALS, REBUILDING EDEN, AND
OTHER MYTHS OF CONSERVATION IN AFRICA

STEPHANIE HANES

METROPOLITAN BOOKS

HENRY HOLT AND COMPANY NEW YORK

Metropolitan Books
Henry Holt and Company
Publishers since 1866
175 Fifth Avenue
New York, New York 10010
www.henryholt.com

Metropolitan Books® and ® are registered trademarks of
Macmillan Publishing Group, LLC.

Library of Congress Cataloging-in-Publication Data
Names: Hanes, Stephanie.
Title: White man's game : saving animals, rebuilding Eden, and other myths of
conservation in Africa / Stephanie Hanes.
Description: New York : Metropolitan Books, Henry Holt and Company, [2017] |
Includes bibliographical references and index.
Identifiers: LCCN 2016034296| ISBN 9780805097160 (hardcover) |
ISBN 9780805097177 (electronic book)
Subjects: LCSH: Parque Nacional da Gorongosa (Mozambique) | Wildlife
conservation—Social aspects—Mozambique. | Wildlife conservation—Social
aspects—Africa, Southern. | Wildlife conservation—Mozambique. | Wildlife
conservation—Africa, Southern.
Classification: LCC QL84.6.M85 H36 2017 | DDC 333.95/41609679—dc23
LC record available at https://lccn.loc.gov/2016034296

ISBN: 978-0-8050-9716-0

Our books may be purchased in bulk for promotional, educational, or business use. Please
contact your local bookseller or the Macmillan Corporate and Premium Sales Department at
(800) 221-7945, extension 5442, or by e-mail at MacmillanSpecialMarkets@macmillan.com.

First Edition 2017

Maps by Jeffrey L. Ward
Designed by Kelly S. Too

Printed in the United States of America

1   3   5   7   9   10   8   6   4   2

For Christopher

CONTENTS

WHITE MAN'S GAME

SOUTHERN AFRICA

DEM. REP. OF CONGO

MALAWI

ANGOLA

Z A M B I A

Zambezi River

Zambezi River

NAMIBIA

● Victoria Falls
■ Hwange National Park

ZIMBABWE

Gorongosa National Park ■

Beira ●

MOZAMBIQUE

BOTSWANA

Limpopo River

Makalali Game Reserve ✕

Kruger National Park ✕

Madikwe Game Reserve ■

Moholoholo Wildlife Rehabilitation Centre

Pilanesberg Game Reserve

Johannesburg ●

★ Maputo

Matutuine

Vaal River

SWAZILAND

Orange River

Laohu Valley Reserve ■

LESOTHO

Indian Ocean

SOUTH AFRICA

Gansbaai ●
Cape Agulhas

AFRICA

Atlantic Ocean

Indian Ocean

Area of Detail

0 Miles   500
0 Kilometers   500

© 2016 Jeffrey L. Ward

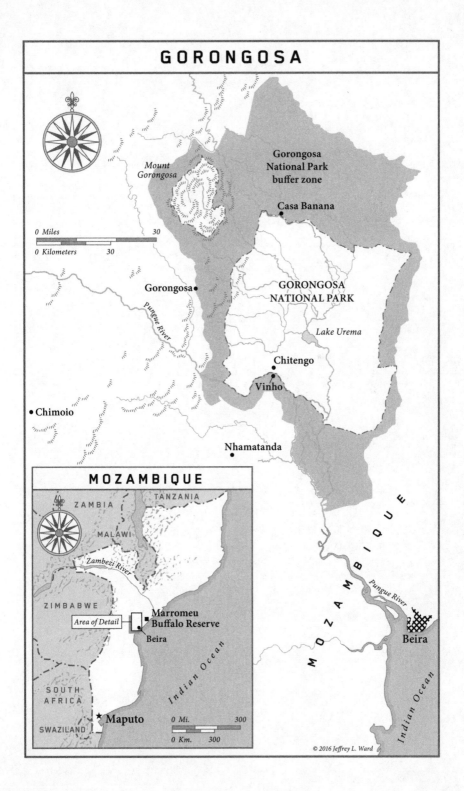

GORONGOSA

Mount
Gorongosa

Gorongosa
National Park
buffer zone

Casa Banana

0 Miles   30
0 Kilometers   30

Gorongosa

GORONGOSA
NATIONAL PARK

Pungue River

Lake Urema

Chitengo

Vinho

Chimoio

Nhamatanda

MOZAMBIQUE

ZAMBIA

TANZANIA

MALAWI

Zambezi River

ZIMBABWE

Area of Detail

Marromeu
Buffalo Reserve

Beira

MOZAMBIQUE

Pungue River

Beira

SOUTH
AFRICA

Indian Ocean

Maputo

SWAZILAND

Indian Ocean

0 Mi.   300
0 Km.   300

© 2016 Jeffrey L. Ward

Introduction

One afternoon some years ago, a red helicopter hovered above the great green folds of Mount Gorongosa. Its propellers whirred against the humid air like the wings of a metallic hummingbird; the rumble of its engine rippled through the massif, which at its tallest point measures some 5,900 feet above the surrounding Mozambican lowland. The pilot, an amicable South African, peered down at the landscape. It was all green: deep green, bluish green, purple green. He was looking for brown, for the clearing he was convinced would be there, somewhere.

The mountain itself was an inselberg, an isolated, steep hill shooting up abruptly from the horizon, island-like. It was some eighteen miles wide, and its topography and foliage made it difficult to see what was happening at ground level. The earth hid from the air, ducking underneath trees and scrub. Even walking on the mountain could be confusing. Trails through the forests and fields twisted back on one another; deep caves had given generations of locals a way to escape or trap their enemies.

The section of the mountain under the whirring helicopter was an area heavily influenced by a man whom the locals considered a rain-maker, a traditional leader who went by the clan name of Samatenje. The helicopter's passengers—particularly the multimillionaire who had chartered the flight, an American who went by the given name of Greg—were well aware of this fact. Indeed, it was the reason they had flown here and were now looking for a landing spot through the trees. This rainmaker, they believed, could help them with a development project they had started nearby, in the national park that sprawled in the mountain's shadow.

This park shared the name of the mountain, Gorongosa. At one time—before being ravaged by two decades of war and another decade of neglect—the Gorongosa National Park was widely considered one of the best safari locations in southern Africa, on the bucket list of desti-nations for the rich and famous of Europe and America. By the time the helicopter was hovering over the mountain, though, it held a dif-ferent attraction. Now the Gorongosa National Park was home to what some were calling one of the most ambitious conservation efforts on the continent, a groundbreaking initiative to restore both environ-mental and human dignity.

Greg Carr—"just Greg," he would say to everyone, with a smile—had listened with keen interest when his advisers told him about Samatenje, and he quickly decided that they should pay the rainmaker a visit. Perhaps, he suggested, this Samatenje might bless their work. Perhaps the rainmaker might even perform a traditional ceremony call-ing on the ancestors to support it. The others had nodded. Yes, that would be worth the journey.

This was not, mind you, because those on the helicopter believed in rainmaking or ancestor spirits. The scientists and conservationists and development experts, educated in the best Western academies, decid-edly did not think that ancient spirits were present all around them, or that any of the other supernatural beings whom rural Mozambicans routinely credited with the fortunes and misfortunes of daily life actu-ally existed. They were, however, familiar with and committed to the best practices of development and human rights. They believed in local buy-in, local involvement, and, at least ostensibly, local input—all those categories newly tracked by the alphabet soup of donor organizations concerned with Africa. So identifying the regional "thought leader," and gaining his culturally appropriate endorsement, was an important part of their work.

The request for a meeting had been made through a chain of African staff members and local contacts. On the appointed day, Greg's team loaded the appropriate supplies into the rented helicopter: gifts of soda and tobacco, beer and cloth. Greg and his top staffers were familiar with the routine. For almost a year now they had crisscrossed this lush district, meeting with local chiefs under mango trees and pitching their case for a new way of living with the earth. Again and again, they handed out beer and asked to have the ancestors bless the park's revival.

The pilot maneuvered the helicopter into another sweeping dip, the arc of a bird from its feeder, looking again for that clearing. There it was: brown, as all the clearings here were, soft brown, reddish brown, tinted like the dust that stuck to bare black legs. It was a meeting place of sorts, large enough for the community to gather, with benches at one side made out of logs smoothed on top for men to sit. There were a few rough-hewn stalls. One displayed a sparse collection of secondhand T-shirts, gathered for resale from the larger market in Gorongosa Town, at the base of the mountain.

A crowd had collected below, the way crowds always seemed to form when Greg's helicopter approached. From the ground, it was impossible to miss the noise. The vibrations shook the mountain itself, which spat them back up through the panga panga trees, through the rattling iron cooking pots with their soot-darkened legs, over the walls of the houses protected by banana and palm fronds. Skinny dogs pawed the ground, nonplussed. Children, attracted as children are by something different in the day, ran to get a better view. The pilot swore under his breath as he saw the space where he could land shrinking. Every time he worried about the onlookers—especially those barefoot kids, all snotty-nosed, running every which way—getting too close to the blades. Their parents, summoned by either concern for the scampering children or their own curiosity, crowded in. The African fabrics and Western T-shirts ("50 Cent: The Anger Management 3 Tour," "New Rochelle

High Softball," "My Kid Went to Florida and All I Got Was This Lousy
T-Shirt") formed a rainbow circle.

From inside the helicopter the passengers looked down, energized.
If there was any nervousness, it was overwhelmed by their usual confidence. From the air, all looked in order. Slowly, the pilot guided the
helicopter to the ground.

What happened next depends on which stories you believe. I can tell
you what I saw: how the helicopter lowered, its blades spinning a white
circle against the trees and sky; how the dirt and dust and twigs of the
landing zone formed their vortex; how the waiting people turned away;
how a man with jagged shoulders tried to lift his torn sports coat—
linen perhaps, a summer jacket in another life—over the back of his
neck as he tensed up. One of his hands pulled the frayed collar as far as
it would go. The other pressed a young boy against his legs.

I can say how the faces looked to me, as the blades stopped spinning
and the crowd turned back toward us. Instead of cheering and grinning,
as people often did when Greg and his entourage emerged from a helicopter, instead of rushing toward the passengers with outstretched
hands and backslaps, they stood stonily silent. They scowled. For a split
second, the crescendo of the grasshoppers drowned out our breathing.

I can go on with my own version of the story, one shaped by my
nationality (American), my profession (journalism), my sex (female),
my age (thirty-something), and my aching desire, then as now, to figure
out why Western efforts to help the environment and Africa—about
which, in more disclosure, I care deeply—so often fail. But there are
many other stories that would emerge from that clearing on the mountain. There is Greg Carr's version, and those of the other staff members
of the Gorongosa National Park, dedicated and well-meaning environmentalists and aid workers. There are the tales that grew in the remote
area where the helicopter landed, where people speak their own dialect
and hew close to the rules of spiritual leaders. There are still other
stories that have grown on the mountain's lower slopes and in the

wider region beyond it, stories that have evolved as the years passed. They are all different.

I first started reporting about Greg Carr's efforts to restore the Gorongosa National Park in 2006. I was a foreign correspondent based in southern Africa at the time, and a source told me that, in central Mozambique, a human rights philanthropist connected to Harvard University was creating a groundbreaking model for helping people through conservation. I visited the park, and ended up spending the next decade reporting and writing about it. From the beginning, I liked Greg, and I fell in love with the breathtaking Gorongosa region. Yet the longer I stayed, the more the stories I found diverged from one another, and I increasingly wondered what was actually happening there. The more I watched the glowing news reports and reverent documentaries about the project—and there have been quite a few of those over the past ten years—the more they bothered me.

For quite a long time, I tried to resolve the competing narratives, to figure out who was right and who was wrong. Many locals insisted that dire events had unfolded after the helicopter landed in Samatenje's territory: violence and destruction, the suffering of people and animals alike. They saw disasters freighted with meaning, ordained by spirits and ancestors. Meanwhile, the Westerners, along with a number of Mozambican park administrators, dismissed not only the supernatural explanations, but the very premise that anything was going seriously wrong. If there were problems, they were just minor mishaps, unfortunate but surmountable difficulties in a clear-sighted plan that would significantly improve the region and perhaps the world. Sometimes it felt as if I were reporting on two different planets.

It was only when I abandoned the quest for the one "true" story that I started to understand what was really happening there, in the lush heart of Southeast Africa. I also started to realize that the contradictory Gorongosa stories are not exclusive to the region, but are representative of what is happening all over the globe in other environmental "hot spots," as the nongovernmental organizations (NGOs, in development lingo) dealing with conservation call them. So many of these

ecologically essential swaths of the developing world are at the center
of a clash of narratives, a collision of truths that has a profound impact
both on the people cast as characters in these dramas and on our
environment.

Now, I am a storyteller by profession, so I admit to a bit of bias when
it comes to the importance of narratives and tales. Yet I am far from
alone in recognizing that the stories we tell—the motivations we ascribe
to ourselves and to others, the ideas we assume people share, the way
we think of our relationship with the earth—dramatically affect our
actions. Our stories are both the foundation and the scaffolding upon
which we construct our worlds.

So my goal is not simply to tell my version of Gorongosa, but to
reveal the hidden conflict that is playing out among the various tales.
Indeed, simply recognizing the *existence* of narratives beyond our own
is an essential first step for reversing what is, frankly, an appalling track
record of well-meaning Americans and Europeans creating unintended
consequences around the world. For it turns out that the reason so
many Western projects in Africa fail is not because of bad planning or
poor investment strategies or any of the other mea culpas presented in
the evaluation reports of the World Bank and other donor agencies. We
fail—although we almost never admit it—because we are stuck in our
own mental framework. We cannot see the other narratives, even when
they actively clash with our own. We certainly do not accept that our
tales are no truer than any others. We simply can't imagine that stories
involving evil spirits and perturbed ancestors are, in many ways, no
more outrageous than our own explanations of the world, with their
all-knowing outsiders and logical solutions.

This book, then, is a safari of sorts through our African stories, a
voyage into how we got here and what we do now. After all, the tales
from Gorongosa mean little out of context. (Imagine trying to analyze
Western literature while knowing nothing of Homer.) To have the
Gorongosa National Park experience add to any greater understanding
of why the Western conservation movement—and Western development in general, for that matter—has struggled around the world, we
must start by understanding how we came up with our ideas of wilder-

ness, conservation, and development; how we built up our notions of Africa, nature, and utopia.

In Swahili, *safari* simply means "journey." In English, however, the word has taken on far more specialized connotations. It is an exploration, an adventure, a quest. And it is central to our relationship with African nature, whether in the realm of tourism or conservation.

The complete safari experience encompasses not just the travel itself, but also the preparation beforehand and the memories that travelers carry with them when they return home. This book has the same three-part structure. Think of part 1 as gathering supplies for our journey into the tangle of stories, getting a sense of how we formed our traditional narratives of Africa, why we are still stuck in them, and how they appear today. In part 2 we will go to Gorongosa, to see both the promise and the tragedy of those stories up close. Finally, in part 3, we will look at what happens when we bring such tales back to our own lands, and consider what they tell us about our role in the wider world.

Imagine the scenes described in this book as sightings in the bush. I do not intend them to be comprehensive, just as there is no way to see an entire ecosystem when you drive through it. Instead, what you get are glimpses, at once connected and disconnected: an elephant here, a lion there, the chirping song of the African warbler somewhere in between. Inevitably, there will be truths that remain invisible, stories missed: an impala hidden by the blond grasses, a rhino blending into the horizon. Someone on a different drive might come back with an entirely different perspective about what's lurking there, off in the palm tree jungles or just behind the knoll on the sweeping savannah. Yet the moments you experience on your own safari are no less real for all that. Putting them together makes your own story—one that, in this case, urges a new way of thinking about nature, conservation, and the pitfalls of best intentions.

Before I left Mozambique, I went to visit one of the local chiefs—known in this part of Africa as a *régulo*—in a community on the lower slopes of Mount Gorongosa. This was a strange outing for me, because I knew

I was shedding some of the rules of Western logic and journalistic objectivity that had long guided my life. After an exchange of pleasantries, I took a deep breath, leaned in, and shared a request with one of the *régulo*'s sons. He turned to consult, in a low voice, with a group of elders. I kicked the dust and waited.

The *régulo*'s son looked me over. I must have been a pathetic sight: a sunburned white woman wearing pants, away from home, without children, mumbling something about writing a book and wanting to know the best way to go about it vis-à-vis the ancestors. As a general rule, Western journalists tend to side with the Western scientists. We do not believe in ancestors or spirits or other sorts of the occult. We like facts, *our* facts. Still, I had spent enough time around Gorongosa to know that, at the very least, it wasn't a bad idea to hedge your bets.

A ceremony was the only way forward, the *régulo*'s son finally responded. He suggested I return the following week, supplies in hand. I knew the drill: cloth, tobacco, beer.

On the appointed morning, the villagers gathered in a clearing. I perched on a reed mat in the dust with the other women, their knees to the side, their skirts lying in kaleidoscopic contrast with the brown-red earth. Imitating them, I tried not to fidget, but it's not a particularly comfortable pose, with your hip falling asleep and your skin baking in the sun.

Eventually the *régulo* himself emerged. Eugenio Canda, a tall man with a glint in his yellowed eyes, on this occasion looked somber in a long skirt of black and white cloth. He nodded at me and ducked into a small square hut that served as a sort of village shrine. The villagers began clapping in unison with cupped hands, the traditional way of summoning the ancestors. I joined in, making sure my palms were perpendicular to each other. That's the way women clap here. Men hold their hands parallel.

Inside the hut, the chief began preparing offerings for the spirits who the people here say live on Mount Gorongosa. He poured some wine into the dirt and glanced up at the sacred massif looming behind us, its blue-green folds hiding secrets that religious figures like Eugenio do not share with outsiders. He started calling out the ancestors' names, and summoned his senior wife to join him as he walked over to a slender mopane tree at the edge of the clearing. The two knelt together and poured more wine onto the ground. That was the female ancestors' spot, someone explained to me. Men and women move in separate spheres even when they're spirits. I nodded. Female ancestors are said to do a better job of looking out for their living sisters, so I appreciated the gesture.

We passed a tin cup full of wine around our circle, and everyone took a sip. When we finally stood up from that dusty communion, the women began to sing. Suddenly I was in a sort of Mozambican conga line—this was a feature I didn't recall from any of the earlier ceremonies I had attended—while the villagers sang in Sena, the local language. The song had Christian-style lyrics about admitting sin and requesting forgiveness. We danced around and around, with a stutter step that I kept messing up and a syncopated clap that I eventually managed to get. The white-hot sun was baking us in the clearing; I wondered if the others were also sweating. Eventually, Eugenio slowed the pace, and everyone clapped, one more time, in unison, with the cupped hands.

Before I knew it, the ceremony had ended. People began to mill around, the men filtering to some chairs in the shade of a mango tree, the women back to the reed mats on the ground. Eugenio grinned at me, gave me a thumbs-up, and asked me to take a picture of him and his family.

"Was that ceremony good?" I asked him as I clicked.

"Yup," he said. "You can do your book."

I couldn't help but laugh. This was not exactly the revelatory experience I had half-allowed myself to imagine.

After a few minutes of photos, Eugenio was satisfied. Shooing off the children and wives, he ushered me toward the shade, where, as a visitor, I was given a stool.

"It's good that you are writing about Canda," he told me, referring to his own last name and also the name of this district on the mountain. "In school, everyone learns about Vasco da Gama." He harrumphed derisively at the name of the Portuguese explorer who, centuries earlier, docked just a few dozen miles to the east of here. "The people of Canda—we were here way before Vasco da Gama. Are you writing this down? We were here on the mountain before the white people. And there have been many who have wanted to conquer this place. It does not work. Not yesterday, not today, not tomorrow."

He checked again to make sure I was taking notes. "Are you going to put this in your book?" he asked.

"Sure," I said. "Yeah."

Now it was his turn to laugh, although I didn't quite know at what.

"A book," he repeated. "So what story are you going to write?"

PART I

ADVENTURERS
AND SAVIORS

1

The Trouble with Painted Dogs

In the arid northern reaches of South Africa, on the edge of the Kalahari Desert, is a sweeping landscape of dust and thorn bushes that many people consider one of the top safari spots in the region. It is called the Madikwe Game Reserve, and by the mid-2000s, when I started reporting from the continent, a growing number of well-heeled international tourists were shelling out a thousand dollars or more per night to stay there. Madikwe offered exclusivity, convenience, and plentiful big game—and it didn't have malaria, a scourge of most African wilderness areas. The surrounding country was stable. The reserve's luxury lodges and game drives were regularly booked to capacity.

Yet Madikwe was also something more than just a trendy new destination for the rich and famous. This land of loping grasslands and cotton candy sunsets, I had heard, was also the location of one of the region's clear conservation success stories. It was the place where one could witness the remarkable comeback of a species that many scientists believed was at the edge of extinction: the African wild dog, also known as the African painted dog, *Lycaon pictus*. The latter name was the one that many of the creature's advocates preferred, since "wild" seemed to perpetuate the canine's bad reputation as a child killer and cattle eater.

I hadn't written environmental stories in years, but I was fascinated by what I heard about Madikwe and its big-pawed flagship species. Over the past decade, the number of wild dogs in Africa had fallen from about a half million to a scant one thousand. With their big ears and cute puppy antics, African wild dogs were beloved by conservationists and animal rights activists, but they were despised by most farmers and villagers, who shot them regularly. Not long ago, experts predicted that the dogs would soon go extinct.

So I pitched to my editors what I figured would be a relatively straightforward piece: I would go to Madikwe, look at the dogs, and write about the good news coming from the reserve. Maybe this place held clues for how to save other big, lovable African animals, I suggested. Maybe the wild dogs could help teach us how to save rhinos, elephants, and cheetahs, all those adopt-an-animal stars back home. My editors agreed, and soon I was driving from my new home in the sprawling South African city of Johannesburg—a metropolis that feels about as far from roaming elephants and lions as you can get—toward the Madikwe Game Reserve.

I was excited. I was (and am) an admitted animal softie. When I was a child, my favorite board game was a "keep the animals from going extinct" product sold by one of the big conservation groups. Those organizations knew a prospect when they saw one, and they kept me in their database. Over the years, I must have received hundreds of brochures about orphaned baby elephants, distressed mama leopards, needy lion cubs, and various other weep-worthy creatures whom I could help for no more than the cost of a cup of coffee a day. (I regularly paid up.) I watched nature documentaries, where I heard more about the dangers facing one species or another. I read the conservation displays at the zoo. Like many Americans, I figured—without thinking about it very much—that the biggest environmental problems facing Africa had to do with threats to the charismatic animals we know and love from children's books.

And why wouldn't one think that? Given the proliferation of photographs of sad-looking elephants and their ilk, most of us could be excused for concluding that the key to African nature preservation is just to love animals, give them refuge, and keep the baddies from killing them. It's a straightforward story, reinforced by generations of explorers and scientists, writers and politicians. It's good versus bad, simple and understandable, the way we think about many things in the developing world. But as I would soon find out, it's also pretty much completely wrong.

The Madikwe Game Reserve lies at the intersection of two types of southern African grassland: the lowveld, a savannah region, and the Kalahari thornveld, which is basically what it sounds like, with bushes and trees regularly sporting finger-length spikes. (One of the first instructions I received in the bush was never to drive over the massive piles of elephant leavings, since the pachyderm stomach can handle thorn bushes that a car's tires cannot.) The earth is reddish brown, with dirt roads curving through scrubland and the occasional wooded patches along a line of rolling hills.

Today the reserve looks like something out of an African storybook: tan impala grazing in the grasslands, an elephant marching regally across the horizon. But this is a new look for Madikwe. As recently as the 1980s, this region was agricultural, though barely so. The farmers' crops regularly died, the ranchers' cattle were often skinny. The land was bad and getting worse, everyone there agreed. The only good thing about it, if you had to pick something, was the view: wide-open vistas framed to the south by rocky, rugged mountains.

In 1991 the local government did a survey of the region and agreed that it was, indeed, unfit for agriculture. So officials, along with some of the struggling farmers and villagers living there, proposed a new use for the land: wilderness. Or, if not quite wilderness, something that we in the United States often confuse with it: a game reserve. To Westerners, this might seem like a strange decision. We tend to replace our farmland with subdivisions, shifting more people into spaces once populated by plants and animals, moving it even farther from nature. We expect basically the opposite of what the people of Madikwe proposed.

Yet their decision was perfectly logical. There was, around that time, the anticipation of a boom in the number of tourists coming to southern Africa, and particularly in the number of travelers hoping to look at animals. Partly this was because of improved travel logistics, with cheaper airfares and better vacation packages proliferating. There was also the approaching end of apartheid, which had previously kept many international travelers away from South Africa. Most important for the farmers of Madikwe, though, was the perception among the wealthiest tourists that wildlife viewing in eastern Africa, the traditional destination for that sort of thing, had become altogether too, well, touristy.

For close to a century, Americans had been scrambling to look at, or shoot, animals in Kenya and nearby countries—ever since Teddy Roosevelt launched the trend with his own, much-publicized safari to East Africa in 1909. (More to come on *that* crazy adventure, complete with thousands of animal carcasses.) At first it was only the very rich who could make the journey. But by the 1950s, going on safari had become altogether democratic, if still fairly expensive. By the 1980s, travel writers were bemoaning the crowds pouring into Kenyan and Tanzanian reserves, and waxing nostalgic about the more private, exclusive safaris of days gone by. They worried—in what I would come to realize is a central theme in our stories of Africa—that the days of African wilderness were numbered.

The search was on for a new destination. Tourists wanted a place more remote, less commercial, more *wilderness*-y. So high-end safari-goers began to cast their gaze southward. The farmers of Madikwe noticed the trend and formed what was essentially a co-op, bringing together some 262 square miles of land. They agreed to let the South African parks board and private businesses build a fence, import animals, and coordinate the construction of high-end safari lodges. In return, the local people would get a substantial cut of any tourism concessions. To stay attractive to moneyed safari-goers seeking a sense of solitude, Madikwe limited the number of lodges and decided not to allow any day visitors inside the fence. Thus was born the "hidden gem," as the promotional brochures called it, of the southern African safari world.

Soon after I pulled through the gates of this new private "wilderness," I met up with a cheerful game ranger named Penny Lombard, who had agreed to help me learn more about the state of the wild dogs. Penny worked at one of Madikwe's game lodges, a beautiful place, complete with a pool and thatched-roof chalets, built on a series of wooden walkways by one of the rivers of the reserve. Other lodges in the area were even fancier. Some explicitly embraced colonial-style comfort and were decorated with old British Empire maps, leather trunks, and zebra-skin rugs. If it was in questionable taste in modern-day Africa to advertise a "return to the graciousness of Colonial times," as one luxury lodge put it, the tourism industry hadn't gotten the message.

Every morning, the guests at Penny's lodge rose early to meet her or one of her colleagues. They were given a tin of coffee or tea along with a few biscuits to tide them over until breakfast, boarded a game drive vehicle, and set off to look for animals. In many ways, Penny was a modern iteration of the classic African safari guide, escorting moneyed visitors through the bush. She was chatty and likable, a perfect host with a keen eye for nature and a knack for driving her guests to the best spots for evening drinks. (She and many of the other rangers would gently suggest the best place for their guests to take a picture, typically a big orange sun dropping behind a baobab or acacia tree.) She ate with her guests at dinner and checked on them at breakfast.

There were significant differences from the safaris of old, of course. Having a female guide was the most obvious, though Penny was still in a small minority of what remains a macho, male-dominated field. The second big difference was the lack of firearms, at least among the tourists. (Game rangers typically carry a rifle as a safety measure in case of rampaging animals.) Though there are still many hunting outfits and hunting reserves across the continent, most safari-goers these days want to capture animals only with a photographic lens.

Still, the pressure to find animals for the guests is the same as ever. The creatures that tourists particularly want to see are the ones most heavily advertised in safari brochures, known as the Big Five: the elephant, the buffalo, the leopard, the rhino, and the lion. The term itself is a throwback to the days of the hunting safari, a category for those animals considered the most dangerous to track on foot. Today, the Big Five are more like the Disney princesses of the bush, characters somewhat randomly grouped together in a very successful marketing campaign.

Penny knew all about tracking down the Big Five, but her job had an extra challenge: finding her tourists wild dogs. Thanks to its conservation successes, the Madikwe Game Reserve had become particularly known for these endangered animals, and the well-heeled visitors definitely wanted to see them.

Like many of the smaller game parks in South Africa, Madikwe is surrounded by a fence, which works to keep animals in and people out. (It's an impressive logistical feat, building a fence that will stand up against animals as varied in size, strength, and digging ability as the elephant, the buffalo, and the warthog.) Still, just because the dogs were somewhere inside the fence did not mean it was easy to find them. "They're tricky, hey," Penny would say, gearing up her Land Rover for another game drive.

The wild dogs rarely stayed in one place; if not contained in a fenced reserve, they might roam twenty or thirty miles a day. Indeed, this is one of the reasons they had fared so badly in modern Africa. Left to their own devices, the dogs will cross dozens of cattle ranches and other farms every week, each one populated by a shotgun-armed farmer quick to target any "vermin" that pose a threat to his livestock.

In most South African game reserves, rangers from the various lodges radio one another on the sly, passing along the coordinates of, say, a leopard, so that every guide can "discover" the animal. Madikwe was no exception. But even with this network, the dogs were elusive. Being constantly on the move meant that they could easily avoid the roaming game drive vehicles, which to the animals probably seemed to swirl aimlessly around the reserve.

Luckily for me, though, Penny had just heard rumors of a wild dog den in one of the far corners of Madikwe. She wanted to check out the scene before she brought her guests there and offered to take me along. So we climbed into her truck and drove for an hour through the bush, past some of the other safari lodges and the remains of an old farm.

We chatted over the noise of the wind, as hot air and the smell of dry grasses wafted through our open windows. Eventually we pulled up to a big old tamboti, a tree with a thick trunk, craggy branches, and wood so toxic that if you cook with it you're likely to get severe diarrhea and may even die. (I had a running gag with one of my colleagues, only half-joking, that in Africa everything could kill you. That spider? Deadly. That snake? You don't have a chance. That tree? Yup, that'll kill you too.) Under the shading branches was a wide stretch of dirt with various holes leading belowground. It was an abandoned aardvark den, Penny explained, that the wild dogs had taken over.

Sure enough, there were the dogs, or at least their pups. They were piled on top of one another, all paws and ears. Now and then one of the buried puppies would decide that it wanted to wiggle its roly-poly body out from under its siblings, causing the whole collection to start toppling over; then they'd wag their tails, lick one another, and readjust. They plopped onto their backs as if looking for a belly rub. Sometimes a couple of them would nip at each other, then nuzzle playfully.

Toward the edge of the den was an older dog. This was the babysitter, Penny explained, an adult who would stay and watch the babies while the others hunted. The dogs had many sweet arrangements like this, she said. Although their hunting style is ferocious, wild dogs' social structure is gentle and caring, atypically so for the often harsh bush. The pack members remain devoted to one another through sickness and health. Unlike many animals, wild dogs even take care of their elderly. All the adults in a pack, male and female, help raise the pups, and the older dogs let the younger ones eat first. Instead of aggression, the dogs use submissive behavior to get food from a fellow pack member, a low-wagging approach not unfamiliar to domestic dog owners. This is quite different from, say, lions, who growl and swipe at one another whenever a carcass is in sight, an arrangement that usually has the big males eating first—even though the females do most of the hunting, as many safari guides will point out. A wild dog who has eaten will even regurgitate some of its meal for a hungry relative. The wild dogs lick one another in greeting, wag their tails, and snuggle up close together.

Such kindness is in contrast, Penny acknowledged, to the dogs' hunting style. Wild dogs are terrifying predators. They pad quietly through the bush, encircling their antelope prey like guerrilla soldiers staking out a target. Suddenly, they will charge directly into the herd, scattering the herbivores in hoofed panic. The antelopes that lag behind—the babies, say, or the older beasts, or the ones who just weren't born with quite the same predisposition to escape—become the targets. Then the dogs work as a team. The pack leaders chase the prey at speeds of more than thirty miles per hour. When those dogs tire, the ones who have been saving some energy take over in the lead spots. Eventually the prey starts slowing down, and the dogs pounce, tearing pieces of flesh from the antelope until it crumples. This is part of why the dogs are treated with such hatred by people who don't understand their sweeter nature, Penny explained: the hunts make them seem brutal.

We sat for hours watching the puppy antics. The pups did not seem to be disturbed by our presence. As with many animals, they didn't appear to notice that there were separate, individual humans within our truck; they just seemed to accept the Land Rover as an unusual but uninteresting presence, quiet now with the engine turned off, and far enough away not to cause alarm. When the adults finally arrived home from the hunt, the puppies pulled themselves up on wobbly legs and ran toward them, tails wagging. It was cute. Beautiful. The hope of new generations. Penny sighed. "It's a haven here for them," she said.

I left Madikwe inspired to write about how this gorgeous reserve was saving some of the last wild dogs on earth, about the hopeful discovery of a new generation of pups.

Then I started making phone calls.

One of my first calls was to Steve Dell, the field ecologist at Madikwe. I began by offering my congratulations on his success in helping save the wild dogs, on the new litter of pups that would surely let this endangered species gain some ground. He laughed at me—in a nice way, I guess.

"The wild dogs of Madikwe will never be viable as a population," he said.

Huh? I asked him to clarify.

The reserve, he explained, was simply too small to allow for a naturally breeding population of wild dogs. The dogs were such effective hunters that if park managers allowed them simply to do their thing in the reserve, they would quickly wipe out the rest of the animals and then die off themselves. In South Africa, he told me, the only viable population of wild dogs was in the country's largest park, the 7,523-square-mile Kruger National Park—and there, scientists estimate that the dogs numbered only 450 at the most. In Madikwe, to deal with the dogs, the park had to either kill a lot of them or move a lot of them. It had done some of the former, and had also been making progress with the latter, but wild dogs are a hard sell. They are notorious escape artists, Dell said; unless a reserve has a "bullet-proof fence," as he put it, the dogs will find a way out. And once they do, they will likely be shot by angry farmers who see them as pests.

In fact, he told me, the people who started the Madikwe reserve had argued for a long time about whether they would allow wild dogs to live in their new park at all. Many of the cattle farmers whose land would eventually become the reserve had no love for the animals; meanwhile, a number of conservationists warned that the reserve wouldn't be able to manage the dogs in such a small space.

Wait, I asked. The conservationists didn't want the dogs?

Dell laughed again.

They weren't only worried, he explained, about the impact on other animals. They also thought that the gene pool of the wild dogs themselves could be damaged. In the wild, the dogs roam such lengthy distances that pups coming to breeding age generally encounter another pack. Then they are able to mate successfully with the other dogs, branch off, and start their own packs. Given the limitations of space and ecosystem, however, the Madikwe Game Reserve could handle two packs at the most. So there was a real danger of inbreeding. Indeed, as planning for the reserve progressed, the tide seemed to be turning against the dogs. Making the switch from agriculture to game park was already risky, and adding wild dogs was looking like just too much to take on.

But it so happened that at around the same time that planners were squabbling over Madikwe, a number of South African conservation organizations formed a Wild Dog Advisory Group (known, perfectly, as WAG), which planned to create what is known as a "metapopulation" for the dogs. A metapopulation is essentially a single animal population split among multiple places. In this approach, rather than let the animals in question live, breed, and die wherever they might wander, the reserve distributes them among different protected areas—acting to ensure proper gene pools, reduce the impact on a region's prey or flora, and manage population growth. WAG knew that wild dogs would not be viable in Madikwe, and would not survive long if they lived only there. If the Madikwe dogs were part of a metapopulation, however, they could survive—living, as a group, similarly to how they would exist in the wilderness. Only with quite a bit of management by humans.

Wow, I said.

This was the future, Dell responded.

Still, he said, not all was rosy in Madikwe. At this point the dogs were running out of places to go. Those cute little puppies I saw? They were a headache for the reserve managers, showing that the metapopulations were almost *too* successful. And it wasn't as if scientists could just put the dogs back into "the wild," Dell said. Farmers would be up in arms if it became known that a game reserve was intentionally releasing wild dogs near their farms. After all, it was the current state of the "wild"—that is, the lack of any real wilderness that suited the dogs— that had made them endangered in the first place.

By the time we had finished talking, I had a headache. In some ways the metapopulation approach struck me as, well, cool: the best use of advanced science and wildlife management to allow for conservation against geographic odds. But it also had a whiff of "The Sorcerer's Apprentice" about it. The magic makers were working harder and harder to try to keep up with their creation's self-replication, and it seemed like they were losing control. Which is partly why Gregory Rasmussen had a totally different perspective on what should happen to the dogs.

Rasmussen, the founder of the Painted Dog Conservation project, is a wildlife conservation biologist who grew up in Zimbabwe and spent years working there. His daring efforts to convince farmers to be friendlier to the dogs—and a near-fatal plane crash he suffered while trying to track animals from the air—gave him quite a bit of cred in the macho world of African conservation. Operating generally without the oversight of the large international conservation agencies, he achieved remarkable success: during the sixteen years he worked on wild dog conservation, the dog population in Zimbabwe increased from three hundred to about eight hundred. And almost all the dogs were outside protected areas—not fenced in, like those in Kruger and Madikwe.

This point was key, Rasmussen said. Places such as Madikwe may be important for preserving the dogs and spreading awareness about them, but the protected-area approach to conservation was simply not going to work to save the dogs, given their range and breeding requirements. To see a true rebound of the wild dog, he said, one needed a real change in the relationship between humans and the canines. That's what had happened in Zimbabwe, where farmers and ranchers gradually altered their views on the animals. Without that, the dogs simply could not have rebounded as they had. Because the fundamental problem for wild dogs isn't genetics or prey numbers—it's humans. To fix their situation, you need to start with people. Sure, Rasmussen acknowledged, it may be even more difficult to change people's entrenched attitudes about wildlife than to fence in reserves, build metapopulations, and manage the dogs' breeding. But it is more sustainable in the long run.

Then again, altering human perceptions doesn't always last, either. Indeed, if changes within the human world were what helped the dogs in Zimbabwe, they were also what threatened their downfall again. By the mid-2000s, Zimbabwe, once the breadbasket of southern Africa, had descended into political and economic turmoil under the increasingly challenged rule of President Robert Mugabe. A spate of farm invasions, in which Mugabe cronies violently seized land owned by whites, had upended the country's agricultural sector, eventually leading to the sort of hyperinflation that would have been laughable if it weren't so devastating for everyone in the country. (I still have a Zimbabwean fifty-million-dollar bill from that time, framed on my bookshelf.) The turmoil led to a host of environmental scourges, ranging from an increase in poaching to an uptick in the illegal trade of live wild animals—and it hit the wild dogs hard.

Rasmussen told me that he knew of cases in which smugglers trapped and sold Zimbabwean wild dogs to reserves in South Africa, and even to American zoos. Hunting also increased, as people became more desperate. This sort of human aggression can quickly have a devastating impact on the socially minded canines. Scientists know that six is the minimum pack size for wild dogs. If a farmer or poacher shoots just one dog out of a six-member pack, the rest will probably die.

So, sure, Rasmussen said, it's great that you saw those pups in Madikwe. And sure, it's fine to have the parks; the dogs are at least safe there temporarily. But for real environmental change to take place, the battle is outside the protected areas, and the wild dogs are just one poignant example of far larger dilemmas. How, in today's world, can we establish a balance between the needs of people and the needs of nature, allowing for the respect and flourishing of both? How do we invest in each but also get away from what has become a devastating dichotomy between the two?

There's a lot of discussion among conservationists about this, Rasmussen told me; you'll see it crop up at the big conferences and in academic papers. We're pretty sure that the old ways of doing things aren't working. But really, he said, nobody has figured out what to do instead.

I put down the phone and sighed. How, I wondered, had we gotten here? How had our stories, which had seemed so clear back in the United States—all those zoo exhibits and National Geographic videos and conservation fund-raisers—come to mask what seemed to be a mess on the ground?

I would carry these questions for a long time, but I would get my first inklings of an answer in a rather improbable place: in a metal cage dunked into chilly water in the middle of a swarm of hungry great white sharks.

2

Swimming with Sharks

The fishing village of Gansbaai sits on the rugged southern coast of South Africa, an hour's drive from Cape Agulhas, the southernmost point of the continent. With a sliver of white sand beach, impossibly blue water, and a rocky shoreline blanketed by the southern reaches of the Cape Floral Region, one of the richest areas of plant biodiversity in the world, the area seems nearly overrun with natural beauty—and that's just the perspective from the land. The waters off Gansbaai hold their own bounty of biodiversity. For generations, fishermen have known the area to be rich with some of the region's most prized catches: species such as the much-appreciated galjoen, now the national fish of South Africa, and the valuable abalone, which sells for sky-high prices to a primarily Asian market. One of the largest whale migrations in the world swims by Gansbaai's cliffs during the summer; one of the most important colonies of South African penguins breeds on the rocky Dyer Island, not far offshore; and a colony of some fifty to sixty thousand seals is not far away.

And then there are the great white sharks.

Scientists still don't know exactly why the great whites come in the numbers they do to a place off the coast of Gansbaai, a stretch of water that has been dubbed Shark Alley. Indeed, they don't know much about great white sharks at all. Scientists have never observed a great white shark mate, nor have we seen a great white give birth; we don't even know where they do it. We don't know where they migrate— although one shark tracked by scientists made her way from South Africa to Australia and back again—and we don't know much about how they communicate. We also don't know why, at this location just off the south coast of Africa, where the Agulhas current of the western Indian Ocean meets the cold Benguela current of the eastern Atlantic, so many sharks seem to hang around for a few weeks and then move on.

Yet they are there. And because of that, so, increasingly, are the tourists.

I had traveled to Gansbaai because I wanted to learn more about both these species, the sharks and their visitors, and because I had heard that one of the more popular things for Americans and Europeans to do on a trip to South Africa was to go "shark cage diving." This involved people donning wet suits, climbing down into a metal cage attached to a boat, and being dunked underwater so that they could see the great white sharks at eye level. The activity had become so popular that Gansbaai was now marketing itself as the "Big Two" town, a play on the Big Five safari market. Instead of elephants, rhino, buffalo, lions, and leopards, Gansbaai offered whales and sharks, with the promise of an equal or even greater level of adventure. And this notion of adventure, I had started to realize, was at the core of our flawed narratives of Africa and its natural world.

Michael Scholl, I figured, would be well placed to tell me about the sharks, the tourists, and the way they were increasingly intersecting off the coast of South Africa. One of the world's leading shark researchers, Michael had spent eight years identifying and counting individual sharks, distinguishing one from another by the unique nicks in their dorsal fins. He recognized before anyone else the way the sharks seemed to crowd into two separate areas of the Gansbaai waters before swimming along on their mystery journey. At the time of my visit, he was also working with one of the town's shark cage diving tour operators, a role he seemed to fill somewhat uneasily.

It wasn't that Michael was reluctant to share with visitors his awe and respect for the creatures. "I want people to get to know them," he told me. But he was bothered by the way he saw many shark cage diving companies perpetuating the *Jaws* stereotype. In order to get the sharks to swim close to the boats—and to the humans dunking themselves underwater—the tour operators had to chum the animals. This basically meant trailing a sickly pink mix of ground-up fish parts behind the boat, so that their scent of blood would attract the sharks. When the sharks got close enough for the tourists to see their telltale fins cutting through the water, the boat staff would throw out a fish head or other bait attached to a fishing line. If the operator was dexterous enough, he could move the bait in such a way that the shark would lunge toward the cage of tourists, jaws wide. The shark had no interest in the humans, Michael explained; it was simply trying to get the food. Tourists loved it, though: it was a rush better than a roller coaster, a photo op to trump all other Facebook posts. The shark, meanwhile, would get the unpleasant experience of crashing unexpectedly into the bars of a metal cage.

"A lot of these operators, they just want to play up the *Jaws* thing," Michael said.

Jaws, I quickly realized, is probably the least favorite movie of all time for anyone who cares about the great white shark. By making the great white, which Michael recognized as an inherently shy creature, out to be a killer, the movie ushered in a generation of people who either feared or despised the animal. And that had resulted in a decided lack of sympathy about the fate of the sharks, who were actually in quite a bit of peril. Over the second half of the twentieth century, the great white population dropped to what scientists estimated to be only 20 percent or so of what it was in the 1960s, although everyone admits it is almost impossible to count sharks precisely.

In 2005, after a generation of overhunting and culling, conservationists succeeded in getting the shark listed as one of the species protected by the Convention on International Trade in Endangered Species. An international treaty accepted by more than 180 governments, CITES essentially puts trade controls on products related to plants and animals at various levels of endangerment. But Michael and other shark researchers knew that to see any real, long-term improvement for the great white shark, the animal needed an image makeover. They wanted people to think of the shark not as a merciless brute, but as something beautiful and mysterious, worthy of care.

So when Michael's research money dried up, he approached the owner of what he believed was the most conservation-minded cage diving operation and asked if he could work as a guide. It would be a win-win, he said. He would offer a new way to attract tourists: a more nuanced, intellectual experience for the visitors actually interested in the species. At the same time, he would get a ride out into the waters of Gansbaai, where he and his research assistants could continue their work. The owner agreed.

Michael was preparing for one such trip the morning I arrived in Gansbaai. In a little boathouse attached to the cage diving operation, he was giving a slide show presentation to a group of tourists, most of whom had come from Europe. Michael himself was from Switzerland, and he had a wiry, windblown intensity that gave extra energy to his biology lessons.

The tourists watched politely as he talked about the identification of dorsal fins, about shark growth and the mysteries of the worldwide migrations. They seemed to really perk up, though, when he got into the logistics of the morning. They would be going a kilometer or so into the ocean, he explained, out to Shark Alley. They would chum the water, and then it would be a matter of waiting patiently until the sharks came. There would be wet suits for the tourists to put on before they went into the cage, which was big enough for five or six people at a time and was attached to the side of their thirty-two-foot catamaran.

Michael flipped to the next slide, which displayed in red letters a simple warning: "Watch Your Hands."

"Now," he said, "there are a few rules on the boat. Number one"— he paused, looking at the group—"no trying to pet the sharks."

The tourists laughed.

"I'm totally serious," he said. "You won't believe the number of people who are tempted to reach out and try to touch them. These are incredibly powerful creatures. They might hurt you without intending to."

I followed along as Michael led the group toward the boat, the *Shark Fever*. One of his assistants asked me if I was planning to go into the cage.

"Maybe," I said. I thought it was a terrible idea. "No promises," I added.

As the tourists chatted excitedly, Michael waxed poetic about the animals we were about to see. The media always describe the shark's eyes as dull, killer-like, he said. Actually, they are blue, luminous, deep—"there's no experience like looking into the beauty of a shark's eye," Michael said. Sharks have six senses, he noted. In addition to the ones they share with us (sound, sight, smell, touch, and taste), they are also sensitive to electricity. On the underside of the shark's snout is a system of pores called the ampullae of Lorenzini, which can sense minute changes in an electric field. Even subtle movements create tiny electromagnetic waves; so when a shark is in deep, dark, murky water, it can still detect the presence of other creatures, be they other sharks or prey. The sharks' electroreception may also help them with their migrations, Michael explained, but we don't really know for sure. Sharks also have yet another sensory system, called the lateral line, which lets them detect vibration and changes in water movement. Scientists suspect that this, too, may help explain the sharks' ability to travel immense distances and then return, again and again, to a specific spot in the ocean—like the one a few kilometers off Gansbaai.

We pulled away from shore, the white sand and green hills shrinking in the distance as we neared the rocky outcroppings of Dyer Island. The island's penguin colony had suffered due to generations of "guano scraping," the harvesting of bird droppings to sell as fertilizer, which deprived penguins of material for their burrows. But there were still some of them out there, diving into the inky blue water. Around the island were the remains of various shipwrecks; the reefs and currents of Shark Alley were as dangerous as the unseen predators swimming beneath the surface.

The boat passed the island and soon slowed, bobbing rather significantly in the current. Seasickness, one of the staff members had told me, was the biggest threat in the cage diving experience. The crew began trailing its fishy chum, and tossed overboard a decoy supposed to resemble a seal, one of the great white shark's preferred meals. Around us was a scattering of similar boats, catamarans with tourists crowding the edges, looking for signs of the sharks.

The *Shark Fever*'s crew lowered a large cage down the side of the boat so that the bulk of it was below the surface. The bars were clearly sturdy, but the spaces between them were larger than I had imagined. A number of the passengers changed into their wet suits. The water off Gansbaai is often around sixty degrees Fahrenheit, perfect for sharks but far too chilly for the tourists who come to see them.

When the first dorsal fin cut through the water, a surge of excitement went around the boat. Michael rushed toward the railing, clipboard in hand. Two of his research assistants scanned the water for the fin, ready to jot down the nicks and gaps that allow the sharks to be identified as individuals. Soon there was another fin. One of the boat's crew members tossed a fish head on a rope into the water, dangling it for a while and then swooping it upward in an arc, as one might do when playing with a house cat. Eventually a shark broke the surface, mouth open in a display of razor-sharp triangular teeth, lunging after the bait. Some of the passengers gasped. A few of the men high-fived each other. Almost all of them rushed to get in line for the cage.

This trend of grown-ups, of apparently sound mind, eagerly jumping into a mass of sharks off the coast of Africa is in many ways just the most recent iteration of a story that burst into the European consciousness in the late 1700s. That's when a wave of explorers made their way from the cities of Europe to the landmass that Europeans would come to call the Dark Continent, promising to return with enlightening geographical and scientific information. "Dark," here, was not just a reference to the skin tone of the local inhabitants. The continent was also "dark" because, to these Europeans, it was unknown: uncharted on maps, unsaved by the Christian god, unapproachable through European languages. It wasn't until the 1770s that Europeans ventured significantly beyond the continent's coastline. So those who traveled into Africa were doing something that their countrymen agreed was breathtakingly daring, exciting, even reckless. The people back home couldn't wait to hear about it.

One of the first Europeans to attempt such a journey was a Scottish noble named James Bruce. His five-volume account of his travels up the Nile, published in 1790, was met with critical disdain but achieved massive popularity. Bruce wrote of eating flesh cut from a live buffalo, of people and animals retreating in terror before an army of flies, of suffering debilitating illnesses and participating in ferocious battles and watching natives anoint themselves with blood. He described riding horses, shooting bandits, escaping pursuing warriors, and challenging numerous opponents in duels.

Bruce's noble contemporaries scoffed at much of his work, saying the tales were bogus. Indeed, many of his stories were discredited, or at least undermined, by subsequent research. But Bruce's writings from Africa were widely read, and helped cement the adventurer-style approach to the continent. After Bruce, almost every European who published an account of African travels wrote of tremendous danger, fantastic exploits, and near misses with natives and wildlife. If they had found a way to go into the water to stare down a great white shark, you can be sure that the adventurer-explorers would have done so, and boasted about it back home—and tweeted and Instagrammed it, too, given a chance.

Academics have written scores of papers about why we regard Africa as a land of adventure. Some have explored this narrative in the context of Romanticism: Africa as the exciting, wild, sensual counter to a buttoned-down Europe that had become disturbingly distant from what many Europeans regarded as the restorative power of nature. Others have looked at it through the lens of Victorianism, which saw Africa as an untamed wild being needing to be brought into the

North's godly order and orbit. More recently, we've had feminist theories (Africa as the woman's body to a male Europe, marginalized and socially repulsive yet exciting and lusted for), capitalist critiques (Africa as the source of raw materials, the wild power harnessed by the free market), and theories that basically boil down to "our lives are privileged but boring, so we need somewhere to get crazy."

In other words, the notion of Africa as a place synonymous with adventure is hardly a new one. And neither is the story of Africa as a place of noble scientific exploration—a story that has long been intermixed with the adventure narrative, as it still is today in the waters off Gansbaai. Michael Scholl's slideshow presentation to the cage diving tourists, the educational veneer covering the thrill-seeking impulse, is part of a tradition that goes back centuries.

Shortly after James Bruce fought his way through Ethiopia, another Scot, a biologist and doctor named Mungo Park, volunteered his services to a group known as the African Association. Its full name was the Association for Promoting the Discovery of the Interior Parts of Africa, and its members included some of London's most prominent elites. (They were led by the botanist Sir Joseph Banks, who advised King George III on the creation of the Kew Royal Botanical Gardens.) Influenced by Bruce's tales of the African interior, they were taken by the idea of performing a scientific survey of what, to them, was an entirely unexplored part of the earth. Each member pledged a hefty sum of money to help finance expeditions. The African Association was particularly interested in the Niger River and the "lost city" of Timbuktu, which was said to be made of gold. But it also wanted to catalog the sort of biodiversity that the patrons, sitting in their London clubs, could only imagine.

Park started up the Gambia River in 1795. Over the next two years, he made his way inland as far as the middle of present-day Mali. During his journey he was threatened by prowling lions, incapacitated at length by illness, and tortured by a Moorish chief who imprisoned him for four months. Many back home assumed he was dead. He returned to Scotland, though, able to report a variety of scientific findings, including an analysis of Africans' large-scale agricultural practices. And he could describe the course of the Niger, long a mystery to European geographers.

Park's book about his adventure, *Travels in the Interior Districts of Africa*, made him a popular hero. Although dated to modern readers— it was first published in 1799, after all—the work is still a page-turner. His descriptions of Africa paint it as a ferocious, magical land, a place where "suffocating heats oppress by day" and "the night is spent by the terrified traveler in listening to the croaking of frogs (of which the numbers are beyond imagination), the shrill cry of the jackal, and the deep howling of the hyæna, a dismal concert, interrupted only by the roar of such tremendous thunder as no person can form a conception of but those who have heard it."

This time the critics did not doubt the stories. Still, though Park's exploration was framed by scientific goals, it was also, in many ways, as swashbuckling as Bruce's. Both men were literally writing the story of Africa for readers captivated by the conquest of the unknown, physical and intellectual. For science and adventure, it was worth risking all.

And those who risked all often lost all. The adventure-science approach frequently proved deadly, both for the explorers and for huge numbers of Africans. Park, for instance, took a second trip to Africa a few years after his return, apparently chafing at the comparative boredom of life as a country doctor. This time he joined a large-scale government effort to map out, and potentially seize, some one thousand miles of coastline in northern Africa. He sailed up the Gambia with an entourage of carpenters, soldiers, and porters. One by one, the Europeans with him died of various tropical illnesses. Most historians believe that by the time he reached Timbuktu, the unachieved goal of his earlier journey, Park had gone mad. After his first trip to Africa, he had written that "whatever difference there is between the negro and European, in the conformation of the nose, and the colour of the skin, there is none in the genuine sympathies and characteristic feelings of our common nature." Yet he ended his second journey shooting at any African who attempted to approach his canoe. He sailed past Timbuktu without stopping and died in the rapids of northern Nigeria.

By 1849, when a Scottish missionary named David Livingstone

traveled north from his post in present-day South Africa, both Africa's fascination and its danger were firmly established as part of the European worldview. Livingstone's case was a particularly interesting one for me as I started thinking about our narratives of Africa, because his place in history, still marked by many a plaque and statue throughout the continent, is fundamentally about well-crafted—and crafty—storytelling.

From the outset, Livingstone was acutely aware that his position depended on how he spun his "discoveries." One of his first, for instance, was Lake Ngami, a shallow body of water in Botswana. It is not a particularly spectacular geographical feature, but Livingstone and his supporters, the London Missionary Society and the Royal Geographic Society, announced the "shimmering lake" with great fanfare, as if it were a momentous scientific finding. This sort of embellishment was good for Livingstone because it helped him keep his funding. It was also good for his sponsors because it helped them with their own fundraising, just as the breathless reports sent out by today's large conservation organizations are crucial for getting people in the United States and Europe to open their checkbooks. Indeed, storytelling, not exploring, was probably Livingstone's greatest skill. He quickly recognized that his British sponsors and their donors wanted a particular sort of narrative, and he was smart enough to give it to them.

Between 1852 and 1856, Livingstone traveled some six thousand miles through inland southern Africa, a region almost entirely unknown to Europeans. He brought back tales of scientific wonder, reporting, for instance, that the interior of southern Africa was not barren and desert-like, as had been assumed, but a place of unimagined lushness, of green hills and shading fruit trees. He described the African tribes as placid and kind—the sort of noble savage narrative that both fit Livingstone's abolitionist ideology and made the locals sound like prime candidates for conversion to Christianity. And he wrote with fantastical detail about Africa's wildlife; one of the opening scenes of his hugely popular book *Missionary Travels and Researches in South Africa* is of him getting mauled by a lion. All in all, it was a portrait of Africa as a place of spectacular beauty, of noble if underdeveloped people, of dangerous but fascinating animals, and of unparalleled adventure. With a few tweaks here and there, it's the same narrative we cling to today.

The catch is that it was never all that accurate. As conservationists Jonathan S. Adams and Thomas O. McShane point out in their book *The Myth of Wild Africa*, Livingstone's personal journal entries show him to be much less impressed with the people and the landscape. Indeed, in the journal and other personal writings, Livingstone finds the climate challenging, describes the land as downright inhospitable, and expresses a good deal of disgust and frustration with native Africans. Recently restored journal entries from the explorer show him being bitter and disparaging about the peoples whom he describes in his public writings as gentle and ready for conversion. Indeed, during all his years in Africa, Livingstone apparently made only a single convert.

Even the massive waterfalls that he would name for Queen Victoria get only a couple of lackluster paragraphs in his personal writings. Livingstone underestimated the height and width of Victoria Falls by about half—something that, once you've been there, you realize is not hard to do, given the amount of spray and fog that often blocks the view. Yet the description that came out later in his book makes it seem that visiting Victoria Falls was a moving, magical moment for him. "No one can imagine the beauty of the view from anything witnessed in England," he writes. "It had never been seen before by European eyes; but scenes so lovely must have been gazed upon by angels in their flight." This, Adams and McShane argue, is basically made up. It just sounded better than a "meh."

All this is to say that even as Livingstone helped solidify the narrative that would shape our interactions with Africa for generations, he himself knew it wasn't quite true. It's doubtful, though, this mattered all that much to him. The actuality of the journey was less important, in some ways, than the story—in the same way that the actuality of jumping into a cage with a bunch of sharks may be, to some tourists at least, less important than the photos of their doing it.

Still, some of the cracks in Livingstone's fabricated narrative started to show even during his own time. In 1858 he led a team of Britons on what many regarded as a disastrous expedition up the Zambezi River, attempting to find a route to the interior of Africa and perhaps the source of the Nile. The team was beset by disease, attacked by locals, and apparently mismanaged by Livingstone, whose underlings found him moody, self-righteous, and generally inept. The British government recalled the expedition in 1864, not wanting to lose any more lives or money. And the public started to forget the man once dubbed a national hero. For some years, nobody heard from Livingstone. His sponsors sent some expeditions to look for him, but eventually London society presumed him dead, and the local papers printed some fairly brief obituaries.

But another good story was about to resurrect the missionary explorer. In 1869 the sensationalist *New York Herald* decided to send one of its foreign correspondents, a self-aggrandizing and journalistically suspect character named Henry Morton Stanley, on a quest to find the missing Livingstone. Two years later, Stanley set forth into the interior of Africa with around two hundred porters, twelve thousand pounds of supplies, and an eager audience back home. It would become one of the most famous African journeys in history. Stanley's narrative of finding Livingstone was exactly the kind of tale that American and European readers expected to come out of Africa, complete with battles, intrigue, disease, duplicitous Arabs, bloodthirsty natives, dangerous animals, and, ultimately, triumph.

"What cared we now for the difficulties we had encountered—for the rough and cruel forests, for the thorny thickets and hurtful grass, for the jangle of all savagedom, of which we had been the joyless audience!" Stanley wrote as he and his war-ravaged cohort approached Lake Tanganyika, where they expected to find Livingstone. Within a few pages (after his men "respond to the exultant cry of the Anglo-Saxon with the lungs of Stentors, and the great forest and the hills seem to share in our triumph"), Stanley approaches the missing explorer, the focal point of the months-long journey. "Dr. Livingstone, I presume?" he says.

It was a great ending to the search—and one that probably never actually happened. There is no record in either man's diary of Stanley ever uttering the famous phrase. Indeed, Stanley tore out and destroyed the page of his diary that would be relevant. The first reference to the phrase came years later, when Stanley wrote up his narratives for publication.

This has given rise to no little debate among historians. But as I was reading about it, I couldn't help but think that it didn't really matter what exactly happened when Stanley finally found Livingstone, or what precisely one white man said to the other. After all, the whole adventure was a contrived publicity stunt. Yet people do care. It matters to them whether Stanley presumed, because the *story* of Stanley and Livingstone was—and is—quite real. It captivated audiences then and it captivates them now, a century and a half later. The image of the intrepid reporter braving dangers and nature and finally finding his elusive target with a triumphant Anglo-Saxon cry still resonates with us.

It is certainly more central to our cultural consciousness than the other, darker, and arguably far more important story of Stanley, which only began with that alleged greeting. Riding on the fame from his Livingstone adventure, which made him one of the Western world's preeminent "experts" on central Africa, Stanley began working for King Leopold of Belgium in the monarch's brutal quest to turn the Congo region into his personal rubber factory. The horrors of that venture were massive. Stanley's efforts gave rise to untold numbers of rapes, decapitations, and murders, the destruction of entire villages and social orders, and the introduction of slavery-like forced labor. That story is still playing out for the land and the people of central Africa. But we tend not to tell it. That story is not our reality. We prefer tales of bravery, danger, and triumph, the same kind of narrative that drives vacationers to jump into chilly seawaters with a bunch of great white sharks.

The *Shark Fever* rocked as I watched the first group of wet suit–clad tourists in the cage. Only the tops of their heads were visible in the water. One of the crew members turned to me. "Are you going in?" he asked.

"I don't think so," I said.

"Eh? You have to go in!" he answered. He got the attention of one of the research assistants. "Do you hear this?" he asked.

After a few minutes of shipboard peer pressure, I relented. I was there, after all. Everyone else on the ship was excited about swimming with the sharks. Everyone was encouraging it. And really, what better way to report about the animals than to see them up close and personal? It was, I told myself, a true scientific and journalistic venture.

I found the last wet suit, which was a size or two too big, and put on my goggles. I moved to the side of the boat, went down a ladder, and entered Shark Alley.

The water was cold. I was half bobbing, half floating, next to a few other tourists in the cage. "Go down," came the order from the ship, and we all took a deep breath and dunked ourselves, pushing farther down in our half-submerged cage. Suddenly we saw a creature coming toward us at our level, milky white-gray, the strange bullet-shaped body, the mouth that always seems slack-jawed until it opens up into red and white. There was the eye that Michael had talked about so fondly, and indeed it was not black or dull but translucent light blue, like a marble. I could see why he called them gentle. Sort of. One of the staffers flicked the bait, and the shark lunged, its mouth open and larger somehow than I had imagined in proportion to the body.

I floated back up to the surface, gasping, realizing I had held my breath too long and also was starting to shiver. The wet suit was too large on me to work effectively. "Go down," someone cried, so I dunked myself again.

For some reason the silence surprised me. It was a strange sensory shift, those sounds that typically fill our days giving way to something else, and as I watched the sharks, I couldn't help but wonder how we appeared to them, these humans in a big metal cage next to a boat that smelled of tuna. Then I realized I was floating toward the opening between the bars of the cage. It was the current, I realized, taking me by surprise, pushing my shivering arms and legs out of the cage in just the way that Michael had warned about. I tried to swim backward, but my limbs felt detached, somehow. I started flailing to the surface.

"Go down!"

What if the cage broke away from the ship? I began to wonder. What would be better, drowning or getting eaten by a great white shark? What if the shark somehow busted through the cage? Improbable, but the questions were in fact not so absurd. A few years after my trip an accident did happen, and three tourists drowned. On another venture a great white shark did get into the cage, although it did not eat any of the humans. None of this has stymied the cage diving industry. If anything, the real danger has only made it more enticing.

I heard one of the crew members on deck talking about me. "I think she's turning blue, eh? We might lose one."

The voice told us to go under again. So we did.

The sharks glided by. They were awesome—powerful but graceful, living in a world to which I was certainly connected, but in which my ill-equipped body clearly did not belong.

And that's the thing about going into a cage surrounded by great white sharks: you get a sense, an intense sense, that you do not belong. It's scary and exciting and beautiful all at once. It is a different sort of adrenaline rush from bungee jumping or skydiving or any of those other daredevil activities, experiences that Africa also offers to the latest generation of tourists. The out-of-place sensation of swimming with sharks is something unique, a feeling that exists only in a certain conjunction of circumstances, circumstances that happen to come together in those parts of Africa we like to call "wilderness." In the cage, in that deafening silence of ocean currents, you can be freed of your past; you simply exist, subconsciously confident of your status as a protected observer in a completely foreign ecosystem. That is what happens to us in nature. That's the attraction Africa has held for generations of adventurers, from James Bruce and Mungo Park through David Livingstone and Henry Morton Stanley, and on to today's shark cage tourists swimming in their wet suits off the shores of Gansbaai. The land, the sharks—all becomes a backdrop for our own discoveries, our own revelations, our own adventures.

President Teddy Roosevelt described this strange mixture of peace, danger, and solitude in an account of his own African experience, a lengthy safari in eastern Africa that he undertook soon after leaving the White House. "There are no words," he wrote, "that can tell the hidden spirit of the wilderness, that can reveal its mystery, its melancholy and its charm." Like the explorers before him, Roosevelt embarked to Africa with great fanfare, scientific promises, and a deep sense of adventure. And like Park and Stanley and others, he brought his countrymen along with him, virtually, through his dispatches.

The first appearance of the word *safari* in the *New York Times* was in 1908, in an article about Roosevelt's preparations for his journey. The newspaper defined it as meaning "caravan," which in Roosevelt's case was quite fitting. The expedition included more than 250 porters, dozens of cases of Roosevelt's favorite champagne, and even a bathtub. Roosevelt's son Kermit was traveling with him, as were representatives of the Smithsonian Institution and renowned safari guide R. J. Cunninghame. The American public was fascinated, and eager to hear of the former president's latest exploits and discoveries.

Like the explorers of generations prior, Roosevelt depicted his adventure as, at its core, a groundbreaking scientific and ecological venture. He promised to collect specimens for the Smithsonian museums, to make a biological sketch of the current state of African wilderness, and to keep the American public apprised of the goings-on through regular written reports. The Smithsonian Institution agreed to underwrite the venture, as did many of Roosevelt's political backers, including Andrew Carnegie.

It was in the name of science, then, that Roosevelt and his group "collected" more than twenty-three thousand natural specimens during the yearlong safari, including more than five thousand mammals. The former president and his son alone killed more than fifty large "exotic" creatures such as elephants, rhinos, and lions. Members of the safari caravan ate some two hundred of the animals they shot, the former president reported; most of the others were brought back to the Smithsonian, where many were displayed for a long time in the well-loved Mammals Hall. Although there were close calls aplenty—Roosevelt once had to be rescued from a rampaging hippo—none of the white men were killed on the expedition, a fact of which Roosevelt was rather proud. And the African death toll was minor, the former president told audiences after his return. Just two black men had been killed by wildlife, he said, one "mauled by a leopard" and the other "tossed by a lion." And only "a very few died of dysentery and fever," the former president said, even though "it is almost impossible to make them take care of themselves."

"I have never passed a more interesting eleven months than I passed in Africa," Roosevelt told a National Geographic Society audience soon after his trip. "From the standpoint of the man interested in geography, in geology, in natural history, in ethnology, I do not know how one could put in his time to a greater advantage."

Roosevelt also began—without irony—to sound a warning that African wilderness was under threat. He feared, he said with some urgency, that the "melancholy and charm" he'd experienced would soon be gone, thanks largely to habitat destruction, human population increase, and poaching by local Africans. (He did not seem to feel that his own collecting exploits had anything to do with it.)

This was an important new twist to the long-standing tale of science and adventure, adding yet another variation to our standard narrative of engagement with Africa. Now an expedition could have not only the pretext of science, as with all those explorers of generations past, but also a moral imperative. We have to go see the animals before it is too late. We have to witness them—which, we somehow feel, will help save them.

But as all those dusty old lion carcasses in the Smithsonian storage rooms show, the journey into African nature has always been about us and our thrills. If you put adventure up against nature, adventure is always going to be the clear winner, no matter how much we try to spin our stories otherwise. That is what Michael Scholl found out with his work on the great white sharks.

Although Michael liked introducing humans to the beauty of the shark, he always cared first and foremost about the animals. It was no small concern to him that his own research had been instrumental in identifying Shark Alley, a spot so chock-full of sharks that tour opera-tors could basically guarantee their clients spine-tingling, adrenaline-filled encounters with the great whites. The discovery had been key for the cage diving business. But now, Michael explained to me, his research was leading him to believe that the waters were not just a migration spot but also a breeding ground for the great whites. If this was the case, he said, he would advocate for the section to be closed off to tourists. He wanted nature to win over adventure.

This did not please the tour operators, and Michael did not make many friends among the businesspeople trying to cash in on the American and European desire to dive with the sharks. Not long after my visit, he decided he was no longer able to continue his work in South Africa. Although increasing numbers of tourists wanted to see the sharks, and increasing numbers of commercial ventures sprang up to let them do so, there was very little money to support actual scientific research on the creatures. Michael moved back to Europe.

This struck me as somewhat sad, but I was not particularly surprised. Our stories about African nature are about us, so there's not much room for those who would like to introduce a different narrative. The same goes for our stories about Africa in general—in particular, the idea that Africa is a place we help. This became particularly clear to me one cold evening in the center of downtown Johannesburg, as I listened to a group of rock stars exhort the world to save African children from poverty.

3

Snapping for Africa

On the evening of July 2, 2005, I drove from my home in the leafy northern suburbs of Johannesburg to a revitalizing, artsy part of downtown called Newtown, where there was to be a large outdoor concert. In some ways this seemed like a rather questionable idea. Although the weather is relatively mild in Joburg (as most people who live there call the city), July can get downright bitter. It is the heart of the Southern Hemisphere winter. The air crackles with dryness, speckled with soot from veld blazes outside the city and from paraffin fires lit in the sprawling shantytowns, where there are few other ways to stay warm. In short, it is not a time of year when you want to stand around outside in a plaza and cheer for musicians.

But this concert was supposed to be a big deal. It was the African component of the Live8 festival, one of the largest international charity rock concerts to be held since Live Aid introduced the concept in 1985. Millions of concertgoers were gathering simultaneously in places like Paris, London, Philadelphia, and Tokyo to watch A-list musicians and to join, as organizer-slash-Irish-rocker Bob Geldof said, in "the long walk to justice." As everyone in South Africa recognized, this was a clear reference to Nelson Mandela's autobiography, *Long Walk to Freedom*. But in this case the justice in question was arguably even more grandiose, if rather mushier, than Mandela's fight to end apartheid. Geldof and his colleagues wanted to end poverty, and all the ills associated with it—which, according to them, included AIDS, hunger, malaria, war, corruption, political instability, violations of women's and children's rights, and environmental degradation, among various other woes.

Geldof and his associates had timed the Live8 festival to take place right before a planned meeting of the wealthy G8 countries, all of whom, activists believed, should be giving more money and other assistance to the poor countries of the world. It also marked the twentieth anniversary of Live Aid, which Geldof had likewise organized.

I was just old enough to remember Live Aid. It was a rock concert—or, rather, two rock concerts, held simultaneously in London and Philadelphia—broadcast to billions of people around the world using a multiple-satellite feed system that was technologically unprecedented at the time. I remember watching it on a boxy television at my mother's house in Baltimore, vaguely wondering what all those people were doing. Later I would learn (or maybe some adult tried to explain it to me) that Live Aid was connected to the famine then devastating Ethiopia.

It was, indeed, a terrible famine. According to scholarly studies, about half a million people died of starvation in Ethiopia and Eritrea between 1983 and 1985; a frequently cited United Nations estimate places the number of deaths at a million. Rain in many parts of the country was scarce, food reserves were tapped out, and communities were roiled by sickness. A news team from the BBC, the first Western outlet to report on the events, described the scene as "Hell on earth." Geldof and his colleagues wanted to force the Western public to focus on the devastation and to raise money to help the suffering people. So, with one of the largest television events in history, Geldof and the others tried to create a new narrative of Africa. Africa was not remote, dangerous, and scary, their story went. Rather, it was poor, sympathetic, and in need of aid. The Live Aid insignia, which the Live8 extravaganza would later copy, was a guitar shaped like the continent of Africa, juxtaposed with the back of an emaciated black child.

Sure enough, when I think back to that original Live Aid concert, I remember seeing terrible images of stick-thin black children and feeling vaguely somber and guilty. I definitely absorbed the idea that things in Africa were pretty bad, that maybe my family should donate seventy cents a day to save someone over there, and that I should eat my dinner because children there were starving. This was an elementary school child's perspective, of course, but it's not far from what many Americans and Europeans of all ages took away from Geldof's successful storytelling. In those hours of music—from the first chords of "Rockin' All Over the World" to Bono's impromptu dance with an audience member, a moment that helped catapult his band, U2, to international stardom—Africa was always present, the central cause for all these voices, yet notably passive and silent. It was just waiting for our help, even as flies buzzed around its eyes.

This story was as lasting and influential as it was simplistic. In 2002 a poll by the British organization Voluntary Service Overseas (VSO) found that almost two decades after the concert Western perceptions of the developing world were still shaped by what researchers called the "Live Aid Legacy." Eighty percent of the British public, they found, "strongly associate the developing world with doom-laden images of famine, disaster and Western aid." Seventy-four percent believed that developing countries "depend on the money and knowledge of the West to progress."

"The Live Aid Legacy defines the roles in our relationship with the developing world," the researchers wrote. "We are powerful, benevolent givers; they are grateful receivers." Plus, we think we know a lot more than we do. "Unconsciously accumulated images of the developing world have led to a certainty on the part of consumers that they have all the facts," the poll takers noted.

Take that Ethiopian famine, for example. Few Americans and Europeans ever learned the nuances of that disaster, including the fact that parts of Ethiopia had more than enough food to go around during this time: the famine was as much a result of civil war and internal political strife as it was of food shortages. And few heard the argument that the aid dollars coming in actually prolonged the conflict and forced villagers to move into government camps, where an estimated one out of six people died. Instead, our narrative started and ended with giving money to help the skeletal children in Africa.

The Live Aid story was still going strong when I stood shivering at Mary Fitzgerald Square in Johannesburg twenty years later. But it had also evolved. In the 1980s the emphasis was explicitly on saving, as in "This pitiful child will die if we don't help her right now." By 2005 the rhetoric had become more about fixing, or even solving. This was a reflection of what was going on in the larger philanthropic world, particularly in the United States, where observers noted a decided shift away from the broad, morals-based giving that had been characteristic of the large donors of most of the twentieth century.

In general, those big-name philanthropists of the 1900s—Andrew Carnegie, John Rockefeller, and their ilk—were basically motivated to give because they believed that if you made a ton of money, it was simply the right thing to do to give much of it away. They wanted to uplift humanity, so they gave huge sums to institutions that they figured were doing that, such as libraries and colleges.

By the end of the century, though, this humanistic giving had been replaced by a much more technocratic approach, one that has been called everything from "philanthrocapitalism" to "social entrepreneurship." No longer did donors and activists find it satisfying or appropriate simply to give money away and assume that a large organization would know what to do with it. Instead, they wanted to use their money, or their star power, to change the world in specific ways. They studied the problems and, for a variety of reasons—which have been linked to everything from the tech revolution, with its emphasis on the individual entrepreneur, to an overall cultural uptick in narcissism—these donor activists often decided that *they* were the best people to come up with solutions.

In the United States this meant that charitable institutions saw a

dramatic decline in unrestricted giving, while more donors were funding or founding specific programs and initiatives. The number of private
philanthropic foundations in the United States skyrocketed: one-third
of the country's family foundations were created in the 2000s. And
there was an awful lot of hope that if we could just set the best minds
of commerce, tech, and entrepreneurship loose on the world's big problems, soon enough we would have a much better world.

This optimism changed how people thought of Africa. Although
many in the West, as that British poll found, still viewed the continent
through the Live Aid lens of woe, it was also becoming a place of hope.
This was particularly true among a growing group of celebrity activists, from Bill Gates and Bill Clinton to Angelina Jolie and Bono, who
regularly appeared on the continent and often talked about how much
they loved Africa. These international A-listers jumped into the sorts
of causes that two decades earlier would decidedly not have prompted
an international benefit concert. Bono, for instance, became a global
celebrity spokesperson for the somewhat shockingly unsexy cause of
debt relief, which involves wealthier countries forgiving loans they've
made to poorer ones. Clinton lobbied for mass access to generic drugs
to treat HIV; Gates pushed for data-driven analyses of maternal and
infant mortality.

These new celebrity activists realized that the suffering they saw
across the world was complex and interconnected, and often involved
causes that did not work particularly well in films or snappy advertisements. (Think access to clean water, another big Gates cause.) This did
not dissuade them from their work, however. To the contrary. At the
heart of all this wonky passion was a belief that we should not just help
mitigate the impact of an immediate disaster, such as a famine, but also
make long-term changes to the structure of society itself. As the Live8
organizers said, we could "make poverty history."

Getting rid of poverty was big that year. Earlier in 2005 the scholar
and activist Jeffrey Sachs, of Columbia University, had published a book
that would become a sort of bible to many in this circle. It was called
The End of Poverty, and its argument is essentially that, without any
really uncomfortable redistribution of wealth, the rich world could give

a bit of aid, make some smart policy changes, help Africans do the same, and more or less eliminate the traumas of being brutally poor. The impoverished of the world could gain better standards of living, better health care, and better lives, all at very little cost to the rest of us.

In that same year, Sachs also founded the Millennium Promise Alliance, a nonprofit dedicated to helping the world meet a series of lofty poverty-reduction goals set by the United Nations. A central project of the nonprofit involved creating Millennium Villages, model sites that would, as the organization put it, "demonstrate the power of practical, low-cost and community-led approaches to poverty alleviation that can be replicated at scale by developing nations around the world."

In other words, the Live Aid story that Africa needed help, and needed help from us, was still going strong. But now it was being augmented by data, economic theory, and real, live test case settlements. Ending something like "poverty"—an abstract noun, mind you, whose very definition would be hotly debated if you got a sociologist, economist, and anthropologist in a room—was seen as totally possible. All we had to do was be smart about it, and act.

Or, as I would soon find out, snap.

As the concert staff performed sound checks onstage, the Johannesburg crowd milled around the plaza. The event was not even close to a sellout, but there seemed to be a modest trickle of concertgoers arriving.

On nearby streets, the city's strange army of unofficial parking attendants—a staple of any commercial area in Johannesburg—ran among arriving cars, waving flags to urge drivers into various lots and spaces and then requesting payment to "watch" the vehicles. To an outsider, the scene could look chaotic, but these car guards, as they are called, actually have an intricate hierarchy, and most people who live in Joburg have an innate understanding of what should be paid to whom to ensure that your car still exists when you return from dinner. The juxtaposition of shiny cars and barefoot hustlers might seem uncomfortable, but that was Johannesburg, a place of red dust and abandoned skyscrapers, hawkers and hedge fund managers, boisterous salsa clubs and bougainvillea-draped gardens locked up behind electric fences. The city sprawled, like a Los Angeles with highways built only for a white, car-owning minority. City officials were working to draw moneyed residents back downtown, which was widely considered to be (and often was) dangerously crime-ridden. The Newtown district, with its theaters and restaurants, a popular art gallery and coffee shop, was a key part of this effort. It was perfect, city officials had decided, for a concert like this one.

Onstage, some local musicians began warming up. Some big African names were scheduled to perform for us that evening, including Zola, the *kwaito* star who became internationally known for his score to the Oscar-winning movie *Tsotsi*, and the reggae star Lucky Dube, who would be murdered two years later in a classic Johannesburg carjacking. The other venues, though, had all the big international stars—everyone from Elton John to Snoop Dogg, Madonna to the Barenaked Ladies, Jay-Z to Bryan Adams. And U2—of course there was U2. The enterprise was, in large part, a Bono production.

We saw some of the scenes from those concerts broadcast on the jumbo screens set up around the stage: massive, pale-skinned crowds gathered in London, Philadelphia, Tokyo, Paris; revelers stripping off their T-shirts and spraying one another with water guns. In Johannesburg, one of the opening bands played a set, and a few people toward the front of the still largely empty plaza began to dance. But most just milled around, chatting.

In the other cities, the concertgoers screamed like crazy for their musicians. In Johannesburg the crowd was generally more muted—until, that is, Nelson Mandela walked onstage. The former South African president and Nobel Peace Prize winner was nearing his eighty-seventh birthday, and he was quite frail. His public appearances had become limited, his privacy increasingly guarded by his handlers and his devoted wife, the former Mozambican first lady Graça Machel. Still, he cut an electric figure as he walked to the podium, white hair framing his familiar face and squinting eyes, which were permanently damaged by decades of chopping blinding-bright rock at the Robben Island prison quarry. The crowd went crazy, dancing and singing, breaking into the sort of spontaneous, amazingly on-pitch harmony that regularly astonished me at public events in South Africa. Some people shot their fists into the air, the antiapartheid gesture that would accompany a cry of *Amandla!* ("Power!") and the crowd's response, *Awethu!* ("To us!").

Mandela's voice brought the crowd to silence.

"Massive poverty and obscene inequality are such terrible scourges of our times," he began. He spoke about how the G8 leaders needed to focus on the rest of the world and address the wealth disparities head-on. He talked about how this inequality was injustice, and how the peoples of wealthy nations needed to recognize the perpetuation of these evils in their own attitudes and lifestyles. "Overcoming poverty is not a gesture of charity," he said. "It is a protection of a fundamental human right."

And then, in his Mandela way, he rhetorically embraced his audience—all of it, from those in the plaza in Johannesburg to the wealthy white crowds across the world.

"Sometimes it falls upon a generation to be great," he said. "You be that great generation. . . . Let your greatness blossom. Of course the task will not be easy. But not to do this would be a crime against humanity against which I ask all humanity now to rise up."

The crowd in the Joburg plaza looked both moved and proud. When the music started up again, it seemed there was a bit more enthusiasm, a bit more verve in the dancing. All were stirred by this black African man speaking to the world with unparalleled moral authority.

But then the music quieted. From Europe, over the jumbo screens, one of the Live8 organizers asked the concertgoers all over the world to snap their fingers. To snap together, once every three seconds. Because that, he and the all-star performers would repeat regularly over the next hour, was how often an African child "died of poverty."

Around me, people huddled in their winter jackets. African people. Some looked around sheepishly, embarrassed. Others stared at the international feeds as if the organizers had gone crazy. Then it started. Snap. Snap. Snap. The people in Joburg joined in halfheartedly. Snap.

Elsewhere, the concertgoers took the job seriously. The white people in Paris stopped twirling their shirts. In Philly they stopped cheering, as if to concentrate on the somberness of the moment. In Edinburgh they looked reflective.

Snap, snap, snap.

Then the music started again on the big screens that flashed pictures of warmer weather and bigger, wealthier concerts. The white people stopped snapping and began to dance again, screaming for Pink Floyd or Mariah Carey or Shakira.

In Johannesburg, the people in the plaza looked at one another again.

We would snap our fingers quite a bit that evening, not without some grim humor. After all, Africans were dying! Right now! Heck, the guy next to you might have only two more seconds to live!

As sophisticated as the Live Aid message had become in twenty years, the basic narrative was still there.

According to the concert's organizers, Live8 was a huge success. "We couldn't have made it clearer that we expect the politicians of this generation to end the scandal of stupid, immoral poverty," they announced on their website. Indeed, the music festival prompted thirty million people to add their names to a list that the organizers brought to Tony Blair, then the prime minister of Great Britain and the chair of the G8. Within a week, the G8 leaders agreed on a series of goals to reduce poverty and suffering in Africa. They promised to double annual aid to Africa by 2010. They said there should be AIDS drugs for everyone who needed them, and care for all AIDS orphans on the continent. They pledged to invest in bed nets to fight malaria. They agreed that all children should have free primary education and basic health care.

It was a beautiful, simple story. The world wanted change, and joining together, snapping our fingers in unison, could truly help end the suffering of the poor.

But as it turns out, things didn't work that way. Only a year later, the organizers behind Live8 and some of the related antipoverty movements were exhorting world leaders to "keep their promises" about tackling the problems of Africa. The nonprofit group Oxfam reported that some of the G8 countries had simply failed to make their promised foreign aid allocations. Those of us who looked beneath the surface found even more of a mess: a spiderweb of international contractors, aid sent with devastating economic strings attached, accounting acrobatics that categorized military assistance as food aid. Overall, the developing world did see improvement on many of the UN antipoverty measures, but a lot of those gains in the standard of living had to do with macroeconomic development in China and India, not G8 aid. And while the total amount of foreign aid did increase somewhat, the aid gap (the difference between the promised amount of aid and the amount actually delivered) was growing, and would continue to do so throughout the 2000s.

None of this was a particularly big surprise to those of us who stood in that square in Johannesburg—clearly the most low-budget and hastily put-together concert in the whole international benefit festival— snapping our fingers uncomfortably alongside Africans who were essentially being told that they were fragile and ready to die. Nor was it a surprise to many of the journalists covering the region. We had repeatedly seen the stark difference between the Live Aid story, in whatever form, and the reality on the ground.

The laundry list of misguided efforts to "help Africa" was extensive. There were massive road projects now crumbling because there had been no money budgeted for repairs. In Mozambique, I reported on the decimation of the country's once-thriving cashew industry, a tragedy that stemmed directly from policies dictated by the World Bank. (The bank later acknowledged mishandling the situation, but by that time the factories were closed and scores of people had lost their jobs.) We saw Western high school trips that sent privileged white teenagers to build houses for South Africans who were professional builders; completely unprepared college students offering to solve the AIDS crisis on their summer breaks; and, one of my personal favorites, a soccer nonprofit offering training in the sport for rural African children. (Anyone who has spent any time in rural Africa knows that soccer instruction is about the last thing anyone there needs from us.)

It was enough to make one more than a little jaded. And indeed, around the same time that we were seeing a rise in the technocratic version of the Live Aid story, a new story was also gaining popularity. This one said that we should rethink the whole enterprise of foreign aid. Economist and former World Bank employee William Easterly, for instance, blasted the fundamental ineptitude of aid efforts. The West spent $2.3 trillion on foreign aid over the second half of the twentieth century, he pointed out, yet impoverished children still can't get twelve-cent medicines that would prevent half of all malaria deaths. He contrasted this with the West's ability, in the same month as the Live8 concerts, to deliver nine million copies of the latest Harry Potter novel to its fans in a single day.

Others took the idea even further, arguing that we shouldn't be giving foreign aid to Africa at all—not because we don't care, mind you, but because foreign aid can actually do more harm than good. According to this story, aid undermines local institutions, disrupts local economies, and often leaves people more dependent than they were before we swept in. The African-born, Harvard-educated Goldman Sachs economist Dambisa Moyo turned this argument into the book *Dead Aid*, a *New York Times* best seller that became hugely popular with neoconservatives and some African leaders. Rwandan president Paul Kagame reportedly bought a copy of the book for everyone in his cabinet.

Many of us who wrote about failed aid projects were open to these anti-aid arguments, and found the reaction from aid proponents a bit histrionic. ("Books like that—they're promoting evil," Bill Gates said of *Dead Aid*.) Still, completely abandoning all aid to the continent somehow felt wrong, even to the most cynical journalists. It seemed a suspiciously convenient match for a neoconservative political stance that idolized the free market above all else. In our view, there just were benefits to, say, providing access to antiretroviral drugs for everyone in AIDS-ravaged countries. Did that solve the very complicated problem of HIV transmission, or necessarily reduce poverty? Was it the very best way to fight the disease? No, no, and no. Still, we saw firsthand that getting people drugs stopped them from dying. The same was true for a variety of aid projects. We saw that a village that got a new, clean drinking well had, for as long as the well worked, fewer cases of diarrhea, one of the leading causes of death among children in Africa.

Even more fundamentally, though, I suspect that giving up on foreign assistance to Africa felt wrong to us because "helping Africa" is part of our own narrative. As journalists, we cherished the sentiment that we traveled the developing world not simply for our own thrills, but because our reporting might, in some way, improve or enlighten or connect. The essential Western story of a vulnerable Africa that needs our support was, after all, woven into the fabric of our culture from the first missionaries onward.

Why has that narrative proven so long-lasting? Some say it is grounded in the religious tenet of helping one's neighbor. Others say it's a convenient cover for our real desires: our lust for adventure and conquest. Still others suggest that the "Africa needs our help" story is a handy excuse to look away from our own inequalities and troubles at home yet still feel good about ourselves, a salve for our culpability in this racially and economically imbalanced world. Whatever the reason, the story is there, and we believe in it deeply. Despite the various arguments against aid, at the time of the Live8 concerts most Westerners concerned with African issues felt that the real question was simply how to make aid more effective.

This was as true in the realm of conservation as elsewhere. While scholars and economists debated the best way to help impoverished people in the developing world, some of the rich do-gooders began to turn their attention to environmental preservation. The big, lumbering nonprofits had not been successful in helping the environment, ran the conventional wisdom in this technocratic group. Maybe it was time for some new, entrepreneurial ideas. For many, Africa looked like the perfect place to test out groundbreaking environmental initiatives—initiatives that, when you stepped back, could sometimes appear mindbogglingly odd.

4

The Eco Barons

I had my first close look at the world of wealthy environmental do-gooders in the starkly beautiful center of South Africa, in a scrub desert land known as the Karoo. There, not far from a sleepy little Afrikaner farming village called Philippolis (whose tourism brochures tout "peace and quiet" as well as the annual "white lightning home-brewed liquor festival"), was a large plot of land newly designated as the Laohu Valley Reserve. This was, I had learned, the center of one of southern Africa's most eccentric conservation efforts: the Save China's Tigers animal breeding and rehabilitation project.

Tigers, mind you, do not live in Africa. And the particular kind of tiger Laohu Valley was to focus on, a subspecies called the South China tiger, barely lives anywhere at all. At the time I went to Laohu Valley, in the early 2000s, conservationists estimated that there might be as few as ten South China tigers still in the wild. But none of this had dissuaded a Chinese-born former Gucci executive named Li Quan and her multimillionaire American financier husband, Stuart Bray.

The two came up with their quirky conservation project not long after Quan, a graduate of the University of Pennsylvania's Wharton

School, quit her fast-paced job in the fashion world to settle down with Bray in London. The couple had wanted to be in the same place, with a less hectic lifestyle, they explained, and frankly, money was not an issue. But soon, Quan said, she found herself with too much time on her hands. Too much time and too much mental energy, she explained. "I'm someone who likes to be *doing* things," she said, fingering the cat necklace I always saw her wearing. She had long been an animal lover, she said, and she had been growing increasingly concerned about news reports she saw on the status of the South China tiger, her native country's cultural emblem. But she didn't have any idea what to do about it until she and Bray traveled to South Africa on a luxury safari. Then it all clicked. What if, she began to think, they brought tigers here from China? They could rehabilitate them, breed them, and eventually return them to China, where Quan and Bray would, in the meanwhile, have built the sort of nature areas that the tigers could live in. As it was, they explained, the tiger's natural habitat in China was almost entirely destroyed.

It was an immensely ambitious scheme. And at first, Bray said, his reaction was something along the lines of "You've got to be kidding me." But Quan started calling her contacts in China, began researching conservation and land in South Africa, and drew up a plan. Eventually, Bray agreed to pay the start-up costs for the Save China's Tigers project. The couple bought and combined seventeen sheep farms outside Philippolis, hired conservation experts and wildlife managers in South Africa, and imported four South China zoo tigers, whom they named Hope, Cathay, Madonna, and TigerWoods. (This was before the golfer's sex scandal, so the name seemed a relatively wholesome pick.) Li and her team intended to "rewild" the big cats: to teach them how to hunt and to prepare them and their offspring for the wilderness that the project hoped to create.

All this, I will admit, seemed crazy to me. But in the story we tell about who can save the world, crazy isn't necessarily regarded as bad. To the contrary: in the tech boom, "crazy ideas" were morphing into multibillion-dollar companies, and entrepreneurs were lauded for thinking far "outside the box." There was a sense that long-shot risks could bring in lots of money or create a better society, and sometimes even both at the same time. Indeed, by the turn of the twenty-first century, the line between commercial and social good was becoming increasingly blurred. Recall, for instance, Apple's Think Different campaign from the late 1990s. This hugely successful advertising blitz put—without irony—Martin Luther King Jr., Mahatma Gandhi, Joan Baez, Jackie Robinson, and various other "misfits, rebels, and troublemakers," as the television commercial said, in the same category as Steve Jobs and the consumer smart enough to buy a Mac. "The people who are crazy enough to think they can change the world are the ones who do," the commercial explained.

The cultural mushiness that put fighting for human rights and succeeding in business into the same "changing the world" category helped fuel the growing perception that those who did the latter could also effectively do the former. By the end of the 1990s, the very fact of being rich seemed to bestow far-reaching credentials. The extremely wealthy—who, thanks to increasing income inequality, were more removed than ever from the rest of the population, in both income and lifestyle—also inhabited their own can-do, change-the-world social class. Both within the vaunted "1 percent" and outside it, the cultural assumption was that if you had made it to the financial stratosphere, you could probably do just about anything. Run for president, perhaps. Or solve world hunger. Or, as with Quan and Bray, save the environment in groundbreaking new ways.

Indeed, around the time that the Save China's Tigers project was getting under way, a number of other do-gooder multimillionaires also decided to make the environment a particular focus of their activities. They bought up vast tracts of land around the world and spoke passionately about the importance of preserving nature. Though they did not coordinate their efforts with one another, they would become known collectively as the "eco barons," thanks in large part to a book of that name by journalist Edward Humes lauding their activism.

Humes's list of eco barons showcases people such as Doug Tompkins, cofounder of the clothing companies North Face and Esprit. After a divorce, Tompkins moved to Chile to live the life of an outdoorsman, and he became distressed by the threats facing the spectacular wilderness there. Eventually, he realized that he could protect land simply by buying it—and that's what he did, plot by plot, until he owned more than two million acres of Patagonia, which he then turned into protected areas.

Other eco barons included Roxanne Quimby, the creator of Burt's Bees, who conserved more than a hundred thousand acres of Maine forest; Dutch business mogul Paul Fentener van Vlissingen, who created the African Parks Network; and even Richard Branson, of Virgin fame and fortune, who exported endangered Madagascar lemurs to one of his private islands in the Caribbean. There were also numerous conservation philanthropists of slightly lesser wealth who were likewise trying to see what they could do, on their own, for the environment around the world.

Part of their motivation was a growing disillusionment with what had become known as Big Green. This was the collective label for the organizations that dominate the multibillion-dollar international conservation industry, such as the Nature Conservancy and the World Wildlife Fund (known outside the United States and Canada as the World Wide Fund for Nature). While these groups are often regarded as the good guy underdogs of the planet—as lovable as the panda on the WWF logo—the Big Green organizations have budgets and public relation machines that often dwarf the resources of many of the countries where they work. The Nature Conservancy, for instance, has billions of dollars in assets, owns two million acres of land in the United States, and has established multimillion-dollar partnerships with governments and corporations. Conservation International claims $165 million in annual revenue. The WWF has projects in more than a hundred countries. These organizations are involved in just about every sort of nature-related program one can imagine, from zoo exhibits in the United States to ranger training classes in Zambia and park development in Taiwan. They fund a dizzying array of research programs; employ an army of scientists, game rangers, and fund-raisers; and lead the way in identifying those spots of the world that should—for the betterment of nature, humanity, and Mother Earth, they say—be protected.

In other words, they are exactly the sort of expansive, bureaucratic, fingers-in-every-pie institutions that were falling out of favor at the turn of the twenty-first century. Indeed, around the time that eco barons were emerging on the conservation scene, Big Green agencies were facing growing criticism, charged with everything from "conservation colonialism" to cozy ties with big business. This latter complaint proved particularly sticky. Many Big Green groups accept millions of dollars in donations from companies such as Shell Oil, Chiquita, and McDonald's, and in many instances they actually collaborate with oil and gas companies on both conservation projects and extraction plans. The conservation groups say these partnerships are important both for funding purposes and to help guide corporations into the most sustainable practices in otherwise dirty industries. Critics, though, call it "greenwashing." After the 2010 Deepwater Horizon disaster, for instance, when a British Petroleum–leased oil rig exploded and sent millions of barrels of oil gushing into the Gulf of Mexico, the Nature Conservancy faced questions about its close relationship with a company that, news reports were revealing, had dismal environmental and safety standards. It turned out that not only had BP bought land for the Nature Conservancy, but at least one of BP's top officials sat on the Nature Conservancy board. A former Nature Conservancy staffer wrote that when she was in meetings, any criticism of the oil company was taboo.

If all that wasn't enough to dull enthusiasm about these green crusaders, there was another, more fundamental problem with their efforts, one that was particularly resonant in our data-driven age. Despite all the hundreds of millions of dollars spent every year on conservation, despite all the land purchases and new national parks and animals brought back from the edge of extinction, the world is still facing the same environmental crises—perhaps even worse ones—as it did when all those groups were formed. Of course, it's possible to make the argument that if Big Green didn't exist, the global environmental situation would be even worse. Still, it's hard to avoid the impression that, in many ways, the conservation industry mirrors the humanitarian assistance industry, with alarmist pledge drives, heart-stirring photos, and admonitions to "act now!"—all to be repeated for the next grant cycle.

In 2011 the National Committee for Responsive Philanthropy received a report from a well-respected consultant named Sarah Hansen. In her write-up, which created quite a stir in the philanthropic world, she urged grant-making organizations to start looking for grass-roots alternatives to Big Green—a position that was picked up and repeated by a number of environmental critics. She noted that in the United States, despite at least ten billion dollars in grants given to environmental causes from 2000 to 2009, there were few positive changes either to the overall environmental situation or to public policy surrounding the environment. Instead, she wrote, despite this massive amount of funding—more than half of which flowed to a handful of Big Green organizations, much of it explicitly earmarked for advocacy and policy purposes—the United States in fact witnessed a significant amount of backsliding in environmental policy over the decade.

Other researchers have made similar critiques of Big Green abroad. Kenya-based conservationist and economist Mike Norton-Griffiths, for instance, has called the Big Green organizations operating in East Africa ineffective, and has dubbed many of the tour operators connected to national parks "tourism cartels." Many of the policies pushed by the big conservation groups have backfired, he says—and, in his view, predictably so.

All this, of course, prompts the question: where else can we turn? If giving money to Big Green doesn't work—if the world is still losing biodiversity, if habitat loss threatens a growing number of species across the globe, if accelerating deforestation is leaving already marginalized people with infertile land and contaminated water, if pollution is continuing to poison our oceans, air, and land—well, then, what else should we do?

The eco barons' answers to that question were often unorthodox, and their projects regularly created controversy. Yet the press about them was almost always glowing. At the beginning of the new century, the eco barons were just what we thought we needed.

When Quan and Bray invited me to see their tiger sanctuary for myself, I was eager to go. I was willing to give them the benefit of the doubt.

So I found myself standing in the back of a truck with a South African wildlife expert named Peter Openshaw, who had been hired as the

Laohu Valley Reserve's manager. His crew had just dumped three springbok carcasses into a clearing in front of us, part of a large fenced sanctuary. (There were multiple enclosures of different sizes on the property, all part of a strategy to gradually increase the tigers' independence, range, and hunting abilities.) The tiger named Hope had died earlier in the project, but the other three were thriving, and Peter wanted to show me how far they had progressed since being brought to South Africa. When the cats first got here, he explained, they were so used to zoo meals of chopped-up meat that they didn't even realize that antelope were prey. Instead of taking a bite out of a carcass, they would just bat it around like a toy. But they were quick learners, he said. He blew a whistle. Next to him, his wife, Ronel, who also worked on the conservation team, held a fire extinguisher, her big cat version of the kitchen spritzer.

Within seconds, the tigers emerged from the thorn trees.

Tigers are beautiful cats. Unlike an African lion's sandy blond coat, which tends to look a bit scruffy when one gets up close, the tiger's fur is stunning: deep amber orange, with thick black stripes down the side and around the eyes like mascara. The fur right next to the eyes is white, which intensifies the iris's yellow-amber glow.

Although it is believed to be the original type of tiger, from which all other tiger subspecies evolved, the South China tiger is relatively small as big cats go. The males measure only about eight feet long and a bit over three hundred pounds, while the females are lighter still. As I stood on the back of that pickup truck, though, there was no mistaking the animals for anything "cute." Their carnivorous skill quickly became apparent. The cats padded slowly toward the antelope bodies, as if taking their time to make sure there was no trick. Tigers are naturally cautious hunters: they like to trap their prey with cunning—ambushing them from behind a rock, say, or cornering them at a reserve fence—rather than sprinting. Within a minute or so, though, they had decided this was, indeed, lunch. The first tiger pounced, locked its jaws around the carcass's death-twisted neck, and grabbed it in a sort of massive-pawed hug. Then the cats stumbled back to the shrubs, dragging their meat with them.

Peter was thrilled. "Look at that, hey," he said. In the wild, tigers kill in exactly this way: after a windpipe-crushing bite to the neck, they carry their prey off to the bushes, where they can take their time eating it. And eat they do—even the smallish South China tiger can consume some ninety pounds of meat in one sitting.

The antelopes that Cathay, Madonna, and TigerWoods were "hunting" that day were, admittedly, already dead. But it was a key first step, Openshaw said. And he was also seeing improvement in the way the big cats tried to approach the living antelope he had stocked elsewhere in the reserve. At first the tigers would run straight at the herbivores, who would in turn bolt and outrun them. Now the cats were getting a bit sneakier. (All this dismayed local animal rights activists, who had already filed legal complaints against Peter and the tiger project, saying it was cruel to allow African antelopes to be practice prey for a foreign species. The case was soon thrown out.)

Peter was the first to admit that he had had misgivings about Quan and her idea when he first heard about it. "I was quite wary," he said. As a bush veteran and longtime wildlife manager, he felt uncomfortable with the notion of introducing any alien species into an environment, even a species as endangered as the tiger. But the more he understood her plan, and the more he accepted that the goal really was to return the tigers to China, the more he felt willing to work with the project. Now, he said, he felt like he was involved in something groundbreaking and exciting.

I spent the rest of the visit driving with Peter and Ronel around the reserve, a pastel landscape of blonds and pinks and blues dotted with the tans and browns of antelope on the horizon. It was breathtaking in its sparseness. We spent a good deal of time at the tigers' smaller enclosures, where I realized somewhat uncomfortably that the male named TigerWoods, who I first thought was just pacing back and forth behind his tall metal fence, was actually mirroring my every move. The hunting instruction had been so effective that he was now keenly interested in the smallest person around: the easiest prey.

By the time I left, I still thought the project was unusual, but I also imagined that it might work. Who knows? I thought. Maybe the sort of executive know-how and energy Quan and Bray had brought to this desperate species could help. The two were out-of-the-box thinkers.

They were changemakers. And everyone knew that changemakers changed the world.

Now, to pause here: I just had to force myself to type that word, *changemakers*. It is one of those words that make journalists cringe, a made-up term that has somehow permeated our culture, showing up everywhere from TED talks to NGO job descriptions, from television advertisements to educational policy papers. It hardly even existed before the 1990s, other than to describe an automated cash register that spat out coins. Today its connotation is a positive, even fawning one: we love the idea of the intellectually superior (and preferably also cash-endowed) savior riding in like Clint Eastwood, shaking up the town, and changing things for the better. It is one of our treasured stories, combining the lure of individualism with a sanitized nostalgia for the countercultural, which is now safely confined within the bounds of capitalism.

There has been quite a bit written about the growing cult of the "good" capitalist. David Brooks's book *Bobos in Paradise* highlights how much the bohemian counterculture movement of the 1960s has merged with capitalistic enterprise—to the point that if you hear about, say, artisans using sustainable practices to transform our mealtime experience, you could equally well be learning about a village of cheese makers in the Andes or the newest plate collection sold at Crate and Barrel. This notion of the beneficent capitalist has made it easy to mistake mere mercantilism for actual altruism.

Take, for instance, another eco baron story, about a certain wealthy American who believed that nature held the answer to the economic and development woes of the country of Mozambique. This is not about Greg Carr, the philanthropist who flew to the top of Mount Gorongosa to meet with the rainmaker. (We will return to his story soon.) This tale is different, and chronologically it comes first. Its protagonist is James Ulysses Blanchard III: adventurer, billionaire, anticommunist, and, apparently, nature lover.

Jim Blanchard was a wheelchair-bound Louisiana tycoon who made his fortune in the 1970s by turning his coin-collecting hobby into a hundred-million-dollar-a-year company. Not only did Blanchard sell rare coins, but he also offered financial strategies and other advice to fellow Americans interested in adding precious metals to their investment portfolios. He was devoted to gold and became one of the leading voices in the United States advocating for "real currency" and for the American public's right to own the metal. (Private possession of gold was outlawed in the United States in 1933, and remained illegal until 1975.) He was also a devotee of the writings of Ayn Rand, even naming his son Anthem after the title of one of her books.

To those on the right, Blanchard was a superhero. Although he had been paralyzed in a car accident at the age of seventeen, he was known as a daredevil, flying planes and going scuba diving. He hired a biplane to buzz President Richard Nixon's 1973 inauguration while trailing a "Legalize Gold" banner, and continued to taunt law enforcement officials for the next year as he held press conferences across the country, holding up gold bars and daring authorities to arrest him.

His biographers and friends describe Blanchard as a man of many hobbies. He collected old guns and built a detailed replica of a Wild West saloon at his suburban New Orleans home. Despite being unable to use his legs, he planned an expedition with his son to the North Pole, so that Anthem could be entered into the *Guinness Book of World Records* as the youngest traveler to the region. He also dabbled in clandestine anticommunist activities, befriending Oliver North and helping funnel guns to rebel groups across the world—including in Mozambique, where the Renamo rebel movement was waging a protracted campaign against Frelimo, the country's Marxist ruling party.

"One of Jim Blanchard's favorite foreign projects was assisting anticommunist rebel forces inside war-torn Mozambique in the 1980s and early 1990s," wrote fellow gold bug Lawrence W. Reed in *The Freeman*, the magazine of the fervently free-market Foundation for Economic Education. "He once sent a colleague and me on a clandestine journey inside the country to live for two weeks with the rebels in the bush and help spread a pro-freedom message. Once the war was over and Mozambique adopted policies friendly to private property and free markets, Jim pitched in to assist in reconstruction."

Reed did not specify what sort of "pro-freedom message" they were spreading, or how they went about doing so. The conflict in Mozambique was remarkable at the time for what observers described as senseless destruction. The Renamo rebel group was best known for employing child soldiers, brutally terrifying villagers, and obliterating every inch of infrastructure in the territories it captured. The Frelimo government committed its own atrocities.

But if the message-spreading mission was nebulous, Blanchard's efforts to "assist in reconstruction" were not. In the early 1990s, after Renamo gave up violent resistance and became an opposition political party, Blanchard approached the war-fatigued Mozambican government with a grand environmental and economic plan. He told officials that he wanted to turn a beautiful but combat-ravaged swath of the country into one of the world's most incredible game parks. The area he focused on was a district called Matutuine, nestled between South Africa, Swaziland, and the Indian Ocean on the southern edge of Mozambique. It was the perfect place for a new eco escape: a quick jaunt from Maputo, the country's capital, with miles of cinnamon-sand beaches, leatherback turtle nests, and an elephant reserve that, before the war, boasted impressive pachyderm sightings. Blanchard's plans were big: he would bring a hundred million dollars in investment to the cash-strapped nation, he said, if he could reintroduce animals to the area and develop a high-quality, high-priced game reserve, complete with floating casino, golf course, rolling luxury train hotel, private residences, and scuba-diving safaris. He wasn't just throwing this money around, he explained. He fully expected to regain his investment and more.

It was a tempting offer for a government that was just beginning its struggle to recover from decades of war and famine. And by this point the Frelimo government had, for various reasons, moved away from its socialist roots and adopted a series of free-market reforms. Still, many within the ruling party had their doubts. Wasn't this Blanchard the neocon, the mercenary enemy?

Blanchard insisted that bygones should be bygones. He cared about the country, he said, and his plan was the sort of venture that would lift up everyone. He promised that he would consult with the local communities to make sure his environmental initiatives didn't negatively affect their livelihoods. He argued that subsistence fishermen or farmers who needed to be relocated for the park would end up living far better than before: he would give them first crack at jobs in the new eco enterprise and preferential shares in the company. And of course, he promised, he would build new schools and health clinics. It would be a win-win all around, he said: for the environment, for Mozambique, for the local people, for investors.

In 1996 the Mozambican government agreed to give the entire district of Matutuine as a concession to the newly formed Blanchard Mozambique Enterprise. The government also turned over to the Louisiana businessman part of the subtropical Inhaca Island, just a short ferry ride from Maputo, home to more than a hundred varieties of coral and more than three hundred species of birds. Overall, the concession was the size of Mauritius. For his part, Blanchard raised the stakes and promised an $800 million investment.

A number of conservationists expressed skepticism about the deal, given Blanchard's political background. But groups such as South Africa's influential Endangered Wildlife Trust quietly endorsed the arrangement, saying that any effort to save the wildlife of Mozambique was better than nothing. It was clear, conservationists said, that the Mozambican government itself did not have the capacity to manage protected areas.

As promised, Blanchard flew to Matutuine to hold meetings with residents, and he made the same promises to them that he had made to the Mozambican government officials. This environmental initiative would help the local people, he said. He wanted to lift everyone up from poverty. Then he contracted with a Zimbabwean company to build a new, electrified fence around the famed elephant reserve. After all, if Blanchard was going to restock the park with a budgeted nine million dollars' worth of game, then surely there needed to be a fence.

The problem, local people said, was that this new fence was in the wrong place. It cut significantly into their traditional areas, isolating villages from one another and preventing access to important fishing spots. The construction also managed to trap a number of elephants on the wrong side of the fence, which meant that a group of frustrated, hungry pachyderms, unable to follow their usual grazing routes, were instead ravaging village crops and tearing thatched roofs from huts to get at families' food supplies. Months passed, and neither schools nor health clinics materialized. And since the park itself (to say nothing of the proposed marina and underwater observatories) was years away, the promised jobs had not yet appeared, either.

When researcher Rosemary Galli traveled to southern Mozambique in the late 1990s, she found a population "in both revolt and despair." In community meetings she attended, residents spoke of being ignored both by government officials and by the representatives of Blanchard's initiative. A number of people said they wanted to leave Mozambique for South Africa, because "in Mozambique animals are treated better than people."

Three years after he signed the agreement with the Mozambican government, Blanchard was found dead in a Louisiana motel room not far from his home. Many international news articles simply reported that the fifty-four-year-old magnate had been killed by a heart attack or a stroke. Louisiana papers, though, noted that the medical examiner's office had found in Blanchard's body a deadly combination of cocaine, an unknown opiate, and the tranquilizer benzodiazepine. His widow acknowledged that he had struggled with addiction and bouts of mania.

Although news reports initially indicated that Blanchard's heirs would continue the eco-paradise project, it soon appeared that they were more inclined to sell the concession. The Mozambican government, which is able to revoke land grants if promised investment does not materialize, shut down the project and reclaimed the land in late 1999. Conservation groups sharply criticized Blanchard and his organization. They bemoaned the waste of years that could have been spent on active conservation, and criticized the American businessman as out of touch at best, crazy at worst.

Richard Fair, an experienced game warden whom Blanchard hired to manage the safari enterprise, insisted that the project had in fact made headway. He told reporters that park administrators had introduced twenty-four kudu and fourteen waterbuck, no small feat given the complexity of animal relocations and the limitations of infrastructure in postwar Mozambique. They built that fence, a significant undertaking, and took steps to rectify the community relations damage that resulted from it. They refurbished derelict ranger posts, supplied uniforms and radios to forty-three scouts, and coordinated antipoaching patrols. Park administrators were also working with local community leaders to hold regular discussions about the park. Yes, sure, Fair told other conservationists and government officials, the project had been slow getting off the ground. But considering the challenges, the efforts could hardly be called worthless.

The new conventional wisdom, though, had already been established. At one time, the park had been written about as the somewhat bizarre but inspiring brainchild of a maverick; after Blanchard's death, it was decried as the misguided, egotistical venture of a fraudster. Journalists took particular delight in mentioning that one of Blanchard's managers had suggested that along with importing elephants and lions, the reserve should also import San Bushmen from Botswana. (Blanchard later fired that employee.) Early on in the project, the development team put together what became known as Blanchard's black book, a thick, glossy, expensively produced brochure detailing the Disney-like attractions to come. Intended to attract investors, the document was now the focus of ridicule. The imagined golf courses and luxury hotels seemed worlds away from the broken infrastructure and community controversies on the ground.

Perhaps, some speculated, the fact that the wheelchair-bound Blanchard flew to his nature concession instead of driving to it altered his perception of what was possible. From the comfort of private jet and helicopter, the landscape looked like a lush green-aqua postcard; perhaps he didn't realize how difficult any travel or construction would be given the unpaved, deeply rutted, often impassable roadways. And perhaps because Blanchard didn't know the local languages, people speculated, he didn't understand the full complexity of the cultural dynamics in the place where he would be building his paradise. Or perhaps he just didn't care. Regardless, everyone agreed, the plan had been outrageous from the start. Given Blanchard's background, they should have known better.

If Blanchard's story is a warning, it is also an example of the chameleon-like staying power of our basic "changemaker" narrative. When something goes haywire, we put the blame not on that underlying narrative but on the characters within it. We don't stop to consider whether there is a problem with the basic plot line itself—with the notion that rich people from the United States can, and should, drop into parts of the world vastly different from their own in order to dramatically reshape environments and societies.

In our mind, the changemaker is so powerful that a project's success depends solely on his or her motivation and abilities. The problem with this, of course, is that when a grand enterprise is built entirely around one or two people it is bound to be shaky.

Which brings us back, for better or worse, to Quan and Bray and their out-of-place tigers. A few years after visiting the reserve, I checked back on the Save China's Tigers project. It had gotten a lot of media attention since I traveled to Philippolis and garnered a growing number of celebrity backers, including Jackie Chan. The overall number of tigers was now up to fifteen. However, none had gone back to China. The ecosystem there simply wasn't ready, the project's representatives explained to reporters. News articles about the enterprise repeated what I had written on my first visit: here was an unusual but hopeful idea, with great potential that might eventually be realized sometime off in the future. Really.

Then things started getting uglier.

Quan and Bray split up. With some one hundred million dollars at stake, according to Quan's divorce papers, the couple shot accusations back and forth, and the tigers featured prominently in the dispute. Bray accused Quan of behaving in a way that undercut their conservation program. He said she talked about the tigers as if they were her children, which made the project's scientists uneasy. He told the court that the couple had argued after Quan set up Twitter accounts for each of the big cats, and had "them" send tweets back and forth to one another. It was the sort of strange anthropomorphizing that gave their critics ammunition. He maneuvered to have her removed from the charity's board.

Quan hit back even harder. Bray, she said in court, had been defrauding Save China's Tigers by regularly dipping into the Mauritius-based trust the couple had established to fund the charity. The money that was supposed to go to the tigers actually fueled the couple's extravagant lifestyle, she testified: expensive dinners and wines, houses in London and the Swiss Alps. Bray was the one who controlled the funds, Quan said, and he regularly told her that there wasn't any separation between the money spent on their personal lives and the money that was supporting Cathay, TigerWoods, and the other tigers in South Africa.

Bray vehemently denied the allegations, and a family court judge in London eventually sided with him. The judge called Quan a liar who had become "blinded by her desire for revenge." Quan's claims about Bray's financial misbehavior, the judge said, struck him as a scheme to gain access to the trust's money. He speculated that Li was so upset about being ousted from the tiger project, the organization she saw as her baby, that she was now willing to destroy it. (At the time of this writing, Quan has been granted permission to appeal this ruling.)

It was tawdry, tabloid-worthy stuff. But in the grand scheme of things, it was also not that surprising. After all, this is what happens with stories of individual saviors. Humans are fickle and disappointing as well as inspiring. So when changing the world, or even just the fate of one species, is intimately connected to the supposed superpowers of a single person the whole project can quickly crumble.

This is why when I heard about another wealthy American coming in to save nature and people in southeast Africa I was initially skeptical.

The tip came to me from a longtime conservationist named Judy Oglethorpe, a scientist with the WWF. Oglethorpe had run some of the organization's most intellectually fascinating research projects, including one exploring the connections between war and environmental preservation. At the time, those working in development, emergency relief, and environmentalism all generally operated in separate spheres. Oglethorpe's work was pushing people to recognize that their concerns overlapped tremendously; that even when there was an immediate humanitarian crisis on the ground, ignoring conservation issues was dangerously shortsighted. Evidence showed that environmental degradation caused by war and attendant relief efforts (situating refugee camps next to a forest, for instance, which often results in deforestation as people cut down trees for firewood) often undermined social stability in the long run. Communities that were left with a damaged environment had a harder time rebuilding after war.

Oglethorpe's work described many of the problems, but it also mentioned some solutions. She told me that if I really wanted to see a place coming back from devastation, I should travel to the middle of Mozambique, to Gorongosa National Park. Interesting things were happening there, she said. An American named Greg Carr had decided to devote his life and treasure to restoring this beautiful park, which had been destroyed in the Mozambican civil war. Lest I be too ready to scoff, she said (perhaps sensing my jaded journalist opinion about would-be Western do-gooders), I should know that this particular benefactor was unusual. His background was in human rights. He wasn't tied to any of the big organizations, so he could approach conservation and development from an unencumbered, fresh perspective. She didn't think this was a vanity project. And he was smart, she said. Very smart.

I was intrigued. Perhaps, I thought, there could be a new answer brewing to the big questions I had encountered while reporting about the wild dogs. Maybe here, in remote Mozambique, someone was figuring out how to truly help people and nature at the same time.

—— PART II ——

GORONGOSA

5

The Five-Act Play

The Gorongosa National Park sits in the middle of Mozambique, where Africa's Great Rift Valley approaches the Indian Ocean. At about fifteen hundred square miles—slightly larger than California's Yosemite—it is by no means the biggest protected area in the region, but it is certainly one of the most biologically and topographically diverse. Flying over Gorongosa, one sees palm tree jungles and acacia trees, a breathtakingly expansive floodplain, and groves of yellowish-green fever trees, their branches tangled in fairy-tale embrace. A large lake in the center of the park, Lake Urema, reflects the sky like a silver mirror, while crocodiles slither along its edges. Powdery white limestone gorges drop hundreds of feet into a slender valley of ancient trees, where crystal-clear streams cascade over time-softened boulders. There are inselbergs and caves, rivers and grasslands.

Decades ago, there were big mammals, too. People called the Gorongosa "the place where Noah left his ark." According to animal surveys conducted in the 1960s, the park was home to some fourteen thousand buffalo, three thousand zebra, and more lions than any other reserve of its size. Along with them went vast numbers of elephants, hippos, sable antelope, and other creatures that attracted tourists from around the world. All told, Gorongosa National Park boasted a greater animal density than even the famed Serengeti Plain.

By the time Greg Carr came to Gorongosa in the mid-2000s, however, those animals were gone. In the civil war that ravaged Mozambique throughout much of the 1970s and '80s, the park's animals were among the many victims. The park itself was a battleground, and soldiers from both sides slaughtered the wildlife for food. Even after the United Nations brokered a peace deal in 1992, poachers took advantage of the postwar chaos to go after the animals with the most marketable body parts. The conservationists who first returned to the park after the war, part of an emergency response team funded by the Africa Development Bank, told me they could smell meat smoking on the floodplain.

This emptiness did not faze Greg, however. He had expected to find trauma when he arrived. After all, that was why he was there.

It is hard to say exactly why Greg Carr decided to spend his time in a devastated African nature reserve, enmeshed in the difficulties of conservation and development. As he often said to me, rather pointedly on occasion, people are complicated. It's impossible to do full justice to someone's thoughts and motives in a few thousand words. But the basic *story* of Greg is easy to tell. Indeed, since I first wrote about him and Gorongosa, it has been told again and again, in newspapers and magazines, in movies and on television.

In the mid-1980s, Greg was a graduate student at Harvard University's John F. Kennedy School of Government. Although he hailed from Idaho, and had received his undergraduate degree from Utah State rather than one of the prestigious East Coast schools that Bostonians seem to favor, Greg fit right in. He had a quick intellect and a knack for making friends. He'd arrived at Harvard fully intending to be an academic, with plans eventually to get a PhD in linguistics. Yet after doing a case study on the dissolution of the AT&T telephone conglomerate, he decided to change direction.

The U.S. Department of Justice had filed an antitrust lawsuit against

AT&T about a decade earlier, eventually prevailing against the monopoly that had long controlled almost all telephone operations in the country. Although Greg began researching the breakup of Ma Bell as a public policy issue, he quickly recognized a business opportunity. In the past, AT&T controlled essentially all the technology used by the phone companies. Now it was an open playing field, a field where money could be made.

Greg found himself obsessed by the idea. That often happened to him: a fever, he would call it. It was how other people described falling in love. Ideas overtook him, and once they started taking shape he couldn't shake them. They slipped into his evenings and weekends, into his friendships and his sleep. He could see the puzzle pieces snapping together, far into the future. Sometimes it seemed that his mind just worked faster than other people's, finding innovative answers to problems that others hadn't even recognized yet. As his brain zoomed ahead, out of sync with those around him, the usually charming Greg would sometimes turn aloof and distracted, as if he had moved on to other thoughts.

Instead of continuing with more graduate studies, Greg joined forces with another twenty-something, a recent graduate from the Massachusetts Institute of Technology, and started a company called Boston Technology. The goal was to create and sell to the emerging regional telephone operators something called voice mail. It was audacious, but Greg and his small team built the first widely used voice mail system in the United States. Greg then sold that service to Bell Atlantic and other phone companies, beating out competitors such as Siemens and AT&T itself. All of a sudden, he was very, very wealthy.

For the next decade, those close to him told me, Greg was a classic entrepreneur workaholic. He expanded Boston Technology. He led the investment group that bought the online service Prodigy, and then turned Prodigy into one of the country's first major Internet providers. He helped create Africa Online. In 1998, just shy of his fortieth birthday, he and his partner sold Boston Technology for $843 million.

But then, in what came as a shock for a number of those who worked with him, Greg decided to quit the for-profit world. He had never

wanted to be a businessman for life, he told me later. He had just recognized that if he made a lot of money, he could go on to do whatever
he wanted.

One thing he wanted to do was read. He picked up works on cogni-
tive psychology and bioanthropology, and he dove into Greek literature. Euripides, in particular, became an obsession. Greg saw in the
poet's tragedies the morality and universal humanism that would form
the foundation of the modern human rights movement, centered on the
revolutionary concept that there were laws higher than kings and rights
higher than laws. He would sit late into the night in his bookcase-lined
library, or on his deck looking out at the twinkling lights beyond the
Charles River, and read about the thin line between greatness and hubris,
love and rage; about characters who were passion-driven in their tumul-
tuous quests to follow a path of righteousness only to realize later that
they were pursuing the wrong god.

About a year into his retirement, he established the Gregory C. Carr
Foundation to support the arts and human rights. Soon thereafter he
pledged eighteen million dollars to endow a new Carr Center for
Human Rights Policy at Harvard, which at that time was the largest gift
from any Kennedy School graduate. He gave half a million dollars to
the Idaho Anne Frank Human Rights Memorial, and then another half
a million to the Idaho Human Rights Education Center. He provided
funds to turn the neo-Nazi Aryan Nations compound in northern
Idaho into a peace park. On a whiteboard in his condo was an ever-
evolving list of other ventures he supported: a theater in Cambridge, a
radio station, and a women's leadership center in Afghanistan. He began
the planning for a new headquarters building in Harvard Square; he
said it would be the town's first totally "green" structure, using geother-
mic energy instead of fossil fuels. He dabbled in filmmaking and started
work on a natural history museum.

"The world is just so chock full of fabulous ideas," he once gushed
to the Harvard student newspaper.

In the midst of all this activity, though, Greg started to feel a growing sense of dissatisfaction. He wanted to really commit to a project, he
told his closest friends, something that would both capture his intel-

lect and produce the sort of sweeping change he would be proud to call his life's work. As he explained it to me, he spent a lot of time thinking about this. He brainstormed about it in Cambridge, contemplated the question at his pied-à-terre in New York City, talked it over at his compound in Sun Valley, where his parents and his six older siblings gathered with their families for summer vacations. His sentiments evolved over time. At first he thought he wanted to do something more with human rights, but he was also becoming more interested in *humanitarian* rights: access to the basic necessities of living, such as food, shelter, and health care. This, inevitably, brought his attention to Africa. And it was around this time, as Greg tells it, that a mutual friend introduced him to the Mozambican ambassador to the United Nations, a longtime diplomat named Carlos Dos Santos.

Dos Santos had arrived in New York City in 1996, only four years after the end of the civil war that had left his country battered. He carried clear instructions from his superiors: go and find new investors, whether individual or institutional, who might assist in the rebuilding of Mozambique. So Greg Carr was a man Dos Santos was more than happy to meet. The ambassador made his pitch to the philanthropist: if you want to help, he said, come to our country.

Before he met Ambassador Dos Santos, the little Greg knew of Mozambique came from television news. A devastating cyclone had hit the country a couple of years earlier, and the related flooding caused a humanitarian disaster. A baby was born in a tree, he recalled—baby Rosita, saved with her mother by a South African medical helicopter minutes after her birth in March 2000, the drama caught on camera.

And then there was the Bob Dylan song from the *Desire* album: "I'd like to spend some time in Mozambique, the sunny sky is aqua blue." A light little apolitical tune that struck some fans as incongruous, given its release in 1976, the first year of Mozambique's independence.

Bob Dylan and CNN. Greg was the first to admit that he simply did not know much about Mozambique when he and Dos Santos began talking. But the more he learned, the more he realized that Dos Santos was on the mark. This country, relatively unknown among the American public, could very well be the place for which he'd been searching.

Mozambique came in close to the bottom on the UN Human Development Index, which measures public health, literacy, life expectancy, economics, and various other factors in some 185 countries. In 2000 it just beat out Sierra Leone and Burundi, but was notably worse than Haiti, Sudan, and Bangladesh. Life expectancy was in the high forties. Almost half the population was considered illiterate. The HIV rates were climbing, with about a fifth of the country estimated to be infected, and even higher percentages in the center of the country. In 2000 the International Monetary Fund estimated that 70 percent of Mozambique's population lived in "absolute poverty," a development term that indicates the lack of basic needs such as food, water, shelter, and sanitation.

At the same time, Mozambique seemed uniquely able to ask for, and make use of, outside assistance. Ever since the end of the civil war, the government of Mozambique had been working diligently with the World Bank and the IMF to make the structural changes they recommended for pulling the country out of poverty. It revised the tax code, eliminated government subsidies for the cashew industry, and implemented financial reforms designed to stem inflation while encouraging investment and private business. The economy was growing by nearly 10 percent a year, and many in the international development world pointed to Mozambique as an example of the benefits of foreign aid. A "donors' darling," they called it. It was the perfect combination of need and possibility, lapped by the waves of the Indian Ocean.

But what could he do to help? Greg wondered, walking to his office past the throngs of undergraduates making their way to the Gap. What could lift up the country, and how? He considered the situation with his entrepreneurial mind. There must be a niche, he thought, something that Mozambique could offer the world. He knew the country had prawns and cashew nuts and even some oil deposits. Foreign companies had made a fortune processing aluminum there. But he had no intention of becoming involved with an extraction industry. He knew far too well how diamonds, coltan, and oil made outsiders rich while leaving local communities destabilized and poor. He also didn't want to start one of those aid projects that his intellectual friends mocked: the road that soon crumbles, the water pump that always breaks. So what, then?

Eventually he came to the answer, one that connected with so much in his life that it seemed almost inevitable, fateful—something out of Euripides. The answer was *beauty*.

Mozambique, he realized when he went to visit, was drop-dead gorgeous. Its long Indian Ocean coastline, a sparkling ribbon of white, stretched some fifteen hundred miles from South Africa to Tanzania. The vast majority of it was undeveloped, with palm tree coves and water so clear that even from a plane you could see straight to the sandy bottom. The interior was lush and diverse, from the scrubland on the South African border to the tropical jungles of the interior and the vast forests of the north.

Beauty, Greg decided, was Mozambique's secret weapon. He came up with an idea that in some ways seemed simple, but was actually groundbreaking. Perhaps, he thought, he could take part of this stunning landscape and turn it into a development engine. Through beauty he could save Mozambique.

The next steps were methodical. Greg wanted to find the right location for his development-by-nature project. He asked one of his employees, a human rights worker named Sidney Kwiram, to help him scout possible protected areas in Mozambique that could serve their goal of alleviating humanitarian hardships on a wide scale.

They flew to Mozambique in 2004. With a group of advisers—from the Mozambican government, from the local office of the U.S. Agency for International Development, and from the Carr Foundation—they toured the country, from the Matutuine beaches that had once been Blanchard's concession to an international park straddling the border with South Africa. Gorongosa was not on the itinerary, Sidney told me. Indeed, as she recalls, it was only a day or so before Greg was scheduled to fly back to Boston that she received a phone call from an American named Bob Snyder, who at the time was a regional director of the faith-based organization Food for the Hungry. Sidney wasn't sure how Bob had gotten her number, but she had been trying to tap into the NGO network in Mozambique, asking people to contact her with thoughts and advice, and word must have gotten to him.

Bob asked her if Greg had considered the Gorongosa National Park for his project.

No, Sidney responded. They hadn't even heard of it.

She recalls that they talked for no more than five minutes. But in that time, Bob mentioned enough of their buzzwords—*poverty, malnutrition, AIDS, political marginalization, spectacular landscape*—that Sidney felt they needed to take a look at Gorongosa, even if it meant postponing Greg's trip home. The other officials were doubtful. Gorongosa Park had been destroyed in the war, they explained. The animals had all been killed. The park barely existed anymore.

But Sidney and Greg were still interested. So the group flew to Beira—Mozambique's second-largest city, halfway up the Indian Ocean coast—and took a helicopter inland.

The landscape of Gorongosa, Sidney recalls, took their breath away. So did the old administrative headquarters, called Chitengo Camp, where they landed the helicopter. Flame trees shaded the bombed-out remains of a restaurant and a semicircle of dilapidated bungalows, made minimally habitable by the emergency response team that had only recently been able to get into the park. The other buildings were in ruins: bazooka-blasted concrete walls, a water tower pockmarked with bullet holes, thatched roofs falling in on themselves. The entourage made sure to stay in the cleared center of camp, knowing it was quite possible that land mines were scattered around its edges. Unexploded ordnance was all over the country, with some experts estimating that millions of mines were still buried nearly a decade after the peace accord.

By the time they boarded the helicopter again, Sidney recalls, Greg had decided that they'd found their place. The combination of potential and loss written on the body of the land was overwhelming. USAID officials in the helicopter that day also noted the philanthropist's remarkably quick decision making. Later, depending on who was telling the story, this was relayed as an optimistic foreshadowing of competence, a sign of the American can-do spirit—or a really bad omen.

I first traveled to the Gorongosa National Park at the end of the rainy season in 2006, and I quickly found myself captivated as well. The land was both breathtakingly beautiful and deeply troubled, and I had the strong sense of something just out of reach, rumbling barely under the surface. It felt similar to how, if your whole body is attentive enough, you can feel elephant calls going through the air, even when their pitch is below the range of human hearing. Later, I would credit this out-of-reach sense as the thing that kept bringing me back there, to the point where Gorongosa eventually became the almost exclusive focus of my reporting. But on my first visit I mostly pushed that feeling aside. I had a straightforward mission: to find a story that I could turn around fairly quickly for my editors back home. Ideally, it would be the narrative that Judy Oglethorpe had previewed for me some months earlier, a story of paradise lost and now resurrected.

My contact at the park during that trip was a Portuguese man named Vasco Galante, who was in charge of the park's public relations. A former professional basketball player and businessman who spoke multiple languages, Vasco was living at the time in a tent at the back of the bedraggled main camp. He was extraordinarily helpful, and among other things he enthusiastically shared some of the old footage the Carr Foundation had collected of Gorongosa. Sitting under the thatched roof of the *boma*, the open-air structure that served as the camp's restaurant and general meeting place, we watched the videos on his laptop. There were home movies of lions twitching their tails, of huge groups of zebra and antelope, of elephants crowding one another at watering holes. It was beautiful—something reiterated by everyone I interviewed on that trip, from scientists and park administrators to rangers and villagers.

"There were many animals," a ranger named Gone Samuel (the first name is pronounced roughly like "John") told me, in one version of the story I would hear again and again. Gone grew up in a nearby village and had worked in the park before the war. "There were buffaloes, there were zebra, everything. All sorts of animals . . . Before the war the park was good. It was giving employment to many people, it was beneficial for the residents here. People who lived on the boundary of the park— when they got sick they were taken to the hospital here. There were lots of benefits."

He paused. "And then there was the war. Everything was destroyed."

This destruction was as ubiquitous as the tales of once-upon-a-time glorious Gorongosa Park. It was there in the nervous glances of taxi drivers who took me and my photographer colleague into the park, hours of driving along menacing, spine-rattling roads. It was there in the ramshackle bungalows where we tossed our bags, and in Chitengo Camp itself, with its eerie feeling of ruins being slowly reabsorbed by nature. It was in the war graffiti and the bullet holes.

We interviewed Gone outside the remains of a park restaurant. There were a few battered sections left of what once must have been an intricately tiled floor. On the walls that had not been blasted away was graffiti of stick figures holding AK-47s. *Viva Frelimo*, someone had scrawled. More ruins by the old airstrip—once a convenience for the movie stars and astronauts who visited Gorongosa—were battered and pockmarked by long-ago gunfire. So were an old, defunct water tower, a former ranger barrack, and various other buildings.

The most obvious sign of the war, however, was within the park itself. We left Chitengo Camp regularly to venture deeper into the protected area, riding in the back of a pickup truck along the recently demined and restored dirt roads. The landscape was dazzling: pinkish-blond grasslands, towering palm trees, miombo woodlands, and that spectacular floodplain stretching for miles toward Mount Gorongosa, a pastel blue trapezoid on the horizon. But there were hardly any animals. Now and then we glimpsed the flash of an impala, one of the common antelope of southern Africa. I believe we might have seen a warthog, and certainly some birds. But there was nothing like the herds of big fauna that drew crowds in the 1960s and '70s.

The available statistics of Gorongosa's wildlife put numbers to the emptiness. Of the fourteen thousand buffalo that lived in the park in 1968, only fifty were left by the year 2000. Of three thousand zebra, none remained. There was only a handful of elephants. Hippos, sable antelope, and other animals had been poached out of existence.

Greg wanted to fix these numbers, Vasco told me, while helping local people in the meantime. And he had made the extraordinary pledge of thirty years and some forty million dollars to do so—a remarkable time frame in a sector where most grant cycles span two or three years at best.

"Basically, the objective of the project is to bring back the wildlife to this park as there was before, especially in the sixties and seventies, when the park was well known for wildlife lovers," Vasco told me. "It was really a special place. But besides that, the other important objective has to do with increasing the life quality of the communities surrounding the park. We strongly believe that this park can change a lot here."

The story was easy: that tale of beauty possessed and lost, with the possibility of renewal through a main character who was white, wealthy, charming, and equipped with exactly the kind of technocratic philan-thropy credentials that our Live8 generation adored. It was familiar to readers, recognizable and easily absorbed. As Greg would say himself, the story of Gorongosa fit perfectly into the Western literary tradition. It could easily be told as a classic five-act play.

For those who have forgotten their high school English classes, there is a traditional structure to the five-act play. It begins, typically, with what is called the exposition, or backstory. In this section the important characters are introduced, the scene is set, and the audience begins to get a sense of what happened before the main plot began. Act 2 is the rising action. It shows the events that build to act 3, the climax, which many English teachers describe as the turning point in the plot. In act 4, the falling action, a series of events shows the protagonist either winning or losing in the climax's aftermath. The final act is the resolu-tion, or denouement. That's where the remaining conflicts are resolved and the knots untied, for good or for ill.

These days, modern literature tends to play with this structure, twisting and subverting it. Many writers critique the control inherent in the very frame of the five-act play. Theorists argue about whether postcolonial stories can ever be told in this way, or whether the form of dominant Western discourse defeats their function before words are even on the page. But Greg found the traditional form compelling. So, to help his team visualize what they were all working toward, he brainstormed with them a Gorongosa Epic Play and e-mailed around a summary.

They titled act 1 "Pre-History." In Greg's document, this begins in 1920, when Gorongosa is designated as a hunting reserve. "People who care about Gorongosa" try to get a stricter conservation status for the area, pushing to turn it into a national park.

Act 2 is "The Golden Age." The curtain rises in 1960, when the national park designation is granted and hunting is banned. "People from all over the world recognize that Gorongosa is a magical place," the plot summary proclaims. "Presidents, prime ministers, astronauts and Hollywood stars visit."

The war is act 3, "The Dark Age." In 1981, the park is closed. As fighting drags on, soldiers from both sides kill animals for food. And after the war ends in 1992, organized poachers slaughter nearly all of the remaining wildlife. "Thirty thousand zebras are reduced to thirty. Gorongosa is a forgotten land."

Then comes the answer to those problems, act 4, "The Restoration." In 2006, the Carr Foundation signs a long-term agreement with the Mozambican government, pledging "to restore animal populations, develop Mozambican management capacity, and to create a tourism revenue stream that will finance the Park's annual budget." When those tasks are accomplished, the park will be considered sustainable, and will be "handed back" to the Mozambican government.

Act 5 is, simply, "Happily Ever After": "After Hand Back the Government of Mozambique will manage this world-treasure ecosystem, tourism paradise and national symbol 'til the end of time."

The end.

I have probably read and reread this outline hundreds of times now.

It always startles me, the way that, right there, in one e-mail memo, story-telling is creating its own reality. The five-act play was all the fund-raising campaigns and conservation efforts and Live8 finger snapping rolled into one. Of course, this particular "Epic Play" was about one particular project. But in broad terms it revealed just how much our engagement with Africa is actually a product of our own Western canon.

From early on, I saw that there would be some complications in act 4. In my piece for *Smithsonian* magazine, the first major story about Gorongosa in the American media, I described how Greg and members of his staff took a small boat across the Pungue River to visit a nearby village called Vinho. (The village's name, Portuguese for "wine," was given by colonialists as a sort of joke; a nearby village is called Bebido, or "drunk." Which says a lot, really, about colonial attitudes and their legacy.) Vinho had about 280 adults and twice as many children, a school that went through the fifth grade, and a water pump that teenage girls used to fill plastic jugs as they jostled babies tied to their backs. Of the fifteen or so communities that directly bordered the park, Vinho was the closest village to Chitengo Camp. And because of this proximity, it was a bit of a test case for Greg's idea of using nature to help people.

That particular day, a meeting was scheduled in Vinho between Greg, some of the local Vinho elders, and the man who ran the entire district, an accomplished politician named Paulo Majacunene. Greg wanted Majacunene, a man known to have quite a bit of power and authority, to help convince the people of Vinho to work with the park on conservation. In particular, he wanted the villagers to stop poaching and to cease setting forest fires, which were a huge problem for the park. (Poachers set fires both to clear underbrush and to herd animals into snares. Some farmers also set fires simply to clear their land for crops, but these blazes could spread in devastating fashion.)

So Greg, several park administrators, and the park's warden at the time, a Mozambican named Roberto Zolho, got into a rickety boat and crossed the crocodile-infested Pungue. They climbed the river's sandy banks, past the homemade fish traps and splashing children, and walked through maize fields to a central clearing near a massive gray baobab tree. A crowd had gathered there for the meeting, and we all waited for what seemed like a very long time for the district governor to arrive.

When he finally got there, everyone sat down to listen to speeches. The park officials and local leaders got some chairs under a tarp; most of the onlookers found places to sit on the ground. Majacunene told the crowd that when the Carr Foundation restored Gorongosa, there would be jobs, health clinics, and money for Vinho. But the community needed to help, he said. No more setting fires. No more killing animals.

Everyone in the crowd nodded. A little girl next to me peed in the dirt.

Majacunene led a series of cheers, thrusting his fist into the air. "*Viva* Gorongosa Park!" he yelled in Portuguese.

"*Viva*!" the crowd answered.

"Down with poaching!" he yelled.

"Down!" echoed the crowd.

Greg, seated next to him, gazed at the crowd and joined in the cheers, looking something between proud and astonished.

"Did you see that?" he said to me as the meeting broke up. "They get it. They really get it."

Roberto was standing near us, seeming bemused. "They're the ones doing it," he said.

"What's that?" Greg asked.

Roberto explained. Those villagers thrusting their arms in the air, shouting about getting rid of fires and poaching? They're the ones doing the poaching and setting the fires.

"So they're the poachers," Greg repeated slowly. He looked around the clearing at the villagers chatting with one another. He smiled, a wry sort of smile that I saw regularly, one that seemed to appear when something struck him as particularly absurd. "Well, we're starting," he said. "You know, it starts somewhere."

This idea, that at least Greg and his team were *starting* something, is essential to the Western canon five-act version of development and conservation. We can stay in act 4, the crisis's aftermath, for a long time, because the pledge to "restore" nature can always be pitched in the present continuous: *restoring* nature. If things are going badly, it just means that we haven't gotten to the scene change yet. We still have our story, and its central focus is still on our efforts to repair a destroyed paradise, on whether the American can take what was broken and make it whole again.

Sure enough, in Gorongosa this *restoring* has gone on for quite a while. In the years since I first wrote about Greg and his ambitious plan, dozens of other journalists have come to report about the man and the project. And just about everyone has returned with the same story. The nuances are sometimes different, of course. But as with my *Smithsonian* article, even the pieces bringing some skepticism to the white explorer-adventurer narrative are fundamentally based on the Western perspective: will he or won't he succeed? Whether shading toward criticism or praise (and virtually all the reporting has skewed to the latter), the story is still the individualistic test of the American eco baron.

Even as I was finishing this book, almost a decade after my first trip to Gorongosa, PBS ran a series about the park called *Gorongosa Park: Rebirth of Paradise.* It was a classic adventurer-explorer story retold for the Live8 generation, full of danger and beautiful footage. Its underlying message: sometime soon, Gorogonsa National Park might be restored to its former glory.

The central problem with all this is that there is no room within the five-act play for other stories. There can be no tales with different characters, different time frames, different points of tension, different logic systems. The structure is set. There is no room to show that the hostile reception Greg got on his visit to the rainmaker, for instance— the scowling, silent faces that greeted his red helicopter landing on the mountain—might best be seen not as a plot point in the restoration of Gorongosa National Park, but as a moment in a much longer story of colonial troubles and evil spirits, a story with far different acts and plot lines.

But those stories are all there. To ignore them, to tell and live in and imagine *our* stories exclusively, is like turning up your Mozart to try to drown out the Megadeth blasting from the apartment next door. It doesn't work, and for everyone around, it just makes things even more confusing and unpleasant.

The longer I stayed in Gorongosa (an unusually extended and committed time, in the end, thanks to a generous journalism fellowship), the more I saw these other stories undercutting and swerving into the canonical five-act play. And the more I recognized how they clashed with our Western tales, the more I suspected that this conflict of narratives may well be at the root of our failure to do good in the developing world, whether for people or for nature.

I kept on reporting my conservation stories, but I started to feel increasingly uneasy about them. It seemed to me that the Gorongosa restoration project would not, could not, do what all those bright minds of conservation and development said it would do. Indeed, I started to worry that, like some character from Euripides, it might end up doing quite the opposite. Even stories of conservation successes—the introduction of new animals into the Gorongosa landscape, for instance— became, from another viewpoint, something far darker.

6

Of Buffalo and Poachers

On a bright morning in the cool of August, I rode with Greg Carr and a few of his staff members to a dusty enclosure outside the administrative headquarters of South Africa's Kruger National Park. There, the head veterinarian of South African National Parks service, a soft-spoken man named Markus Hofmeyr, was standing on top of a large metal truck used for transporting wild animals, testing its doors and ladders. Another half dozen scientists were waiting in the thin winter sunshine. Carlos Lopes Pereira, one of the top veterinarians in Mozambique, whom Greg had recently hired, was double-checking the tranquilizers he had mixed the night before. And somewhere just out of sight, in the interconnected animal pens with towering stick walls, two herds of carefully chosen buffalo pawed at the dust.

It was a key moment for the Gorongosa project, and arguably for conservation overall. The scientists gathered at Kruger that morning were going to take the first steps in what some of them suggested could be one of the most ambitious animal relocation and restoration efforts ever attempted at an African national park. As some of the more breathless press reports would put it, this was an effort to rebuild Eden.

For some time, Greg and his staff members had debated whether they should try to speed the recovery of Gorongosa by importing animals to the park. Some conservationists warned against this, arguing that it would be more prudent to simply protect the environment and allow the ecosystem to rebuild itself naturally. Change one little part of the system, even with good intentions, they said, and you never know what sort of ripple effect you might unleash. But Greg and his advisers concluded that they could not wait for nature. The gene pools of the few animals remaining in the park were dangerously small, and it was unclear if the mammal population could ever rebound unassisted. Besides, they needed more animals quickly, in order to implement their plan of bringing in ecotourism dollars to help the surrounding communities.

The park administrators therefore decided to import a variety of species into Gorongosa Park. This was not a simple proposition. Besides the sheer difficulty of moving wild animals—think about the struggles of getting your house cat into its carrier, and multiply that by about a million—there is, as those wary conservationists warned, a particular fragility to ecosystems. Even the right animals, if added at the wrong time or in the wrong order, can make the whole environment go haywire. But the Gorongosa scientists believed they needed to take the risk.

One of the ecological problems that had resulted from the animal slaughter in Gorongosa was a breakdown in the way grazers worked their way through the grasslands. In a healthy grass-based ecological system, a few large species eat and trample the tall, coarse grasses, making way for the more tender grass varieties that are eaten by a variety of smaller grazers. Those smaller grazers then attract carnivores, which help control the overall animal population. It is this sort of delicate balance that crumbles when one species disappears, and helps explain why conservationists around the world are so concerned by the accelerating loss of biodiversity. Everything, they know, is connected.

In the Gorongosa ecosystem, the best habitat shaper is the hippopotamus. A hippo passes his days lounging in the water and on muddy riverbanks, but he spends much of the nighttime trampling and eating his way through grasslands. Weighing up to eight thousand pounds, and with a mouth that is almost two feet wide, the hippo is one of the most efficient grazers around: every night he eats his way through a loop up to six miles long. But hippos are not good travelers. Their weight and need for constant moisture make transporting them through southern Africa particularly difficult, and the success rate for hippo translocations in African game parks is markedly low.

Buffalo, the scientists decided, were the next best choice. Buffalo are essential to grassland ecosystems. They are big animals, with stocky legs and massive, horned heads, and can weigh up to two thousand pounds. A herd of these creatures will flatten the tall, rough grass of a savannah, and eat quite a bit of it as well. But buffalo, too, presented a problem for the Gorongosa park officials. The vast majority of available buffalo in southern Africa were infected with bovine tuberculosis, and the Mozambican government had strict import regulations on animals that could be carrying the virus. Greg's team worried that they might not be able to find any disease-free animals to import.

Bovine tuberculosis is not native to southern Africa. European settlers and their infected cattle brought it with them when they flocked to the continent in the late 1880s, determined to turn bushveld into farms and ranches. Ever since then it has been a major agricultural problem, but it was not until 1990 that conservationists in Kruger realized they would have to deal with the disease as well. That year, park rangers stumbled across an emaciated buffalo bull near Kruger's southwest border. When park veterinarians inspected the animal, the test results were clear: the bull was a victim of the pathogen *Mycobacterium bovis*, which causes lesions on the lymph nodes of the animal's head, tonsils, and lungs and eventually leads to death. Bovine TB had passed from domestic cattle to the African buffalo.

It was only a matter of time, scientists worried, before the disease spread throughout the park and infected all one hundred or so buffalo herds in it, each comprising around three hundred animals. This would be a disaster, conservationists warned. Not only could bovine TB damage the park's buffalo population, but it could easily make the jump back into cattle living along the northern border of the park. That might severely affect the local agricultural industry. Some feared that it might even exacerbate an already devastating human tuberculosis crisis in the region, since some studies claimed that drinking unpasteurized milk from TB-infected cows could transfer the infection to humans.

And this was not all. By the late 1990s and early 2000s, conservationists across southern Africa had started the process of trying to rebuild or create new wildlife reserves. Some of these were business ventures, led by entrepreneurs trying to cash in on the region's safari boom; others were nonprofit environmental efforts. Some, such as Quan and Bray's tiger reserve, were built on reclaimed farmland, in an attempt to reverse the centuries-old pattern of taming the bush into grazing land for cattle; others were more like Greg's project, restoring protected areas that had been abandoned or destroyed. Whatever their focus, these new reserves almost always needed animals—and for the same reasons as Gorongosa, they particularly needed buffalo. Kruger National Park would usually satisfy this demand, but there was no way it could export animals infected with tuberculosis. The bovine TB crisis in Kruger had the potential to derail conservation efforts across the region.

Markus, Kruger's head vet, and his colleagues decided they needed to act. Working with the South African Department of Agriculture, Forestry and Fisheries, they assembled a pool of disease-free buffalo, using a double-fenced quarantine area and a fenced 2,200-acre preserve within the park. When these buffalo gave birth, the calves were whisked away from their mothers early, to prevent the natural transmission of disease, and were closely monitored by the region's best veterinarians. They were regularly dipped for ticks, inspected for signs of parasites, and subjected to blood tests. They associated only with other buffalo that had been equally sheltered.

By 2006, when Greg Carr was looking for animals to relocate to Gorongosa, Markus's program had been declared a success. But its intense management was costing Kruger Park hundreds of dollars a day, and there was now a large enough pool of genetically diverse TB-free buffalo roaming South Africa—some twenty-five hundred of them—that the veterinarians felt comfortable discontinuing the effort. They were planning to phase out the Kruger program, and were looking to either sell or relocate the last of their animals.

On the open market—and because of all the new private nature reserves, there was quite a business in wildlife trade—these buffalo would be worth about $9,000 to $15,000 each. For a conservation project like Greg's, however, Markus and the other officials were happy to make a deal. South Africa would sell disease-free buffalo to the Gorongosa National Park for about $1,300 a head, Markus told Greg.

Greg was elated. He would take as many as he could, he told Markus. Markus offered him fifty-six.

Six months or so before we gathered in the dusty clearing by the animals' enclosure, Markus had divided the buffalo into two groups to be transported separately to Gorongosa. Buffalo are hierarchical. While the herd size varies, there is always a linear order of dominance among both males and females. Each herd has one dominant bull, who will tolerate younger males until they are old enough to go off and form their own "bachelor herds." There is also a smaller group of top females, who typically enjoy each other's company. Once a herd is formed, its members are incredibly protective of one another, and will fight off even lions or crocodiles to save one of their own.

The day before the trip, Markus and Carlos, Greg's veterinarian, went one more time to inspect the animals. The men wanted to make sure the buffalo were all healthy enough for the journey: some eight hundred miles in a cramped transport truck. Two of the females, the veterinarians determined, were too sickly to make the trip, but all the others were in good shape.

Carlos then spent the evening working on what he called the "juice," the drug cocktail with which the veterinarians would inject the buffalo as they crowded into the metal trailers. First would come a tranquilizer, to calm the animals as they started their voyage. This would last for two or three hours. Then there would be a mixture of two antipsychotic drugs, Haldol and Acuphase, which would kick in as the tranquilizer wore off. In human medicine, Haldol is used for the most difficult schizophrenia cases, while Acuphase is used to sedate psychotic inpatients. In a buffalo, the vets believed, the drugs would last forty-eight to seventy-two hours, calming the animals enough to keep them from killing each other in the cramped containers. "They'll be on their feet, but they will not be motivated to fight or get in trouble," Carlos explained to me.

By morning, there was nothing left to do but herd the animals into the transport trucks. The park scientists were ready with their tranquilizers. They took up positions on top of the trucks, looking down through openings in the roofs. (There had been some worry that the two vehicles were a bit small, but the team decided that they'd make them work.) Greg waited in the shade, chatting now and then with the various scientists and officials who came over to him.

"This is exciting," he said when I wandered over to him myself. The buffalo were only the start of his plan, he explained. Next would come zebra and wildebeest, and after that rhinoceroses, assuming the park had a strong enough antipoaching team to fend off the well-armed illegal hunters that rhinos always attracted. Then cheetahs, perhaps, and maybe other species too.

If you look back at scientific surveys of the park from the 1960s, Greg told me, you'll see records of tens of thousands of these animals. "When I was first talking about this project, I showed those to a friend of mine who taught biodiversity at Harvard," he recounted. "He said, 'Greg, this is one of the great conservation projects of the world.'"

When the Kruger scientists determined that everything was in place, they released the buffalo. The mass of bovine bodies surged through the funnel of pen enclosures, slipping through gate after gate as staffers herded them toward the ramps of the transport trucks. They stormed forward, kicking up a tornado of dust in a whirl of hooves and horns and bellows. Buffalo are fierce. They are herbivores, but they're known as one of the most dangerous animals in the bush, because they are unpredictable and often ill-tempered when surprised or agitated. According to bush lore, a buffalo wounded by a hunter will not run away. Instead, she will circle her attacker, monitoring his movements. When the chance arises—when the hunter is looking away, perhaps, exposed as the weak and vulnerable human that he is—she will charge, horns down for goring.

Hundreds of people in Africa are killed by buffalo each year. Local nicknames for the creature translate roughly as "the black death" and "the widow maker." Some people claim that the buffalo kills more people in the bush than any other animal, but you hear the same of crocodiles and hippos—as well as about the mosquito, which spreads malaria. There was our joke again: everything in the bush could kill you.

The Kruger veterinarians were razor-focused as they balanced themselves atop the transport trucks, shooting their medicine downward as the buffalo rushed inside. The sound of hooves on metal echoed across the dry winter landscape; from inside the trucks came thuds and bangs, as if someone were receiving a tremendous beating. The containers shook. More and more animals swarmed through the gates and up the ramps, pushing into the trucks. It was as if the enclosure had been turned into some strange African rodeo.

Within minutes, the buffalo were locked in the vehicles. They snorted and snarled, bucked and kicked in the dwindling space. There was little room inside the trucks, and the animals were panicking. Then, just when it seemed the stress would reach intolerable levels, the herds started to calm. The frantic struggling began to fade into tranquilized sleepiness. It took some minutes, but soon the clearing became quiet again, and we could hear the birds.

The staffers double-checked the metal locks on the truck doors. When they were confident that all the buffalo were secured they gave the go-ahead to the drivers, who revved the engines. Slowly, the massive trucks pulled away from the animal pens and into the bush. Soon they drove out of the Kruger reserve, where the buffalo had spent their entire lives, and toward the international African highway.

The park scientists recognized that some of the animals would probably die as the trucks made their way north across South Africa, up through Zimbabwe, and into Mozambique. One or two buffalo in any translocation almost always succumb to the stress of the move, to the lack of fresh air and the strange movement underneath, to angry bulls and dominant cows and fear. The park staff just hoped the deaths would prove minimal until the trucks arrived, two days later, at the newly built, USAID-funded Gorongosa National Park wildlife sanctuary.

———

The twenty-three-square-mile wildlife sanctuary at Gorongosa National
Park was designed by some of the top biologists and veterinarians in
the region. They had looked for a spot that would have the best ecosystem and topography for new animals, a nice air flow to keep the tsetse
flies at a minimum, and a location practical enough for monitoring but
remote enough that it gave the animals some peace and did not unduly
tempt poachers. Once they settled on a place, they had to ensure that
the area was clear of land mines. And then they needed to build a fence.

The sanctuary fence was important. Without it, the newly imported
animals would likely scatter throughout the entire park, making it hard
for the park scientists and rangers to track them. They might even
leave the park altogether, since unlike Kruger or Madikwe, Gorongosa National Park was not fenced off from the surrounding lands.

Partly the reason for this was practical. Building and maintaining
a game fence is incredibly costly and labor-intensive, and putting one
around the whole park would have used up quite a lot of Greg's budget. But there were also other, more philosophical issues. Local people
lived within the park's borders, for example—not many of them, and
fewer than during the war, but they were there, fishing in Lake Urema
and insisting they were on their home turf. It would have been troubling, from a human rights point of view, to essentially cage them in.
There were also disputes with border communities about where,
exactly, the park's boundaries lay. I spent one morning sitting on the
ground in a village next to the park as elders drew maps in the dirt with
sticks, arguing with a park administrator about where their land stopped
and the protected area began. In short, fencing the entire park would
have been far too expensive and complicated.

For the wildlife sanctuary, a fence was more manageable, though it
would still be a massive undertaking. The sanctuary's perimeter was
almost twenty miles long. The park had to import the material from
somewhere, transport it over sketchy roads, and then use significant
manpower to install the barrier in a way that would withstand the
charge of an angry two-thousand-pound buffalo. If administrators

wanted to electrify the fence, they would have to fight a constant battle against the rapidly growing grasses creeping up around it.

But all these challenges, Greg realized, actually created a golden opportunity for his project. Constructing the wildlife sanctuary fence would take the better part of a year and require dozens of workers. From the very beginning of his involvement in the Gorongosa project, Greg believed that the park could become an economic engine that would help the people living around it. And here was a chance to offer local people jobs.

His team put the word out in the local communities, and eventually the park hired a group of laborers who chopped the bush away from the fence line, dug holes for the metal posts, helped install the fencing, and cleared trails for scientists to monitor the sanctuary. It was the perfect example, Greg and his team said, of how saving an ecosystem could provide benefits to the local community.

One of these fence construction workers was a young man named Tomás Jeremias. Tomás had gotten the job because of connections. His brother, Salazar, was a ranger at the park and had put in a good word for Tomás when people started to talk about the park hiring laborers. "That's how it works," Tomás said with a shy smile when I asked him about it.

By all accounts, he was a hard worker. He was on the sanctuary fence project for nine months, living in temporary workers' lodging in Gorongosa and toiling in the bush heat. He listened to stories about the American man who was going to bring in new animals from far away, and about how those creatures would find a new home in this enclosure that he and the other laborers were building. Scientists would monitor the new buffalo in this sanctuary for some time, Tomás learned, as the animals grew accustomed to their new habitat. Before the park released the Kruger animals into the wider ecosystem, scientists wanted to test Gorongosa's small collection of native buffalo who had survived the war, to make sure they were not harboring bovine tuberculosis themselves. The last thing they wanted was for the carefully bred disease-free buffalo from Kruger to become infected after their arrival.

So Tomás watched the rangers make their rounds of the sanctuary, preparing their antipoaching patrols, and listened to the locals talk about a renewed Gorongosa National Park. And he received a paycheck. He rushed to buy cooking oil for his wife, who was waiting for him with their three young children in their home near the Bué Maria River, a half day's walk from the sanctuary. The pay meant that he could buy school supplies and a school uniform for his five-year-old son. It meant he could buy some dried fish at the local market. And it also meant that Tomás no longer needed to trap animals inside the park to smoke and sell along the main road, which is how he had survived before the Carr Foundation came calling.

"Now that I had other income," he explained to me later, "I no longer needed to be a poacher."

This was exactly the kind of outcome Greg and his team had hoped for. Local people would choose not to damage the environment if they had other options, the park staff said repeatedly, following the conventional wisdom of the international conservation movement. Once locals recognized the potential of the park—recognized that if nature were preserved, treated kindly, respected, and nurtured, it would offer far more economic opportunities than the short-term gain of a slaughtered antelope or monkey—they would no longer poach or set fires or otherwise damage the ecosystem. Tomás Jeremias was the hopeful face of the new Gorongosa.

Tomás's contract with the park ended in December 2006. The sanctuary was complete, and the temporary laborers were let go. This was not a great concern to the park managers. After all, they figured, they had demonstrated with a year's worth of salary the type of living that locals might gain from a profitable, ecologically and financially sustainable Gorongosa National Park. The park administrators expected that those people who had gotten jobs working on the sanctuary—as well as those who had been hired for other short-term projects, such as clearing grasses after a particularly fertile wet season or helping to renovate the Chitengo Camp villas—would go back to their communities as friends and supporters of the park. As Tomás himself had said, cash was hard to come by in these parts. Surely the local people who had benefited from the park would not damage it by poaching.

This underlying bargain—give up poaching in return for some direct or indirect benefit from the park—was of supreme importance to the Gorongosa project. Without it, I realized after dozens of interviews, there would be a poacher in pretty much every household in the region.

It took me a while to stop being instinctively judgmental about the idea of near-universal poaching. In our American culture, the word *poaching* carries a severely negative moral charge. Even if we don't mind *hunting*, we don't like poaching. It's bad.

Indeed, this value judgment is inherent in the very concept of poaching, which is a decidedly European notion. Originally, "poaching" referred to the behavior of rascals who would dare hunt deer on the king's land; think Robin Hood and the like. Europeans then brought the concept of "poacher" to Africa, and—fairly predictably, given the racial attitudes of the time—quickly applied this term to black people who hunted where the whites didn't want them to hunt. Africans who killed animals in new European-delineated hunting territories (or, later, in newly designated "nature areas") were poachers. Europeans and Americans who shot hundreds of elephants and other endangered animals—Teddy Roosevelt, for example—were hunters. It is a linguistic distinction that has lasted to the present, despite protests from indigenous groups who point out the inherent unfairness in the categorization.

Today, many conservationists agree that *poaching* is perhaps an overly broad term, and they have tried to distinguish among different kinds of illegal hunting activity. Subsistence poachers—poor locals who hunt game illegally because their families need protein—typically get the most sympathy from environmentalists. Commercial poachers selling bush meat, for whom (at least in the eyes of outsiders) hunting is a matter not of survival but of profit, receive a lot less sympathy. Trophy hunters, who kill elephants for their tusks or rhinos for their horns, are the most reviled of the lot, since the animals they kill aren't even used for food. (Rhino horn powder gets sold in Asia as a drug, though officials say that its use as an aphrodisiac is an urban legend; the horns are more often packaged as a cancer cure. Their efficacy for either use, Western scientists say, is nil.)

In much conservation literature, these three types of poachers are now presented as distinct. But none of them is portrayed as particularly good. So it surprised me when one of my favorite park employees, an energetic man named Tatu Alexandre Jorge, told me quite unabashedly that poaching was simply a way of life around Gorongosa.

"Miss Stephanie, *everybody* here poaches. Everybody. Unless they are a ranger, or have another good job at the park." He looked at me and grinned, and waved a hand to encompass the open-air restaurant. "A good job like mine."

Tatu was one of the first Gorongosa Park employees I met when I came to Chitengo. He was the restaurant's all-around waiter, bartender, soda provider, and, later, wait staff manager. He was also in charge of the beer, which was not only a hugely important job here but one that required a great deal of trustworthiness, since you can be sure that everybody was leaning on the beer man for some off-the-books favors.

"So everybody is a poacher, Tatu?" I asked. "Or at least was, before they got a job with the park?"

"Yes!" he said. "Even me!"

"You?"

"Yes!" he exclaimed, gesturing. "I was the most feared poacher of them all. Everybody knew me."

He was clearly quite proud of himself. And I started to realize that here, poachers and rangers were not in a battle of good versus evil, but in a game of cowboys and Indians, where they were often willing to switch sides. As Tatu told me, it was precisely because he was such a well-known poacher that park rangers were so eager to hire him when Greg's project began. The ranger in charge had moved his name from ninety-ninth on the list of job applicants to third.

This was good news for Tatu and his family. Poaching is a tough job. The animals he caught earned him seventy-five meticais, or a few dollars, per kilo of meat. It was a fairly set price, he explained. He had a few customers who would visit him regularly to buy whatever he had caught and then take the meat to Beira, where it sold for a hundred meticais per kilo. Most of the bush meat would get eaten by the city residents: it was less expensive than beef sold at markets, and certainly cheaper than whatever you could buy at the grocery store.

While seventy-five meticais is better than nothing—and certainly better than any other work Tatu could have found in these parts—it was still a struggle to support his mother, his wife, and fourteen children.

"Wait, you have fourteen kids that you're taking care of?" I asked, somewhat aghast.

He shook his head in that beleaguered way parents across the world would recognize. "It is a lot of children," he said.

Seven were his own, he explained. (He and his wife had never lost a baby, he told me proudly.) The other seven were children of two of his deceased brothers—one shot by a Zimbabwean soldier during the war, one killed in a car crash. Many of his other brothers and sisters had died too, he added matter-of-factly. And as the oldest brother remaining, Tatu was responsible for the descendants.

Anyhow, he said with a shrug, things had gotten much better since the Carr Foundation came here.

A year after the Kruger buffalo stormed their way out of the transport trucks, shaking their massive heads and huddling up with other herd members, they seemed to be feeling comfortable in Gorongosa. The two herds had settled into grazing patterns throughout the woodlands and grassy parts of the sanctuary. The water pools managed by Gorongosa Park staffers were plentiful enough to quench the buffalo's thirst; the tsetse flies, which do not exist in Kruger Park, were still bothersome but no longer shocking. Lions had not made their way through the sanctuary fence, so the transplanted animals lived basically without predators.

The buffalo cow, then, could not have expected the wire.

It was draped expertly around a tree trunk: strands of steel wrapped into a circle and tied with a noose-like slipknot that would slide closed when the wire was pulled. Hidden by brush, grasses, and foliage, the wire loop was all but invisible. It wasn't until the buffalo stepped into its circumference and pulled her leg forward that she realized something was wrong. Something was tugging her back. She kicked, but the wire that had closed around her leg just squeezed tighter. She kicked again, even harder, pawing the ground with her other hooves, bellowing. The wire dug into her skin.

Conservationists and animal rights groups have called snares one of the most inhumane hunting methods. Snares are indiscriminate, as likely to trap the paw of a lion or the trunk of an elephant as the neck of a buffalo, and they kill slowly and painfully. The more an animal pulls, the tighter the snare digs. Some antelope have gnawed off their own legs trying to free themselves; others have died of hunger, thirst, blood loss, or infection.

Snares are also the cheapest hunting tool around. Poachers can take wires from telephone lines or electricity cabling or building sites. If no metal wire is easily available, they can use fishing line wrapped multiple times to form an unbreakable noose. A poacher walking through the bush can quickly drop dozens of snares along a game path (a route through the bush that animals have trampled regularly enough that it looks like a hiking trail) or next to a popular water hole. The poacher can then disappear unnoticed, returning some days later to check on his traps. In a park the size of Gorongosa there are thousands of snares scattered throughout the bush at any given time. Across Africa, they are uncountable.

The Sheldrick Wildlife Trust, a conservation nonprofit that runs desnaring efforts in the Tsavo Conservation Area in Kenya, says that poachers typically expect 5 percent of their snares to catch an animal per day. Even if there were only a thousand snares in their Massachusetts-size park at any given time, the trust points out, that 5 percent rate would mean more than eighteen thousand animals killed per year. Other conservation groups have equally alarming figures. Scientists reviewing data from Zambia's Luangwa Valley, for instance, calculated that 20 percent of the conservation area's adult male lions were snared, while wild dogs and elephants were also regular victims of snaring.

If such an animal, not desirable for food, gets caught in a snare, the poacher will simply leave the creature to die. It is collateral damage. Likewise, if there is some reason the poacher cannot come back to check his traps—if business has taken him elsewhere, or if he suspects a ranger patrol has moved too close for comfort—he will leave even the bush meat animals, the impala and warthogs and buffalo, to rot. There will be more animals caught tomorrow.

In the case of the buffalo cow in Gorongosa, though, the poacher did come back. He crept into the sanctuary, avoiding the ranger patrols monitoring what was supposed to be a wildlife safe zone, and made his way quickly to his snares. The buffalo was almost dead when he found her. He finished the work, quickly cutting her throat. It is nearly impossible to drag a buffalo through miles of bush, so the poacher skinned and butchered her on the spot. He packed everything—the valuable meat of her haunches and sides, which he would smoke at home and then sell to bush meat traders for about a dollar a kilo; the tongue, which he would boil; and the stomach, which he would use himself in stew. He hauled these remains of the conservation masterpiece through the wildlife sanctuary, out of the Gorongosa National Park, and to his home near the Bué Maria River.

Tomás Jeremias knew exactly how to avoid the rangers patrolling the wildlife sanctuary. He had spent months watching them as he carried construction supplies through the tall grasses, while working on the sanctuary fence.

I first met Tomás a few months later. He was walking among tables of tourists on an unusually busy night at the Chitengo *boma*, playing a sort of instrument I had never seen before, something that appeared to be a Mozambican cross between a violin, a maraca, and a whistle. He was well scrubbed in the way of the local Mozambicans, who, without running water, always seemed to be far cleaner and more put together than I. His short-sleeved, patterned button-down shirt hung crisply over pressed khaki pants; he walked in rubber sandals with the gait of someone who had spent a lifetime on his feet without arch support. The instrument he played consisted of a wooden bow, the ends of which were connected by a palm frond, and a stick with a gourd on it filled with stones that rattled. He played the palm frond with his mouth and moved the stick along it to change the pitch. It produced a haunting, if somewhat repetitive, melody.

Now and then one of the tourists would glance up as Tomás walked around the tables, with the earnest, not-quite-comfortable look of travelers new to Africa who want to make it clear that they are appreciating the local culture. Most of them looked away, however, with consciously nonchalant avoidance. Tomás's pace was slow and respectful; he kept a peaceful, private half-smile on his face as he moved through the restaurant.

I had spent dozens of evenings by that point in the Chitengo *boma*, but this was the first time I had seen a musician.

"Who's that?" I asked Vasco, the park's PR chief, who was typing on his laptop at one of the plastic tables the staff had set up on the new patio.

He followed my gaze. "I don't know," Vasco answered. "Let's ask him."

When Tomás walked our way, Vasco called over to him and unrolled a couple of meticais. "Good evening!" Vasco said.

Tomás's smile lit up his face, glowing through his shyness.

"What is that you're playing?" Vasco asked.

"*Nhacajambe*," Tomás answered softly.

"*Nhacajambe*?"

"Yes."

It was a traditional instrument of the area, Tomás explained. Once upon a time, many people in these parts would play the *nhacajambe* at parties and other gatherings, especially where beer was being made. These days, though, it was a disappearing art, he said. With development had come generator-powered speakers and music CDs pirated from China; he was one of very few people left in the region who still could—or wanted to—play the instrument. Most young people are not so interested in traditions like this, he said with a shrug.

"Do you live in the park? In Vinho?" Vasco asked.

Tomás smiled again, but this time sadly.

"*Não*, I am a poacher," he said.

The presence of the poachers was one of the odder aspects of Chitengo Camp in its early days. On my very first visit, some two years before, I had stumbled across the camp's jail, located somewhat incongruously next to the *boma* where we ate our meals, but conveniently, I guess, near both the ranger headquarters and the police station. This was not a jail as you might imagine one in the United States, though. There were no visible guards or locks, just the same cinderblock walls and laundry hanging from the windows that you could see at the rangers' housing.

During the day, the poachers left the jail in their own clothes, carrying their own machetes, and embarked on what I understood from administrators at the time to be a kind of forced work duty, a penalty assigned by the camp's police officer after suspected poachers were caught. It was not ideal, park administrators admitted to me at the time— and sure, due process would have been nice. (Greg was a human rights philanthropist, after all.) But I should understand, they said, that prosecution through the formal legal system here was impractical. Remember, this was a country barely returning to some functionality after a devastating civil war. The park had neither the resources to drive poaching suspects for hours to the closest magistrate, nor the manpower to designate rangers to hang around a courthouse. Prosecuting poachers that way would, in fact, cause the park to lose money, because any fines imposed on them would either be minimal or go unpaid. Most of the poachers had no extra cash—it was one of the reasons they were poaching in the first place.

Besides, most of the rangers knew most of the poachers: they all came from the same villages, and often even the same families. So the park management decided that the most practical way to address the problem of poaching was to do as people in this region often did when dealing with personal disputes: they would handle things on their own, outside the formal legal structure of the state.

So they came up with the system of work duty. It was a simple concept: if we catch you taking the park's property, we're going to make sure you pay us back in a way that actually counts. The work duty could last for weeks or months. Sometimes the rangers would have the poachers clear weeds and encroaching brush from the park's road system. Sometimes the poachers would help the rangers fight bush fires. All the men cutting grass with machetes around the park were poachers, I was told.

This forced work duty, the park managers believed, would both ensure fair restitution and discourage further poaching. It also fit in with what was happening all around the continent, as conservationists increasingly took the fight against poaching into their own hands—sometimes with violent results.

In the world of conservation, poaching in its various forms is considered one of today's biggest threats to animals and ecosystems around the globe. It sits alongside habitat destruction and climate change at the top of environmentalists' list of major concerns; it has been the focus of advocacy and prevention campaigns, international fund-raising and documentaries, and millions upon millions of dollars spent on in-the-field law enforcement.

In the world of law in many developing nations, however, poaching is often a mere property crime, sometimes lower down on the pecking order of offenses than pickpocketing. It often falls under civil "damage to property" statutes, and the fines are generally light, if courts bother to hear the cases at all.

This has created a conundrum for park managers and conservationists. In order to protect their natural resources, park rangers must vigorously defend against poachers: they must patrol their reserves, remove snares and other traps, and gather intelligence at local markets where bush meat is sold. Rangers must cultivate informants, learn how to protect themselves against sabotage, and be skilled enough with a gun to defend themselves if an armed poacher begins shooting at them—something that happens rather frequently in southern Africa's protected areas. (The Thin Green Line Foundation, a nonprofit dedicated to supporting park rangers, estimates that, over the past decade, a thousand rangers have been killed in the line of duty.)

Yet once the rangers manage to run this gauntlet, once they uncover a group of local poachers or even catch a poacher in the act, the result is often a letdown. In much of southern Africa, rangers are supposed to turn poachers over to the police, and often the case ends there. The police might feel that the evidence connecting an alleged poacher to a dead animal is just too sketchy, or they might simply be uninterested in pursuing a mere property crime. Even when a police department does bother to investigate and charge a poacher, the next steps—going to a judge or magistrate, making a case, and seeking a sentence—are likely to be unrewarding. Convictions are infrequent, and for those who do get convicted of poaching, the penalty is typically a small fine. (In Kenya, for instance, until recently the penalty for being caught with a game trophy was around one hundred dollars.) There is often the statutory threat of a year or two of jail time, but in most places this has rarely been applied in sentencing.

Even the United Nations has weighed in on the issue, describing poaching as one of the world's more serious international criminal enterprises, but to little avail. Wildlife groups call antipoaching laws some of the least enforced statutes in the world. And sometimes frustration with such toothless enforcement can boil over.

In Swaziland, for instance, Ted Reilly—a bush-weathered white African whose father established one of the most profitable farms in the country—once loaded a mutilated rhinoceros carcass into the back of his truck and hauled it to the residence of King Mswati III.

This was in the midst of what became known as the Rhino Wars, a spate of relentless poaching from 1988 to 1992 during which at least two or three of Swaziland's rhinoceroses were being killed every month. Reilly had already earned a reputation as a staunch conservationist: decades earlier he had turned his father's farm into Swaziland's first protected area, and had worked with the monarchy to painstakingly restore the wildlife that had once called the land home. Reilly had imported elephants and rhinos, zebra and buffalo, and King Mswati's father, King Sobhuza II, had blessed the project and worked closely with Reilly on issues of tourism and conservation. The king had even donated animals from his own vast land reserves. But now the Rhino Wars were threatening to unravel everything.

Reilly was convinced that lack of law enforcement was at the root of the problem. As was common in the region, Swaziland's decades-old Game Act, which outlined the legal codes around wildlife use and damage, framed poaching as just a minor, individual property crime. The law needed to get tougher, Reilly told his friend King Mswati repeatedly. Rangers needed more legal backing. They needed more fire-power. And when he saw yet another rhino murdered on his land, the horn slashed away from its forehead and the meat left to rot, Reilly deci-ded he had had enough.

Mswati was moved by the conservationist's delivery of the dead rhino. He urged legislators to amend the country's laws on wildlife crime, and soon Swaziland increased the penalty for poaching from a fine to a mandatory prison sentence of five to fifteen years. It gave rangers immunity from prosecution for actions taken to protect wild-life, and—perhaps most aggressively—gave rangers the authority to shoot and kill poachers if necessary for self-defense. Ted Reilly bought his staff semiautomatic weapons. And soon, the Rhino Wars were over.

Many conservationists hailed the Swazi government's tough approach. But the people who lived around Ted Reilly's game reserves had a rather different opinion. Villagers protested that Reilly's rangers had shot and killed a number of men simply *alleged* to be poachers—impoverished men who may or may not have been trying to bring a little meat home for their families. Amid the controversy, international conservationists began to back away from Reilly's Big Game Parks organization.

In 2010, in a move that outraged Reilly and the Swazi govern-ment, the board of the Goldman Environmental Prize—a prominent award for grassroots environmental activism on each continent—gave its Africa honor to a Swazi lawyer named Thuli Brilliance Makama. Makama was not your typical environmentalist. She did not plant trees or turn snares into bracelets; she did not start campaigns to stop deforestation or save the gorillas. Instead, she worked on behalf of poachers. In the mid-2000s she'd started hearing stories about commu-nities terrorized by Big Game Parks administrators and their highly armed ranger force. By that point, Reilly's private company had become the de facto police force where wildlife laws were concerned. The human rights impact of this, Makama argued, was extreme.

Makama won a significant legal victory when Swaziland's high court ordered the government to include an environmental NGO on its management board dealing with game parks and reserves. It was a move, her group said, toward lessening Reilly's control over the lives of the people living around his protected areas, although just a preliminary one. There was as yet little progress in the cases filed on behalf of the alleged poachers and their families. Even so, Makama and her family started to receive death threats.

This multisided war among conservationists, human rights activists, heavily armed trophy hunters, heavily armed antipoaching teams, and poor subsistence poachers has only gotten more violent over the years. And, arguably, suffering most from this arms race are people like Tomás.

By the time I met Tomás, Gorongosa park officials told me that there was a new, formal system in place that better regulated their dealings with poachers. But although it nominally involved the Mozambican legal system and an actual court, in practice it did not look much different from before. Park staffers told me that instead of simply assigning work duty, rangers now brought suspected poachers in front of a magistrate, who imposed fines upon those who were convicted. But because everyone knew that most poachers would not be able to pay these fines, the park and the Mozambican government had agreed upon a system whereby convicted poachers could pay off their penalties with work. The magistrate, largely relying on the recommendations of park rangers, would convert the fine into man-hours and come up with a penal labor sentence. Four months of labor, for instance, for fourteen snares.

That was Tomás's sentence.

I spent a good bit of time interviewing Tomás over the next few days. He was shy but unfailingly gracious. He let me pester him with questions about his life, and answered patiently. After all, he wasn't going anywhere.

He had spent more hours than he cared to remember, he told me, swinging his machete under the hot Mozambican sun, a conscript in that impossible fight against the weeds creeping into Chitengo Camp and onto the park's road network. Nature was always trying to take back Gorongosa, it seemed. As soon as the rangers and staff had finished clearing an area, they had to start again, because the grasses and thorns would already be devouring it once more. At night, Tomás and the other poachers went back to Chitengo Camp. They played cards, or tossed dice, or washed their clothes in a bucketful of suds. Tomás played his *nhacajambe*.

He was playing the instrument one evening, the sounds wafting into the thick darkness, when the cook working at the *boma*—only a few dozen yards away, after all—walked over to him. He asked if Tomás would be willing to play for tourists in the restaurant. It would be entertainment for the guests, the cook suggested, and perhaps a way for Tomás to earn a little bit of extra cash. Tomás agreed, and since then he had been coming to the restaurant in the evenings, walking his slow walk around the disinterested tables.

Sometimes the children paid attention to him, he said. Vasco's young daughter, for instance, would jump up and down, moving to a rhythm that those raised on Western sounds couldn't understand. But most of the white people were quiet and still. Back in his village, one of his younger brothers owned a bar, and when Tomás played there the people would laugh and dance and move, enjoying themselves in the soupy evening warmed even more by palm wine.

He didn't much enjoy playing in Chitengo Camp, he admitted. But it helped to take his mind off his predicament, to distract him from the thoughts of his wife and the young children who depended upon the little bit of cash he brought in with his hunting. Yes, he knew that this hunting was against the rules, he said with a shrug. Of course he did. His brother, after all, was a ranger. But what else was there to do? He needed some way to make a few meticais.

Outsiders might characterize the people around Gorongosa as "subsistence farmers," but subsistence farmers needed cash too—even people like Tomás, who grew sesame, corn, and sorghum on their own small plots of soil. There were school supplies to purchase, and cooking oil. Every year or two someone would need clothing, perhaps from one of the vendors in Gorongosa Town, where rainbows of secondhand garb hung temptingly in thatched stalls. Supplemental food supplies, whether sardines or tomatoes, cost money, as did access to the mill where peasants would grind their corn into flour. And in the main market in the town, a collection of makeshift cinemas offered movies—usually a pirated DVD played on a television in a small, mud-walled room set up with benches—for the equivalent of a few cents a showing.

Not that Tomás had much of a chance to watch movies. Like Tatu, the waiter at Chitengo, Tomás was supporting an extended family: in addition to his own children, he was responsible for his older brother's two wives and six children. This was the brother who had taught him how to play the *nhacajambe* in the first place, Tomás explained to me, and who had taught him how to hunt in this bush. In 1992, the year of the Mozambican peace accord, this brother stepped on a land mine. Tomás came back from Beira, where he'd been living as a servant boy to the local political leader of his village (most of these leaders had fled to the city during the war), and took up his new responsibility as the man of the compound.

For a long time, nobody made much of a fuss about his hunting. There were far bigger problems to attend to as far as poaching was concerned. In those early years after the war, well-armed hunters from South Africa and Zimbabwe swarmed the great Urema floodplain, picking off whatever animals the soldiers hadn't killed. Those poachers came with AK-47s and helicopter gunships. They took rhino horns and elephant tusks, or piled trucks high with corpses of antelope and bush pigs, destined for the lucrative bush meat markets on the coast or back in their home countries. The air smelled of blood.

There was hardly any ranger corps to speak of at that time. The few park administrators could do little but watch. Tomás and his snares were not a priority. After all, if the park officials were going to arrest him, they would have to arrest basically everyone who lived around the park.

So, after decades of poaching, this was the first time Tomás had gotten caught. Someone had told the rangers that he was setting snares, and when they confronted him, he admitted it. There was no point in denying the obvious, he said with a shrug. Everyone knew he had been hunting here. All that had changed was the park's management. Greg had gone through a number of wardens by then, and at that point the man in the post was Carlos the veterinarian. Carlos had put a new incentive system in place to fight the rampant snaring: every month, the rangers would get a certain amount of money per snare once they collected twenty to forty of the wires. (The exact numbers varied by month.) And at the end of the month, the ranger post with the most effective antipoaching efforts got an additional sum of money for the men to divide among themselves. The incentives had their effect: so far, the rangers were on track to arrest twice as many poachers as the previous year. The only poachers who escaped arrest, Tomás said, were the ones cutting deals with the rangers, which he could not afford to do.

The park managers were pleased when Tomás showed up at the restaurant with his *nhacajambe*. Here was yet another way for the park to help local people earn much-needed cash. Ecotourism could help locals in all sorts of ways, they said.

On one of our last conversations before Tomás was supposed to go back home, I asked him about some of this directly. He had been arrested just for setting some snares, not for killing the buffalo cow; though he'd mentioned the buffalo to me matter-of-factly in conversation, as far as I could tell nobody at the park was aware he'd perpetrated that particular crime. I wondered: did he realize the value of the creature he had killed, in terms of both dollars and effort? Was there any chance, given the growing park project and the possibility of more jobs down the road, that he would stop hunting the animals?

He smiled at me sadly and said nothing.

I lost track of Tomás after he finished his work duty. The next time I came to the park he was no longer around, and at least during the time that I was there he did not return to play his *nhacajambe*. I asked some of the other park staffers if they had heard from him, but they had not. They assumed he was home, working his fields. I couldn't stop thinking about him, though. There was something about his story that troubled me, beyond the painful details of his life and situation, beyond the waste of his killing, for pennies, a buffalo that represented tens of thousands of dollars in conservation and scientific investment.

What nagged at me was the fact that the officially delineated "buffer zone" around Gorongosa National Park was home to about 150,000 people, a number that was only growing. As Tatu and others had told me, almost all of them either worked for the park, poached from the park, or lived with someone who did one of those two things. And although Greg and his administrators believed in the power of the park as an economic engine, there was clearly no way for it to provide jobs for *all* these people.

The park team evidently did not see this as an insurmountable obstacle. In part that was because the people behind the Gorongosa project believed in their version of trickle-down economics: if some locals got jobs in the park, other businesses would grow to make use of that increase in regional income, and everyone would benefit. More generally, though, the conservationists just deeply believed that a healthy park—protected by more efficient antipoaching measures, attracting more tourists, distributing more revenue—would clearly help those who lived around it. That was the heart of their story, and they expected that soon the local Mozambicans would understand it too. The people around the park just needed to see the light.

Tomás's story shows something different, though. With his paid fence-building employment, he seemed to be a perfect exemplar of the optimistic narrative path the conservationists had outlined. But for him, however, the plot was not so simple. For Tomás, Greg's project was a destabilizing arrival, giving him little but demanding allegiance with the threat of harsh punishment. Tomás did not perceive himself to be in act 4, the untangling of the park's troubles. Instead, in his story, he was the victim of yet another traumatizing development in a centuries-old tale that had been shaped by far different forces—forces the conservationists barely recognized.

7

The Disorder

In 2006, when I first visited it, the town of Gorongosa was bustling. Minibus taxis crowded the main road, squeezing past schoolchildren and farmers who walked along the shoulder. Pickup trucks drove by, their truck beds crowded with passengers, goats and luggage strapped to the cab. Groups of religious women dressed in matching robes walked serenely to worship at one of the many Pentecostal churches that now dotted the mud-brick neighborhoods. At one end of town, construction workers were busy building a commercial gas station, which would be the region's first. (As it was, motorists who were short on gas could buy fuel only at an unmarked corner, where vendors would run down an alley and return with a plastic funnel and bottles filled with mystery liquid. It worked, but made those of us accustomed to Western infrastructure a bit nervous.)

Park staffers regularly visited the town, whether to check in with family members, meet with regional administrators, or work on aspects of the community building that Greg and his team saw as central to their project. I often grabbed a ride, or drove into town myself in my rickety old 4×4, and wandered around the shops and the central market. An overflowing crowd of vendors there sold everything from dried fish and tomatoes to tissue packs and made-in-China plastic sandals. Overall, the town had the feel of a place on the upswing, part of the general economic and infrastructure development taking place throughout Mozambique.

Or, at least, that's how Western analysts saw it. "In 1999, Gorongosa was virtually deserted," officials with USAID wrote in a 2005 report. "Today, the market offers electronic equipment, food, clothing and other necessities, and a new school nearby serves 500 students. Farmers are opening new land to cultivation of corn, cassava, cotton, beans and oilseeds now that they have access to a dependable trade route."

The development officials took a good deal of credit for this transformation. In the late 1990s, USAID and other donor groups proposed rebuilding the battered EN1, the country's major north–south highway, which cuts through Gorongosa. It was essential to the county's postwar restoration, they told the Mozambican government. Without high-quality roads and railways, there would be no way for farmers to transport their crops to city markets, no way for businesses and industries to move supplies and products. They pointed to study after study showing the link between good transportation systems and economic development. If repaired, the EN1 could become a lifeline, helping to lift struggling Mozambique out of poverty.

The government agreed. Soon, word started to filter out across the region that the foreigners were planning a big project, and that there would be jobs. To residents of Gorongosa, whose primary source of income had been low-yield farming, this was welcome news. They were not the only ones eager for the opportunity to collect a salary, though. Between 2000 and 2005, thousands of people from outside the region moved to Gorongosa with similar hopes of getting work on the road project, or with plans to set up businesses catering to those lucky ones hired to lay tar in the blistering sun.

The EN1 project was only the first of several infrastructure developments that big donor groups had in store for the Gorongosa region. In the fall of 2005, engineers working with the Mozambican government completed a line carrying electricity to the town of Gorongosa from the country's main power-producing dam. The work, funded primarily by KfW, a German development bank, put the town on the grid for the first time. A person could turn on a television or heat up water in an electric kettle. Local officials held a celebration attended by the Mozambican president himself, who gave a speech about the end of poverty. He also warned residents against splicing wires and taking electricity without paying, a common theft in southern Africa.

With the road, the electricity, and a new a cell phone network, the economy in Gorongosa bloomed. So did the population, with an inflow of new arrivals attracted by the town's growing convenience and comfort. Gorongosa was still considered a bit of a country bumpkin backwater by more cosmopolitan Mozambicans, but the time it took to get from there to Beira, Mozambique's second-largest city, was now just three or four hours. Young, ambitious businessmen and -women could move to the town and still keep in touch with relatives and friends elsewhere in the country.

This was success for rural Africa, according to the development agency mind-set, and by the early twenty-first century that kind of success was to some extent spreading throughout the continent. According to a 2010 McKinsey report on the African economy, for instance, Africa's real GDP grew by $235 billion between 2002 and 2007, with the transport and telecommunications sector accounting for a full 10 percent of that growth. At the same time, private infrastructure investments had tripled since 2000, averaging $19 billion from 2006 to 2008. Meanwhile, the rapidly growing number of Africans living in cities—rising from some 28 percent in 1980 to 40 percent at the time of the report—could mean a whole new generation of urban consumers, the analysts wrote with some excitement. "By 2030 . . . , Africa's top 18 cities will have a combined spending power of $1.3 trillion," they predicted.

Gorongosa Town, with its population of about forty thousand, felt quite different from Africa's big cities, including Mozambique's capital. But the trend of infrastructure development, increased urban density and trade, better access to regional markets, and improved telecommunication all fit the general McKinsey-endorsed trend. The Gorongosa

Park project fit into that narrative as well. Greg's vision—as he explained it in the mid-2000s, at least—was to use the park to create jobs, provide the impetus for increased educational capacity, and ultimately turn the Gorongosa region into a "middle class" society. Judging by the buzzing beehive of commerce that I saw, this transformation was indeed under way.

As I talked to people throughout the town, however, I got the clear sense that many of those who actually lived in Gorongosa felt far more ambivalent about the changes all around them. Many, for instance, were troubled by an increase in class distinctions, as the influx of material goods made it immediately apparent who had more wealth. Even the town's new connection to the electric grid created its own divisions. The large meters that the electricity company attached to the outside of the cinderblock homes of its customers distinguished those families who could pay for electricity from those who couldn't. Likewise, the people who could purchase televisions or other goods were allowed to hang out under the awnings of some of the new shops in town, but others were shooed away.

And often it was the longtime Gorongosa residents who were on the losing side of this new divide. They tended to be poorer than the new immigrants. Academic research looking at the Gorongosa market vendors, for instance, found that most of them came from elsewhere. They were mobile businessmen, ultimately taking their profits home with them, but hanging around long enough to make local youth envious of their fancy clothes and electronics.

This bothered many older Gorongosans. They worried that urban value systems were seeping into their own families. Some complained to me that young people were more interested in saving money for televisions than for *lobolo*, the traditional bride price paid to the woman's family. Long-held customs, they said, were beginning to crumble.

By itself, of course, this grumbling might sound like complaints from elders anywhere confronting potentially scary progress. But there were other problems in Gorongosa as well. In the mid-2000s, aid workers noticed, for instance, that despite the economic progress and the fertile landscape, hunger in the district was increasing. People were sicker, too. The development agencies put forth various theories to explain these strange facts, ranging from land-use practices to market forces. Part of the drop in health metrics, they speculated, was because of a rising AIDS epidemic. But some of the hunger and sickness could not be explained, other than as a combination of bad water, bad nutrition, bad luck, and, as the Live8 organizers would put it, simple poverty.

Many local residents, however, had their own explanation. And although at first it struck me as absurd, I came to realize that it was of crucial importance—both for the park project and for understanding other happenings throughout the region. As far as these Gorongosans were concerned, the increasing sickness and poverty in their lives was the result of angry spirits. Some of these spirits were relatively new, and particularly destructive. But others had been around for what to Westerners would seem like a long time—at least since the beginning of Portuguese colonialism. In other words, in the view of many Gorongosans, spiritual discord had been upending local life for generations. What they were experiencing today was just the latest version of this lengthy struggle, and "development" was merely the current iteration of what many of them had begun to call, simply, the Disorder.

Now, as a caveat that would be completely obvious and unnecessary if I were writing about an American city, it's important to mention here that the people of Gorongosa are not all the same. They are young and old, educated and illiterate, old-fashioned and forward-looking. They hold a tremendous variety of views about social trends, so it's impossible to say that all Gorongosans "like this" or "oppose that." A significant percentage of the population has renounced the ancestral spirits and the authority of traditional healers, turning instead to one of a rapidly growing number of Pentecostal Christian churches in town. But the spirits still serve as a sort of shared baseline cultural history, as stories of the Founding Fathers might in the United States. And in some places, such as the higher slopes of Mount Gorongosa, the spirits are clearly the dominant current organizing system for people's narratives

about and understanding of the world. Faced with trouble and disorder, these people naturally look for explanations in the spirit realm.

From this perspective, much about the Gorongosa Park project
began to look very different. Indeed, the more I learned about the spirits and Mozambican history—which, I would come to realize, were in
many ways the same subject—the more the various puzzling moments
from my reporting began to snap into place.

One day, for instance, I'd gone to the lower slopes of Mount Gorongosa to visit Eugenio, the *régulo* of Canda, the chief who would later do
the spirit-blessing ceremony for me. I remember asking him how long
he had been in charge. I was looking for some number of years: five,
maybe, or thirty. But he answered in centuries. He had ruled, he said,
ever since his people moved into the area from the land that is now
Zimbabwe (which historians put somewhere in the sixteenth or seven-
teenth century), ever since his clan's *mhondoro* spirit appeared as a lion
on the western slopes of Mount Gorongosa and indicated that this region
was theirs.

I looked at him. Perhaps, I thought, Eugenio hadn't quite understood my question. I wasn't interested in legends at that moment. I
wanted facts.

But what about you? I asked. How long have *you* been in charge?

He sighed, and started to give the exact same answer—only more
slowly and a bit louder, in the same unfortunate way we Americans
tend to speak to people who don't seem to comprehend English.

In fact, once I started learning more about the spirit world, I realized that Eugenio had been answering my question quite literally. It was
just that he'd been answering for the spirit, in which his ruling authority lay, rather than for himself as an individual man. The *mhondoro*—
the clan spirit that protects the land and the social norms of his
people—had indeed ruled for centuries. And without the spirit there
would be no *régulo*.

In Gorongosa, the ancestors are actually here, now, in a not-quite-
parallel world that regularly touches our own. This may not seem
believable to a Western reader, other than as an exotic anthropological

detail of a "traditional" society in a place far away. But the way Eugenio answered my question is not "traditional," or "unmodernized," or any of the terms thrown about in development lingo to describe the world's poor. It is his current, twenty-first-century life. And whether one believes more in the power of the spirits or in the power of Western economic theory—both, after all, have their share of doubters—it behooves a visitor to at least recognize that Eugenio's *story* is true: it is the dominant macronarrative shaping the landscape where Greg's five-act play is attempting to take place.

Even better is to try, for a moment, to take Eugenio's story as literal truth: to start from the assumption that spirits who lived long ago still live today, connecting past and present in an embrace that makes former wrongs far more tangible than they are in our society, where "history" is something we tend to regard as being permanently gone. (We give nice lip service to the importance of remembering history and making sure we're not doomed to repeat it, but we generally keep tight limits on its ability to play an active present role. One sees this in the widespread dismissal of those seeking reparations for slavery or other ills; one hears it in the skepticism directed toward those who speak out about the lasting impact of a decades-ago assault. Let bygones be bygones, we say, a phrase that makes little sense in central Mozambique.) Once you take this intellectual—and, ideally, emotional—step, it's clear how the different stories playing out in Gorongosa can clash.

If the story of Gorongosa is a five-act play, with 1920s "prehistory" as the opening act and the main drama centering on the park's development in recent decades, then everything that happened since Greg's arrival—from his attempt to get the rainmaker's blessing to Tomás's experience of penal labor—appears in a certain way. But take a different, longer read of history, with an understanding of how spirits fit into and shape the main events, and you will start to recognize another script, in which the same incidents are interpreted quite differently.

In this other story, Gorongosa does not start with the delineation of a hunting reserve in 1920. (To call that *prehistory* would seem as fantastical to Eugenio or Tomás as a lion spirit making territorial designations might seem to us.) It does not proceed in a classic literary arc, through conservation milestones and administrative triumphs. It is not easy to describe journalistically, and certainly does not fit into the nice, clean, optimistic narrative I was seeking when I first visited central Mozambique in 2006, or into the tidy tale that many other Western writers and film producers have told since. Just the opposite. In this other story, Greg Carr's effort to turn Gorongosa into his version of an ecological and human development utopia is yet another twist in a long, troubled history that revolves around outsider incursion and spiritual unrest.

Before the 1800s, when the European powers began to divide up Africa, Portugal was only one player among a number of different factions contending for control over the land and trade routes of Mozambique. The Portuguese explorer Vasco da Gama had reached Mozambique in 1498, and the traders who followed him over the centuries maneuvered along the Mozambican coast, making pacts with various African, Arab, and Indian merchants. Inland, Portuguese overlords controlled feudal-style districts called *prazos*, which operated in roughly the same way as African chieftaincies. Kinship bonds and daily interaction among the different ethnicities created a distinct Afro-Portuguese culture. But after the Berlin Conference of 1884–85, which codified the "scramble for Africa" among the European countries, the Portuguese began to implement a more invasive sort of authority.

The conference agreement formally divided up the African continent among the various European powers—at least according to the Europeans, who traced their new territories on maps that most Africans never saw. The Portuguese, like other Europeans who asserted their control over regions rich in everything from rubber and cotton to gold and diamonds, were eager to claim the African resources for themselves. But unlike Britain or France, which dedicated a huge amount of money, time, and manpower to their colonies, Portugal did not have the governmental capability to set up the necessary colonial infrastructure. So it outsourced its version of extraction to a group of quasi-public, for-profit companies.

In the Gorongosa region, the private entity in charge was called the Mozambique Company. Financed primarily by British investors, the Mozambique Company had a charter from the Portuguese government to administer the rich central swath of the country in return for a hefty percentage of its profits. In theory, it was supposed to act as a de facto colonial government, establishing banks, law enforcement organizations, and educational systems, and tending to the needs of the small number of Portuguese settlers. In practice, though, the company focused its efforts on making money and on repressing the Mozambican population.

This repression was often brutal. The Mozambique Company did not set up the large-scale agricultural or mining ventures that were the norm in nearby districts. Instead, it made money through a crushing tax system, which required rural homesteaders to pay the company in cash—something that was all but nonexistent in the region. If a family could not produce this "hut tax," it had to "donate" a few months of service to nearby gold mines or agricultural lands, with the Mozambique Company collecting the pay. Backing up this edict was a feared police force called the *sepais*, made up of African mercenaries from other districts. Armed with *samboks*, the whiplike clubs that are a common and feared weapon of southern Africa, the *sepais* would sweep through the villages with free reign to terrorize.

During the first years of the twentieth century, an average of twelve hundred men a year—18 percent of the Gorongosa population—were made to labor in the gold mines and plantations of nearby districts. Still others were forced to work closer to home. When the Portuguese decided to build a new road system to better administer the difficult colony, the companies forced both men and women into construction duty for weeks at a time. The conditions were harsh, as was the recruiting. Women were made to leave young children behind at home while they went to work on the roads, where they were regularly victims of sexual assault. Men were taken away from their fields during harvest time, with dire consequences to their families' food security. Violent crime increased throughout the area.

According to anthropologist Christy Schuetze, this period is particularly noteworthy within the Gorongosa region because it marked the birth of a new type of spirit: the *npfukwa*. The Gorongosans were already familiar with spirits who came from people with violent lives, such as the *sepais* or those in the warrior bands that sometimes swept through the region. But those spirits were generally tamed in the afterlife, and their powers could be harnessed through human spirit mediums. The *npfukwa* were different. Many of them came from murder victims, innocent people killed for their belongings. As spirits, they were angry and seeking revenge, and appeared randomly to destroy whole families. To the local population, the *npfukwa* were a clear example of the evil that comes when material possessions are favored over human life and the social order. And they are believed to remain active to this day, roaming the spirit world that coexists with the human world in Gorongosa.

In 1916, after a long holdout, Portugal entered the First World War on the side of the Allies. With the Germans just one colony over, in neighboring Tanganyika (now part of Tanzania), the northern border of Portuguese Mozambique became an important front in the war. Britain and France agreed to send their armies to fight off a German incursion there, while Portugal pledged to provide porters to support the campaigns. As it had done for years, the Portuguese government outsourced the task of "recruiting" to its charter companies. Researchers estimate that more than thirty thousand Mozambican men were conscripted to serve as porters.

Many in Gorongosa fled. Others disappeared into the upper folds of Mount Gorongosa, dodging the tax collectors and occasionally ambushing company officials. In 1917, the leaders of Gorongosa joined a diverse group of African communities, led by a neighboring kingdom called Báruè, and revolted. Coordinated attacks by peasants and warriors across the region caught the Portuguese off guard. The South African general Jacob van Deventer, who commanded the British imperial forces in East Africa at the time, worried that the unruly Gorongosans could provide an opening for the Germans. He sent insistent telegrams to Portugal, urging government officials to take "all measures" to put down the rebellion. The Portuguese officials, for their part, frantically called the administrators of the Mozambique Company.

Within weeks, company officials mobilized large bands of mercenary forces that marched into the Gorongosa district, burning villages and fields as they went. The Portuguese overseers motivated their troops by giving them free reign to rape any women they wanted from the rebellious villages; men and children could also be seized as slaves. Peasants who surrendered could avoid slavery but would still have to serve a year of forced labor. Within the year, nearly twenty-six thousand Mozambicans died within the company's territory. Many communities saw their populations cut in half.

"The old villages are mainly gone," wrote the Mozambique Company's new administrator, Vicente Bandeira da Lima, as he toured the area. The people were "hidden as much as possible, each group as far away as possible from the others in every way." Hollow-eyed children stood with their ribs showing; many of the adults wore bark cloth or sacks because they had no clothes. Family members separated during the rebellion did not know the fate of their loved ones, and were too scared to try to find them. People worried about venturing too far from their huts; many did not realize that the war with the Portuguese was over.

But if Lima was impressed by the devastation, he was not particularly sympathetic. All this, he told the Mozambicans in community meetings around the mountain, should teach them a lesson about fighting against the colonial powers.

The Mozambique Company soon reapplied with new vigor its policy of taxation and forced labor. After the rebellion, nearly a third of the male population of Gorongosa was forced into mining or plantation labor outside the region, and another 10 percent performed forced labor within the district. Many other Gorongosans left to seek work in Rhodesia. But even this held serious dangers. On their way home, these migrants, carrying their savings from months abroad, were often robbed and killed. The *npfukwa* spirits multiplied.

It was around this time that Mozambique Company officials decided to turn some four hundred square miles around the Urema floodplain into a hunting reserve for the pleasure of administrators and their guests. It was a spectacular landscape, after all, with the sort of game that would make a decent shooting holiday for Portuguese settlers in need of some recreation. The lions and elephants may have been a nuisance for the people who lived in the area, but for hunters they were satisfying trophies. Portuguese officials informed the people living there that they needed to move.

Thus Gorongosa Park was born. After a few years the reserve's boundaries grew larger, with yet more people displaced, moved away from their ancestral land and spirits. In 1960 it was named a national park. This, according to Greg's account, was the golden age.

To people in the district, Mozambique's violent struggle for independence and the subsequent civil war were the next logical, if brutal, markers of a world of growing spiritual displeasure. A guerrilla war against the Portuguese, carried out by a group calling itself Frelimo—the Frente de Libertação de Moçambique, or Mozambican Liberation Front—gained increasing momentum in the early 1970s. Around Gorongosa and elsewhere in the country, the colonial government arrested and tortured suspected Frelimo sympathizers. Colonial officials also forced villagers off their rural plots and into crowded communal villages. These *aldeamentos*, the Portuguese said, were for the peasants' own protection. But most people saw them for what they were: a way to keep locals from banding with the rebels, and a brutal disruption to a social system that centered on connection to ancestral land.

Archival footage of that era from the Gorongosa National Park shows frolicking lions, glorious elephants, and white tourists happily sipping beer by a watering hole. But in 1973, Frelimo stormed the park's main administrative center, and the park closed down.

The next year, a coup in Portugal ushered in a new Portuguese government, which vowed to get out of Africa. Its representatives met with Frelimo officials to discuss a power transfer. The people around Gorongosa Park and the mountain triumphantly returned to their land, ready to repair the ecological damage brought about by the fighting and by the spirits' anger at what had happened during it. (Focus, for a moment, on that latter point. As the historian Todd French points out, Gorongosans regard problems with the earth as a direct result of spirits being angry with people. This is different from our Western viewpoint, where we regard ecological degradation as something that *we* do and thereby offend our gods, however defined. These two approaches end up at about the same place—in both, people need to take good actions that result in a healthy earth—but the difference between them is striking.)

The joy of return, however, did not last long. Violence simmered throughout the country, as Portuguese citizens rioted against the new regime. Faced with destabilization, the new Mozambican government gave Portuguese settlers ninety days to become Mozambican citizens or leave. Across the country, Portuguese families began smashing their china, killing their livestock, and burning their supplies. They melted their jewelry and poured concrete into the sewer systems. They were not going to leave a speck for the Communists, they told one another. By 1977 a full 90 percent of the Portuguese in Mozambique had emigrated.

They left behind not only a battered infrastructure but also a country that was, in many ways, woefully unprepared for self-governance. Unlike the French and the British, the Portuguese had shown no desire to "civilize" the local population. Although Portuguese dictator António de Oliveira Salazar and his followers had long insisted that the African territories were part of a transcontinental Portuguese empire, the primary use of Mozambique was merely to offset Portugal's debts. Lisbon invested almost nothing in Mozambique's educational system or in training African professionals. At independence, in the country of ten million people there were fewer than a thousand black high school graduates. There were six economists. The illiteracy rate was 90 percent.

As if that weren't enough of a challenge, the country was still so rural (with 80 to 85 percent of the population living outside the cities) and the transportation network so rudimentary that many Mozambicans had no idea they were now living in an independent nation. This was no accident. The Portuguese colonizers had deliberately repressed any burgeoning sense of national identity within the African population, worrying that it would fuel popular resistance to Lisbon.

Along with striving to establish a nationalized economy, then, the Frelimo government quickly began expanding the country's educational system and working to minimize any potential ethnic and regional differences that could divide the new nation. It encouraged Portuguese-language instruction in all the country's school districts, believing this would be a good way to create a sense of national unity. The Frelimo government opened its offices to various ethnic groups and outlawed ethnic jockeying, repeating the mantra that all people living in Mozambique were equal. The new government, according to some observers, was also remarkably tolerant of dissenters—except, that is, when it came to those who believed in spirits and religion.

In the Gorongosa region, the delight at shedding colonial overlords turned to dismay as Frelimo began working to implement what it saw as the ideal socialist state. It outlawed many religious institutions, including Catholic parishes and schools that had long held a dominant place in the social structure of Gorongosa. It arrested spiritual leaders and mediums. It tried to dismantle the traditional lineage system of governance (in which the *régulo* acted as the representative of the *mhondoro* spirit, with an intricate network of rulers under him) that had continued throughout the colonial period. And if that weren't enough, soon Frelimo was suggesting to peasants that they leave their traditional farming plots and begin working together on communal farms, a notion that felt an awful lot like the hated *aldeamentos*.

The spirits cannot have been pleased by this. So it was terrible, but not much of a surprise to the people of the mountain, when the Disorder reappeared.

Historians disagree about the true causes of what would become known to the outside world as the Mozambican Civil War. Some say it was prompted almost entirely by outsiders—an attempt by the white-governed countries of Rhodesia and South Africa to destabilize their

newly independent, black-led neighbor, supported by neoconservatives
in the United States who saw the fight as a Cold War proxy. Others
point to the outrage and disillusionment in the more spiritual areas of
the country, and say that Frelimo intolerance of deeply held beliefs
naturally led to violent resistance. In Gorongosa, many people believe
the war came because the spirits were angry.

What is clear is that sometime soon after independence, a shadowy
fighting force took up residence on Mount Gorongosa. Later, Rhodesian military intelligence officers would acknowledge that they had
helped form and train this "pseudo-terrorist" group, made up of a collection of criminals, former Portuguese secret police officers, and out-
cast Frelimo fighters. They called it Renamo, the Resistência Nacional
Moçambicana. While it was initially created to combat independence
fighters in neighboring Rhodesia, its duties soon expanded to include
attacking Mozambican infrastructure. Renamo fighters blew up water
treatment plants and power lines, raided communal farm projects,
attacked buses, and dismantled railroad tracks. And, many peasants
said, they worked with traditional healers, *curandeiros*, to secure magic
powers before battle, washing their bodies with herbs that made them
bulletproof.

Renamo's first leader was a disgraced Frelimo army officer named
André Matsangaissa. Convicted of stealing a Mercedes-Benz, he escaped
a Mozambican work camp and joined the Rhodesians' effort. He was
killed in action in 1979, but his death turned into a legend repeated
throughout the war. According to the story, he was on a mission to
attack a government post near Gorongosa when a Frelimo soldier
shot him, point-blank, with an automatic rifle—but Matsangaissa was
unharmed. Another soldier then fired a bazooka at him. That finally
killed the Renamo leader, but the man who had fired the bazooka soon
went mad, felled, it was said, by a Renamo spell. After Matsangaissa's
death, his lieutenant Afonso Dhlakama took over. He also sought the
guidance of *curandeiros* and other spiritual leaders, including the rainmaker of Mount Gorongosa, Samatenje.

In reports found later at Renamo headquarters are multiple
matter-of-fact references to spiritual interventions during the war. There

are accounts of spirits confusing the enemy so that Frelimo soldiers shot at one another, and of Renamo fighters morphing into rocks, birds, and trees when Frelimo forces approached. Many of those on the Frelimo side believed the stories as well—particularly when it came to Mount Gorongosa, one of the focal points of the war. They believed they were unable to defeat Renamo forces there because the rebels had Samatenje's protection. At one point, according to mountain legend, government troops even flew to Gorongosa with the goal of capturing Samatenje, landing their helicopter far enough away that its rumble would not alert the rainmaker or his family. They were stopped by a local *régulo*, however, and ended up instead negotiating with Samatenje to create a sort of demilitarized zone around his homestead.

Some hoped that the collapse of Rhodesia in 1979 would end the fighting in Mozambique, but apartheid South Africa quickly took up the rebel cause. In the weeks leading up to the official transfer of power from the white Rhodesian government to Robert Mugabe and his black liberation coalition—who would rename their country Zimbabwe— South Africa sent a fleet of military transport planes to fly the Renamo fighters southward. The brutal apartheid security machine trained them in the ways of terrorism, supplied them with arms, and helped them recruit more members. Renamo's campaign of destruction in Mozambique became official, if publicly denied, South African policy.

As the fighting continued, Mugabe offered his own troops to help Frelimo battle the apartheid-supported enemy. Other neighboring countries supplied troops as well, and Mozambique became the center of an international war, where regional powers played out their Cold War acrimonies. The Soviet Union and Cuba helped the Frelimo government; neoconservatives in the United States, such as the would-be conservationist Jim Blanchard, funneled money to the rebels. Mozambican villagers were caught in the crossfire.

Foreign journalists who visited Mozambique wrote with shocked bewilderment about the level of destruction and trauma throughout the country. There were towns where every single windowpane had been smashed, maternity wards where every woman and child was slaughtered. There was no clear political reasoning behind the war, no articulated, conflicting philosophies. It was just chaos. Disorder. And out of this disorder was birthed yet another kind of spirit: the *gamba*.

Gamba spirits were an important force in the Gorongosa region by the time I arrived there in the early 2000s, a decade after the end of the civil war. As Mozambican anthropologist Victor Igreja explained to me, the *gambas* were typically spirits of soldiers who had been killed far away from home and never given a proper funeral. Sometimes the soldier's body, after death, was used by people living in the war zone for their own "protective medicine." This sort of black magic is not uncommon in southern Africa, although people do not like to talk about it; it is what happens when the darker sides of the spirit and human worlds intermix. Because a man's remains were not reunited with the land of his ancestors, the *gamba* wanders—furious. He wants revenge.

The people around Gorongosa recognized this new spirit from the violent, inexplicable hardships that began to befall them after the war. Families were shattered by sickness and death, husbands and wives quarreled, crops failed. The spiritual mediums who typically intervene in such situations, finding out which angry spirit is behind a particular problem and what must be done to appease it, were unable to help. At the same time, village women were becoming possessed. They would say angry things to their neighbors and family members. They would curse, and speak in foreign tongues—often the languages of the troops who had traveled through Gorongosa during the war.

In time, some of the women who had been possessed became healers themselves. They performed dangerous ceremonies, taking on a spirit exorcised from another woman's body to allow the *gamba* to reveal his wishes. Sometimes the spirit was content with reparations: a family would offer him back his boots, the weapons taken from him, even parts of his body. But sometimes the *gamba*, yearning for the sort of connection and lineage ties denied to him by his violent death, wanted something else: a wife.

And so women across the Gorongosa region began to become *gamba* wives—going through real marriage ceremonies, building marital huts, and earning the sort of respect reserved for married women. They could begin relationships with human men, too, if that were approved by the *gamba* husband, but any of their children were considered part of the spirit's lineage. They could also become healers, working to help other women and families who were targets of a *gamba*'s anger.

But these sorts of healers and *gamba* wives were not the only new figures to emerge in this age of the *gamba* spirit. The *gambas*, it turned out, were powerful not only in vengeance but in business. A *gamba* could help secure political power or commercial success far more effectively than other spirits. In other words, if you wanted to be rich, one clear way to the top was to harness one of the dangerous *gamba* spirits and get him to work for you.

Soon enough, a new group of mediums—men, primarily, in a telling case of gender disparity—arose not to rescue people from *gamba* clutches, but to help them use a *gamba*'s power for personal gain. There was a dark twist to this particular sort of sorcery: the *gamba*'s price for such assistance was blood. Usually it was a child who would die—often, but not always, a relative. More and more children began to sicken and die around Mount Gorongosa, while more and more individuals— many from out of town—became increasingly wealthy. It was the work of the *gamba*, people said. Like the angry *npfukwa* born in colonial times, the *gamba* spirits showed the clear, terrifying danger of valuing material goods over social traditions.

The spiritual and political background of this one remote district, in a country that is itself only a minor player in the world of international policy and economics, perhaps seems a bit too narrow a subject to take up so much attention on our larger safari of conservation in Africa. But I would argue that this particularity—the detailed history, the current reality, the local understanding of how life works—is central to the question of why our conservation efforts in the developing world often fall short of expectations. Large-scale projects and big aid ideas rarely delve into this level of specificity. Yet Gorongosa *is* incredibly specific. It is also specifically different from all other regions, which are themselves unique and peculiar in ways that often make no sense to a Western understanding of the world. Yet we regularly attempt to implement policies that change only infinitesimally from one region to another, while remaining all the time within our own narratives. In this regard, what happened in Gorongosa is quite representative.

In the Live Aid, five-act-play development narrative, Gorongosa was building its economic capacity, following World Bank–approved and McKinsey-endorsed plans for improving infrastructure. Development officials were helping pave the way, literally and figuratively, for new markets and consumers. On the conservation front, Greg Carr was embarking on a bold new humanistic approach to environmentalism that offered a real chance of helping people and nature at the same time. Everything in the region was looking up.

In the narrative of the *gamba* and *npfukwa*, however, with a history of outsider incursions that both angered traditional spirits and bred new, even more damaging ones, all these developments looked like the newest phase of disorder. And it was *this* story that Greg Carr and his team of conservationists—backed by some of the best academic and strategic minds of the West, motivated by the most benevolent of intentions, welcomed by the power brokers of Maputo—dropped into, coming out of the sky in a helicopter painted red. The color everyone on the mountain associated with the *gamba*.

8

Beware the Mountain

The Gorongosa ecosystem is the result of a perfect intersection of natural forces. Wet Indian Ocean air sweeps inland from the coast and eventually hits the eighteen-mile-long Mount Gorongosa, towering escarpment-like above its surroundings. The rising air cools into blankets of rain clouds, which feed a series of springs and streams and rivers, which in turn flow down the mountain and into the park's Urema floodplain. In the wet season, the lake measures seventy-seven square miles, a source of water that supports an intricate chain of living things. In the dry season, it shrinks to just four square miles—leaving much of the central part of Gorongosa Park looking like a golden-blond grassland—but it never vanishes entirely. It is this expanding and contracting wetland, Greg's scientists knew, that allowed the great animal populations to thrive naturally in Gorongosa Park, whereas most protected areas in Africa need man-made watering holes to keep herds alive in the dry season.

Trees on the mountain are essential to this hydrology. Their thick canopy absorbs sunlight and keeps the air cool; their root systems prevent erosion and allow those springs and rivers to exist. Which is why, not long after he began his project, Greg and a few of his scientists took a helicopter ride to check on them.

The conservationists had heard some rumblings that deforestation was increasing on top of Mount Gorongosa. This was no small concern—and, it turns out, not a new one, either. Back in the 1960s, scientists working at Gorongosa National Park had already noted both the vital importance of the mountaintop forests and the fear that local people might destroy the entire ecosystem if they did not stop chopping down trees. "One particular water holds the key to life . . . the perennial water from Gorongosa Mountain," wrote Ken Tinley, a South African biologist hired by the Portuguese government to take a comprehensive ecological survey of the park. "Protection of this mountain catchment island is therefore of prime importance to ensure its copious, but at the same time tenuous, harvest of water."

Tinley worried that locals were cutting down too many trees, too high up on the mountain—a practice he believed threatened the entire park. He urged his Portuguese higher-ups to expand the park's boundaries to include much of the mountain. This, he said, would let scientists regulate land use and slow deforestation. The Portuguese administrators agreed with him. But then the independence uprisings began, and all such plans were abandoned along with the park itself.

The day he boarded the helicopter for a better look at the mountain, then, Greg knew that the forests there were under threat. But nothing, he would tell me, prepared him for what he saw. Looking down, the conservationists spotted swath after swath of forest newly cleared for small agricultural plots. Trees hundreds of years old lay felled on their sides; stumps smoldered in charred fields. Although they had heard about deforestation worries, the conservationists had also been told by local leaders that the mountain was sacred, and that traditional prohibitions kept peasants from clearing farmland on the upper slopes. The extent of the problem was a shock.

Greg's scientists quickly looked up old satellite images of the mountain and confirmed what they had feared: deforestation on Mount Gorongosa was increasing rapidly. They determined that if nothing changed, within five years the ecosystem of Gorongosa National Park would be damaged beyond repair. All Greg's plans, all their work, all the hope of helping Africa would be for naught. "You're talking about one of the most mysterious, magical mountains in the world, and it's got two or three years left," Greg told me, shaking his head.

Still, as one of his business associates recounted, Greg was a "consummate optimist." He quickly decided that the need to save Mount Gorongosa could add a whole new dimension to his project. The mountain was already known in some bird-watching circles, thanks to the rare avian species endemic there. But its extraordinary beauty held the promise of much wider appeal. Going there was "like stepping into another world," park officials wrote on their website. Towering forests gave way to montane grasses and mist-covered wildflowers; waterfalls tumbled hundreds of feet down rock faces; orchids dripped from tree branches. Vistas opened up for miles over the blue-green valley.

All this, Greg realized, would appeal to many of the tourists visiting the national park. If his project created a series of culturally sensitive ecotourism opportunities on the mountain, with local communities gaining the revenue, it could give alternative economic opportunities to the peasants slashing down the forest, and preserve the ecology of the entire Gorongosa ecosystem. It was an extension of the original concept for Gorongosa Park, now reaching into one of the most culturally and biologically important places in the region.

But to do this, Greg knew, he would have to get local buy-in. Which is why he and his team flew over to visit Samatenje, the rainmaker.

Although the villagers on the ground did not look particularly happy to see them, the people in the helicopter slid off their leather seats, jumped out the open doors, and walked—heads ducked under the still-whirring blades—toward the crowd. And soon the first breach appeared in the brittle wall of silence. The low murmur did not have the same timbre as the chatter in other communities, but it seemed to the Western visitors, who did not speak the language, that perhaps all would soon return to normal. Nobody was aggressive or threatening. Perhaps, they thought, the people of the rainmaker simply did not understand why these white foreigners had arrived. This was a remote place, after all. Perhaps it was so remote that visitors were not only unusual but a little scary.

The Mozambican staff members of the park, though, understood the whispers. The evil ones had come, the people in the crowd told one another, glancing at the helicopter. It was an omen. The color red represented blood and war; it was the color of *gamba* spirits who roamed across the land, taking over the bodies of women, forcing the repayment of debts through pain and suffering. And the red chopper had landed *here*, near the sacred space of Samatenje.

The murmuring became louder, until suddenly the crowd shattered. People began running outward, as if fleeing a bomb that had been placed in the center of the group. Snake! they shouted. A snake!

It was coming up from the earth, with no warning, emerging from the ground as an ancestor would claw his way up from death. Never had a snake appeared like this before, they said. It was clearly another omen. Fear spread, invisible but unmistakable, electric.

A biologist from the Netherlands named Bart Wursten, one of Greg's staff members who had accompanied him on the helicopter, pricked up his ears at the mention of the reptile. He pushed through the crowd, eager to see which particular species had caused the commotion. Bart appreciated most creatures creepy and crawly, and was often eager to share his knowledge with those not equally attuned to the reptilian kingdom. "It's not a snake," he shouted in English, as he neared the center. "Not a snake at all but a legless lizard! Totally harmless!" The crowd gasped as the biologist tried to pull the creature from the depths to show them. It was totally safe, he shouted again.

They watched, eyes wide. It was a battle between the white hand grasping to show them logic, to *prove* logic, and the black body flailing to get away, to return to its earth, down into the depths of a world invisible to those above. Whether it was a lizard or snake or an ancestor, it clearly did not want to be in the scientist's grasp. When it finally escaped, wriggling and slapping its tail this way and that, a frantic display, the scientist was left empty-handed, kneeling in the dust. "It's safe," Bart said again, to the now-silent crowd. And then, slightly subdued: "Perfectly safe."

The crowd on the mountain appeared stunned. Roberto, then the park's warden, crossed his arms over his chest, standing somewhat to the side, watching as the people began to murmur.

"What are they saying?" Greg asked him.

Roberto kept his eyes on the crowd. "They are saying," he explained to the philanthropist, "that we are evil spirits. And some of them do not want to take us to Samatenje." He glanced at Greg. "And they think we want to steal their mountain."

Greg sighed. "They need to understand," he said, almost plaintively. "We're here to help."

A barefoot old man with a scowling, angular face was pacing back and forth in front of the crowd, yelling. He wore a tweed sports coat discarded years ago in another world, too long in the sleeves and too broad in the shoulders, and fraying gray shorts. The crowd watched him intently. He was recounting the evidence, pointing out the danger signs, urging the others to prevent the visitors from meeting with Samatenje. Some stepped up to debate him, respectfully. A strong-looking young man with his T-shirt torn in the back cast his eyes downward as the scowling old man turned on him. Members of the park staff spoke up, along with one of the *régulos* who had come for the meeting. Others took the side of the old man.

Eventually the crowd decided that Samatenje himself should be the judge of what to do with these outsiders. So everyone headed out from the clearing, walking through maize fields for the better part of an hour, the men carrying the beer and soda and other offerings that the park administrators had brought for a potential ceremony.

Suddenly the line of walkers stopped. Word filtered from one person to another: everyone should take off their shoes. Already the outsiders had trod too far into the pure region of Samatenje with their feet covered, yet another affront to the rainmaker. The park staffers sat down, apologizing and glancing at one another, and took off their Keens and Merrells to find the warm traction of the dirt.

It was late afternoon by the time we reached the rainmaker's homestead, which to an outsider looked similar to the other homesteads I had visited on the mountain. There were a few thatched buildings around a swept dirt clearing, and reed mats laid out for visitors. A man with dreadlocks was sitting on a bench. As the crowd settled, he began talking—shouting, really, although it was unclear if he was angry. Roberto whispered to Greg that the man was recounting all the mistakes the visitors had made, although he purported not to be upset with the outsiders, since white people wouldn't know better. He was angry at the locals who had not fully instructed the visitors in how to respect Samatenje.

"Wait," Greg asked, gesturing at the dreadlocked man. "Is that Samatenje?"

No, someone told him. Samatenje is in his hut. He never leaves the hut. This man is just interpreting his thoughts.

"Wow," Greg said.

The sun dropped, the orange glob falling behind the trees in that rapid way it does in southern Africa. The light blue of dusk turned to navy, then black. Flickers of dagga blunts started to appear, like stars sprinkling the velvet darkness. The place smelled of marijuana and warm earth. The dreadlocked man began scolding one of the younger *régulos* for wearing his Portuguese-style uniform to the meeting—a social misstep—and ordered him into the maize field to change. Greg looked on, incredulous.

After an hour or two, the dreadlocked man invited the other *régulos* to go to the rainmaker's shrine, and the crowd waited again. Greg leaned back on his reed mat and looked at the stars. Tosh, the helicopter pilot, whispered that he hoped the villagers hadn't torched his red chopper, waiting back in the clearing some miles away. My photographer colleague Jeff decided that it was too dark to keep shooting pictures and tried to take a nap. I doodled in my notebook.

An hour or so later, the people began to stand up and dust themselves off. Greg looked around.

"That's it," Roberto said.

"That's it?"

"Yes. No ceremony."

The rainmaker, apparently, had declined to bless the park project. But he'd asked to keep the beer.

I remember clearly the walk back to the helicopter. Some of the people who lived on the mountain guided us, using the lights on the back of their cell phones to show us the way. (Although there was no electricity on the mountain, by that point mobile technology existed even in the most rural parts of southern Africa.) Of course the rainmaker wouldn't give the park a blessing on the first ask, Greg said as we walked. That would have been too easy. Now, when the rainmaker *did* decide to help the park, it would mean more.

And besides, Greg continued, maybe we don't even need the rainmaker. Did you see how he embarrassed that young *régulo*, making him go into the bushes and change clothes? I bet if we go and meet with that young guy and show him a lot of respect, make friends with him, we might get his support. And this whole thing with the helicopter and the snake and the shoes and the spirits—it will all blow over soon, and we'll come back and get Samatenje on our side.

A legless lizard, Bart said. It was a legless lizard.

Greg continued to spin this cheerful take on the evening throughout our entire walk back to the clearing. By the time we arrived there, he was all but calling the evening a smashing success, the consummate optimist in full force.

The helicopter was still there, much to Tosh's relief. And back in Chitengo Camp that night, Greg and Bart and the others who'd been on the flight recounted for the rest of the staff their story of the crazy meeting on the mountain.

But their story was not the only one. According to dozens of people I talked to, both park staffers and others living in the Gorongosa region, Greg's visit to Samatenje did not blow over. Indeed, in this other story, when Greg landed in his *gamba*-colored helicopter, he not only committed a spiritual faux pas but also stepped into a long-running war—a war that, unbeknownst to him, he would continue fighting for years.

This war was not just about the lingering Frelimo-Renamo tensions in the district, although those clearly affected how people on the mountain perceived the park restoration project. (Gorongosa was, after all, a *national* park—an operation of the ruling Frelimo government—while the Gorongosa region was still friendly to Renamo, now an opposition party.) This conflict was something bigger. It was between the generations of outsiders who have tried in various ways to control the land and the local people—and spirits—who have long resisted.

"You have to understand," one of the local elders connected to the ruling family of Canda told me. "It's in the very name."

"The name?" I asked.

You see, he said, once upon a time a group of Ngoni fighters arrived at the base of the mountain. These were feared warriors. They had broken away some years earlier from the kingdoms of Shaka Zulu and migrated with their cowhide shields up through the misty hills of eastern Zimbabwe, plundering and fighting as they went. They swept through Mozambique, toward Malawi. And people knew to fear them.

When they saw the Ngoni coming, the people of the mountain fled up its blue-green slopes. They hid and took up their positions. Some of the others who had stayed behind tried to warn the outsiders as they approached: *goro ngosa*.

The elder looked at me, expecting me to understand. It was a Bantu language phrase, he finally explained. It means "the mountain is dangerous." Or, in other translations, "beware the mountain."

As the fighters got closer to the mountain, the peasants who had been hiding there pushed a barrage of boulders down its magic slopes. The Ngoni were crushed, and the mountain remained unconquered.

The moral of the legend was clear, the elder said. Nobody can take the mountain. And though many may try, they always suffer in the end.

From this perspective, Greg's actions—both his visit to Samatenje and, later, his efforts to get mountain residents on board with everything from tree-planting campaigns to ecotourism ventures—were not cultural slipups. They were attacks. The conservationists were outside invaders, trying to seize control. This aroused the *mhondoro* clan spirits, whose job it is to protect the land. And these spirits—who, like the *gamba*, are present and real forces in current events—began to fight back.

The mountain is dangerous. Beware the mountain.

One of the first victims was Bart, the scientist who had tried to pull the ancestor out of the ground.

On a particularly pleasant day a month or two after the unsuccessful trip to the rainmaker, Bart and his wife, Petra, climbed into their Carr Foundation–issued 4×4 at Chitengo Camp and started on the long drive out of the park. They were headed to a city a few hours away to pick up some tourists for a birding expedition. The air had the thin blue hue of a morning in the dry season. Sunlight filtered through the tall palms and miombo leaves, an almost pure white.

To the casual observer, Bart and Petra made a funny couple. The Belgian Petra was soft-natured and calm, while Bart was bombastic and brash, his loud Dutch-accented English often sounding indignant. One of the first times I saw him was after Greg had distributed printouts of the park's new website to the staff members. Almost immediately, Bart went into a tizzy, stomping across the dusty driveway, shaking the pages, and muttering to anyone who happened to cross his path.

"Lantana!" he sputtered, spitting out the word as he marched up the stairs to confront Greg, who was sipping coffee at a table in the *boma*.

Greg looked up. "Yes, Bart?"

"This," Bart said, barely able to contain himself, "this here is a picture of . . ." He took a deep breath and pointed to a photo of a shrublike plant with yellow flowers, captured against a bright blue sky. "Lantana."

Greg looked at him.

Frustrated with the silence, Bart threw up his hands. "Lantana!" he exclaimed. "One of the most noxious, invasive plants around! It's all over the mountain. This is terrible! And here we are showing it on our website."

"This is a weed?" Greg asked, looking closer at the yellow flower.

"A weed? A weed?" Bart was sputtering again. "It's lantana!"

"So we have an invasive plant featured on our home page," Greg said slowly, as a grin started to make its way across his face. "This is funny."

"It's terrible!" Bart grabbed the printout back from him and turned on his heels.

"Sorry, Bart," Greg called after him. "We'll fix it."

When Petra heard about this she sighed. "Oh, Bart," she said.

The two of them had spent years working together. A decade earlier, they had decided to build a small guesthouse and hiking business in what they thought was the most beautiful place they had ever seen, the Vumba Mountains, in the misty blue highlands of eastern Zimbabwe. Their lodge looked like something out of a fairy tale, with a thatched roof and flowering bushes enveloping its walls. It was rustic, beautiful, and friendly. They never had any desire to leave the place, but the political and economic situation in Zimbabwe deteriorated to the point where operating a small business without connections to the ruling regime became all but impossible.

So when Greg Carr offered the two of them jobs with his project, and said that he wanted them to design a sustainable tourism business on Mount Gorongosa, it seemed to Bart and Petra a fortunate opportunity. They would be close enough to Zimbabwe to keep the guesthouse, and they would earn a reliable salary while working in another breathtaking region. They'd stay immersed in wild flora and fauna, which they often found far more appealing than people.

They knew that they had a tough task ahead of them. There was no tourism infrastructure on the mountain, and quite a bit of community resistance. But everyone figured that to convince locals to work with conservationists they needed to get tourists—and their money—to the mountain as soon as possible. So Bart and Petra quickly set about identifying a location for a base camp, arranging for local guides, scouting out trails, and managing the sorts of dizzying complications that come with starting any venture in rural Africa.

They were up for the challenge. And they enjoyed getting to spend some one-on-one time together, even if it was on the rocky, bumpy road out of Chitengo Camp.

The first two-thirds of that road is in the park itself, from Chitengo to a gate at the park's border manned by a team of rangers. The rest of the road, from the ranger post to the paved highway, is outside the park, and at that time it was in particularly bad shape. According to whispers among park staffers, the government and the Carr Foundation were in a bit of a showdown: Greg was insistent that the Mozambican government maintain its own infrastructure, while the government figured that if it neglected the road long enough, the Carr Foundation would eventually pony up the money to make the passage more pleasant for tourists. The result was a horrendous ride, with handmade wooden bridges that groaned as cars drove over them, slick gravel, and dangerous ridges deepened every year by the rushing waters of the rainy season.

It was around one of the bends in this part of the road that Bart's truck began to skid. As the wheels spun hopelessly on the loose, sandy gravel, the momentum of the vehicle pushed it sideways toward the edge of the road, which dropped abruptly into a three-foot-deep ditch. Bart tried to steer away, but that only caused the truck to fishtail further. Within seconds the truck careened off the road and flipped. Bart flew up and sideways, smashing his skull against the top of the cab and crushing his back. Petra was propelled forward into the shattered windshield, her ear ripping away from her head.

They would certainly have died there, everyone agreed, had it not been for a truck of rangers that happened to drive by a few minutes after the crash. The park called for medevac helicopters.

Taken quickly to a well-staffed Johannesburg hospital, Bart and Petra survived the accident. Despite his injuries, Bart was even able to walk again. But their troubles did not end. Not long after Bart returned, in limited capacity, to his work around Gorongosa, a mysterious fire destroyed his and Petra's beloved Vumba Mountains guesthouse. Then the couple did not get another contract with the Carr Foundation. And in 2008, with political violence roiling Zimbabwe, a gang of young Mugabe supporters invaded and ransacked the home the couple had kept near their former lodge.

Without a home, a job, or any foreseeable way of earning a living, the couple, with heavy hearts, left sunny Africa for Belgium.

On the mountain, few people I talked to were at all surprised.

By a year or so after the misguided visit to Samatenje, Greg was getting rather tired of the red helicopter story. I had written about it in one of my pieces on the park, and every reporter who came afterward seemed to ask him about it. It was a blunder, Greg was the first to admit that. But there were inevitably going to be some mistakes along the way on this ambitious and massively complicated project. He had sent word to his assistant that when arranging rental helicopters, the color red was unacceptable. And besides, he assured the growing crowd of journalists eager to hang out with him in his spectacular African park, everything had worked out just fine.

For one thing, the Westerners' confusion about the dreadlocked man at the rainmaker's homestead had been cleared up. "Samatenje," it turned out, is both the name of the spirit and a family name. In other words, as with most spiritual mediums in central Mozambique, the human being who goes by the label of Samatenje at any given time is essentially an interpreter, channeling the spirit. There have been generations of Samatenjes living on top of the mountain; when one dies, another takes over. This is why the dreadlocked man both was not and was Samatenje.

So they gave Samatenje a little bit of time and then returned with another offering, Greg explained. Greg's representatives apologized profusely for offending the ancestors. As a display of goodwill, and an effort to show that they simply wanted to help the ecosystem and the people, Greg offered to host Samatenje at Chitengo Camp and to give him an aerial tour of the park (in a blue helicopter, this time). They were not pressuring the rainmaker for a ceremony, the administrators assured him. They were simply making the humble request to be allowed to demonstrate that their goals were in line with his. They would show him from the air those patches of destroyed forests; they would talk about how they wanted to help preserve the rainmaker's land. Samatenje could decide, in his own time, whether he wanted to support the project.

Samatenje's advisers warned him against accepting. The spirits had been very clear about this, they told him. The outsiders involved in the park were dangerous; Samatenje should not leave the sacred homestead to go with them.

The medium disagreed. He left with the Mozambican park staffers in the helicopter and landed in Chitengo, where Greg was waiting. The park staff had prepared a sumptuous meal, and as they ate in the *boma*, some of the higher-level Mozambican staff members gave their pitch about environmental preservation. Greg escorted Samatenje personally on the aerial tour of the park. And by the end of the visit, Greg told me, Samatenje had agreed to support the Carr Foundation's restoration project.

Greg had someone take his picture with the rainmaker, who grinned into the camera with one arm draped over the white man's shoulder. Greg made this his Facebook profile photo.

The next time I was at the park, though, one of the younger staff members told me that this Samatenje had died suddenly. People on the mountain seemed uncomfortable going into any detail. He'd been sick, was all they said.

There were two possible explanations. For the Westerners, it seemed likely that the rainmaker had died of AIDS. The HIV infection rate was on the rise in Mozambique, and was particularly high around Gorongosa. And from what was known about the fairly young Samatenje—including what people said about his enjoyment of town pleasures, and the fact that in Gorongosa a man this powerful would typically have multiple sexual partners—this diagnosis was not particularly surprising.

For many locals, however, the explanation was different. Ever since that helicopter trip to Gorongosa National Park, people had started to whisper that this Samatenje was betraying his spirit and being corrupted by the money of the white man. Family members wondered if he was even the correct person to hold the title. So when he died, many assumed it was clearly the work of the spirits.

The new Samatenje, the dead man's brother, was far less amicable to the park project. He was not, he told park staffers, going to make the same mistakes as his brother.

The list of odd coincidences revolving around spirit life in Gorongosa got longer the longer I stayed there. One story, which I heard a number of times from both Mozambican residents and park employees, was about a young park staffer who ignored local prohibitions and climbed up a rock that was known to have connections to a fire spirit. When he was driving back to the park, his new 4×4, which had never had any mechanical troubles, randomly burst into flames.

A while later, a lioness somehow made her way into the locked and fenced Chitengo Camp—just a few hours after a spiritual leader had performed a ceremony summoning the *mhondoro* spirit of the old leader Chitengo, for whom the camp was named. According to local legend, Chitengo, a magician-warrior in life, had turned into a lion after death. When the intruding lioness left the camp, she walked directly to the spot in the woods where the old warrior was buried.

It was enough to make even the most secular Westerner raise an eyebrow now and then. Still, I'd have a hard time arguing that the spirits actually caused Bart's accident, or Samatenje's death, or that the legless lizard was actually an ancestor provoked by the color of evil spirits. In my world, spirits do not cause car accidents. Bad roads and bad luck (in as nonspiritual a sense as possible) do. Spirits do not bring death or set 4×4s on fire. AIDS and malfunctioning engines are far more likely culprits.

But what I *would* argue is that there are multiple self-consistent narratives of Gorongosa. And if somehow you were able to shed your cultural baggage and your ideas of how the world works, if you were able to listen to both stories of the mountain from a totally neutral, just-arrived-from-Mars perspective, I'm not sure you would go with mine. You'd probably decide that both Western and local stories make equal amounts of sense, and have equal-size gaps. Or maybe you'd even lean toward the spirits. After all, our Western stories require us to chalk up an awful lot of things to chance. They even, it turns out, require us to ignore a lot of evidence—including facts from within our own logic system.

Take, for instance, the conservationist story of local people destroying their own land and needing outsider help to change their ways. This narrative is hardly unique to the Gorongosa project. (It is not even unique to conservation—remember Livingstone and his fellow missionary adventurer-explorers, and their modern-day counterparts.) But in the case of Mount Gorongosa, it turns out, it is a particularly well-worn tale.

Tinley, the South African scientist who made the first ecological study of Gorongosa, worried about the behavior of the mountain's residents back in the 1960s. So did a Portuguese botanist named José Margarido de Aguiar Macêdo. Surveying Gorongosa around the same time that Tinley was doing his work, Aguiar Macêdo concluded that African villagers were "attacking" the mountain by moving their farming plots to higher altitudes. Both scientists warned of devastating, immediate consequences if local behavior did not change.

The mountain's hydrology, however, was still in decent shape as the twenty-first century began. A 2006 survey of Lake Urema concluded that despite the dire predictions the floodplain lake had seen more or less the same seasonal water heights from 1979 to 2000. This did not stop Greg and his administrators from repeating the same arguments that their predecessors had made four decades earlier, though. Once again, according to park officials, local behavior on the mountain was about to destroy the environment.

A number of academics familiar with central Mozambique and its history were concerned about the Carr Foundation's position. Some saw it as part of a pattern of hyping up "crisis" situations, where the West exaggerates the risk of imminent catastrophe in order to justify extraordinary interventions into foreigners' affairs. Others, more charitably, regarded it as yet another instance of well-intentioned but misguided "helpful" Western intervention.

The anthropologist Christy Schuetze lived on Mount Gorongosa in 2004, and initially believed the alarming Carr Foundation reports about its deforestation. She worried about her friends on the mountain and what was happening to their livelihoods. Once she returned to Mozambique, however, she found the "crisis" to be not quite as advertised.

"I was anxious to return and see the situation first hand," Schuetze wrote about a 2006 visit. "I expected to now be able to see in person what the video and reports described as 'denuded hillsides' above my host family's fields. But as I gazed up at the top of the mountain that loomed over my host family's home, the dark edge of the montane rainforest looked just as it had two years before. There was no sign of crisis, no visible clear cuts, and no barren hillsides as Greg Carr's e-mails had led me to imagine. The fields here were just as they had been since I began visiting the area in 1999."

Over the next few years, Greg and the park administration would launch a series of interventions to, in their words, "save the mountain." They started ecotourism initiatives, embarked on tree-planting campaigns, and talked to local leaders about more strictly enforcing laws against chopping down trees at high altitudes. By several independent accounts, however, these efforts flopped. The park eventually abandoned its plan to bring tourists onto the mountain. The tree-planting campaigns aroused much anger and controversy: in rural Mozambique, planting trees is a way of marking one's ownership of the land, thus many peasants vehemently opposed the project. In fact, by the five-year mark—that supposed deadline for the park's ecosystem being damaged beyond repair—a number of local people had responded to the park's efforts to protect the mountain by choosing to move *higher up* on its slopes. They told researchers that this was a form of protest: they expected that the white outsiders would try to force them all off the mountain soon enough anyway, so they were going to farm the rich soil while they could. Even after that, though, the park's hydrology remained intact.

So did the increasingly calcified opposing narratives. As far as many Gorongosans were concerned, the park officials appeared to be invaders, trying to illegitimately control their ancestors' land. Bart's near-fatal accident, the staffer's car fire, the mysterious lion appearance in the camp—all these were signs that the locals' narrative was, indeed, correct and that resistance was justified.

As far as the conservationists were concerned, the Gorongosans simply did not understand how the park's plans for reforestation and biological harmony would help them. They were risking long-term damage to a spectacular ecosystem that supported all sorts of life in central Mozambique; they were threatening both the park's biodiversity and their children's economic futures. At various meetings and in a slew of reports, park officials discussed how they could overcome this resistance—how they could, as Greg had said on that first visit to Samatenje, make locals see that they were there to help.

At no point did I ever see the park administration consider that the people of the mountain might be right. There was no imagining that their position, their story, might actually be as valid as that of the conservationists, that the Gorongosans might simply not want the outsiders there, regardless of their well-reasoned arguments. For Greg and his team, local opinion was just another obstacle to deal with if it did not fit the project plan. The locals did not have a vote in the matter.

Looking at it this way, it was hard to shake the troubling sense that Greg's initiative, birthed in the human rights movement, had moved away from some of its original ideals. And the problems with this went beyond the theoretical. In practical terms, lacking the support of many of those around the park meant that even the supposedly more straightforward part of the project—bringing animals back to Gorongosa— would become immeasurably complicated.

I would witness this myself in the saga of one elephant, who went by the name of G5.

9

Elephant on the Run

Something in the way that Carlos stormed across the dusty driveway made him appear even more agitated than usual. He gave a curt salute to a ranger walking toward the camp's main gate, and flicked some brushfire soot from where it had settled on his sleeve. He strode to the *boma*, that thatched-roof café and park staff meeting place, and sat down hard in one of the green plastic chairs, tossing his walkie-talkie onto the table.

I was sitting a few yards away, drinking the camp's sticky coffee as ants formed their conga line across the table to the sugar bowl. I exchanged glances with Jonathan Retzlaff, one of the park's guides, who was sitting nearby. Carlos was the warden now, and he always seemed to be managing a crisis. His ragtag army of rangers was in constant battle with an ever-shifting combination of poachers, potholes, wildfires, baboons, politicians, and river-poisoning gold miners.

"It's the elies," Jonathan explained in a low voice. Jonathan was a young Zimbabwean whose family's farm had been taken over by Mugabe cronies a few years back. He talked softly, and watched more than he talked.

"The elies?" I asked.

"The big bulls we got from Kruger. They're gone." He lit another cigarette.

"Gone?" I exclaimed, incredulous.

He gave a short laugh, took another drag, and said nothing.

I glanced toward Carlos again.

The elephants had arrived just a few weeks earlier. There were two old males and four juveniles, all from South Africa's Kruger Park, all with the large tusks that attract tourists and photographers and ivory hunters. The park staff was particularly excited about the two old bulls. These were the elephants most likely to mate, which meant they might introduce their genes for attractive tusks into the resident Gorongosa herd. For a hundred years in Gorongosa, hunters had picked off the elephants with the big tusks, so a sort of accelerated evolution by poaching had taken place: the local elephants were almost entirely tuskless, a genetic condition that occurs in only about 3 percent of natural, unstressed elephant populations.

The old bulls might also calm the skittish locals, staff members had said. Many of Gorongosa's elephants, having survived brutal war and intense poaching, were fearful or aggressive around humans. This was understandable, but not particularly helpful for guides hosting safari tourists—especially given that the older Gorongosa elephants were now passing their wary values down to their young. The park staff had hoped the bulls from Kruger, accustomed to shutter-snapping visitors, would be a good influence.

Greg had made a point to be at the park to watch the bulls' grand entrance, and his public relations staff had made sure to let journalists know about the animals' arrival. So there was a crowd looking on as the transport trucks rumbled into the park at dawn, and the park scientists sedated the bulls and sealed gigantic radio collars around their necks. The park staff wanted to be sure to keep track of these important animals. Every weekday, GPS data would be transmitted to an environmental data company, which would then e-mail the bulls' coordinates to Carlos. The creatures would be known in the park by their frequencies: G4 and G5.

As the anesthetic wore off, the bulls took their first wobbly steps and caressed the unfamiliar air with their trunks. Soon they directed their massive strides away from the hushed collection of onlookers, northeast across the savannah and toward the yellow fever tree forest. They were headed directly toward the park's existing herd of elephants, whom the rangers had spotted grazing some five miles away.

It was one of those elephant mysteries, Carlos remarked at the time. Somehow, the new bulls knew where the local elephants were hanging out—whether by smelling the air, or by feeling earth tremors through their feet, or by some other method of communication that humans don't yet understand.

That night, the scientists and film crews and other onlookers celebrated at the *boma*. Local news reports were breathless. "Elephants to Restore Gorongosa to Former Glory," declared the *Pretoria News*. "Kruger Elephants a Hefty Boost for Mozambican Park," wrote the *Star* of South Africa.

But that was then.

Now, with the spectators no longer around and the dry season fires blazing, there were problems. According to the radio collar signal, G4 had gone out of the unfenced park to the north. He seemed to be heading straight to the Zambezi River—a path that followed an ancient elephant migration route along an outlet of the Great Rift Valley, which now crossed into privately managed hunting reserves.

The situation with G5 was even worse. The last radio frequencies seemed to indicate that he had left the park to the south—into a populated area with villages and farms, highways and railroad tracks. But the park staff could not pinpoint exactly where he had gone. All they knew from the GPS was that potentially deadly human-elephant conflict was imminent. An animal the size of G5 could easily kill people, and terrified villagers might be quick to attack the bull.

I walked over to Carlos's table.

He looked up at me with narrowed eyes. "Yes, the elephant," he glowered. Then he sighed, leaned back in his chair, and gestured for me to sit down. Carlos was tough but unfailingly polite.

We were silent for a moment.

"This," he said softly, "could be a disaster."

Carlos decided to look for G5 from a helicopter. He told me that I could come along, so I climbed into the backseat of the small chopper and strapped myself in. The doors were off so that Carlos could hold the radio antenna out the window, hoping to pick up the signal from the elephant's tracking collar. We lifted over Chitengo Camp and flew toward the coffee-colored Pungue. Below us the land was charred, a palette of browns and crunchy blacks dotted by the withered green of the tops of palm trees.

It was the end of a particularly bad dry season.

The rains here stop every year during the Southern Hemisphere winter, and every year fires start in the parched bush. Some fire is an essential part of the ecosystem, of course: it burns overgrown grasses and shrubs, making way for new, sunlight-seeking plants. This young growth feeds grazers such as zebra and sable antelope, animals that have difficulty munching their way through thick, thorny, dried overgrowth.

Although park managers in Gorongosa recognize the ecological importance of fire, they still try to control these dry season blazes, just as the American park service controls late summer wildfires in Yellowstone. In Gorongosa, the warden arranges deliberate burns that eliminate the most flammable vegetation, and his rangers build fire barriers around Chitengo Camp and some of the particularly ecologically sensitive sections of the park. This way the bush fires serve their purpose, but there are still safe areas for wildlife and enough vegetation for the park's animals to survive until the next rainy season.

Lately, though, many of the fires had been man-made. Some started because neighboring slash-and-burn farmers lit their fields on the wrong day and wind spread the flames into the park. But more often, Carlos told me, the fires in the park were set intentionally. Poachers are the primary arsonists, he said. The flames make it easier for them to hunt. Fire clears out vegetation that might be hiding an elephant or a lion, and thus make it safer for hunters to sneak through the bush. The fires also send fleeing animals into traps and snares.

I had also heard whispers that villagers angry about the park's policies were setting fires as a kind of revenge. That year, Carlos estimated, over 50 percent of Gorongosa National Park had burned—more than before Greg started his project here. The result was the charred landscape we were looking down at, a land that had very little food for the animals remaining.

We dipped and darted in the way of helicopters and spotted the resident herd of Gorongosa elephants huddled in a small grove of palm trees, trying to find leaves to eat. Carlos shook his head. These Gorongosa elephants must be accustomed to the annual fires, he presumed, even if they found the blazes stressful. The new arrivals from South Africa, though, had always lived in the well-managed Kruger Park; they'd never had to deal with this sort of environmental trauma. It's quite possible that the fires spooked G5 enough that he had decided to go home, Carlos said. After all, the latest coordinates suggested that the big bull was charting a course directly back to Kruger.

"He was peacefully living here," Carlos said. "And suddenly he just disappears."

We flew away from Gorongosa Park. Carlos scanned the scattered collections of thatched-roof huts; the wide expanses of brown that might blossom again when the rains came; the dusty, weak greens of stubborn maize fields; the occasional baobab tree, with its thick scarecrow arms reaching outward.

We did not see the elephant. Carlos sighed and told the pilot to turn back to camp. Tomorrow, he said, the company that manages the elephants' radio collar data would e-mail G5's current GPS coordinates. Until then, we would just have to wait.

Carlos knew a lot about G5, at least as far as facts and figures were concerned. In the portable trailer that served as his warden's office, he had stacks of manila files holding information about the animal. He knew, for instance, that G5 measured ten and a half feet from the ground to the shoulder; that his ankles were three feet around; that he weighed approximately fourteen thousand pounds. The elephant's tusks—the main reason for his journey to Gorongosa in the first place—extended four feet out of his skin, and the part of the tusk under his gray flesh was equally long. He was about forty years old. The only way to know the exact age of an elephant is to examine his teeth closely, which is not something you do unless there is a dire need, so "about forty" was fine for Carlos.

The Gorongosa Park staffers had been thrilled with G5's addition to the landscape. He had been mellow, contentedly munching on palm leaves while tourists snapped pictures.

The Kruger Park officials were happy, too. They were reveling in their role as regional environmental benefactors: the South African park had given the elephants to the Gorongosa rehabilitation project for free. They also hoped to score some points on the home front. The animal donation was proof that Kruger was working creatively to solve what many beleaguered South African officials had started to refer to, simply, as the Elephant Problem—a drama that had roiled the highest levels of government in Africa's most developed country. When Kruger officials sent G5 and his companions to Gorongosa, with much fanfare, they put the bulls in the middle of one of the most contentious conservation fights in recent African history.

To understand the Elephant Problem, you need to realize that what happens in Kruger Park affects environmental efforts across the entire southern part of the continent. As South Africa's flagship national park, Kruger is the focal point for some of the world's most adventuresome conservation work. It is also one of the oldest national parks on the continent, and has for decades exemplified both the problems and the potential of African conservation.

Kruger's creators, a collection of expats and white South Africans, believed that South Africa's northeast corner was an ideal spot for a game reserve. The area had never been particularly good for farming, thanks to the cattle-killing tsetse fly, which is prolific there, and it made a convenient stopover point for travelers en route from booming Johannesburg to the sexy seaside city of Lourenço Marques (now Maputo),

the capital of Portuguese East Africa. In the late 1800s, these early conservationists managed to get much of the land designated as "protected." Then they received an extra boost from that central figure of
our conservation narratives, the man who keeps popping up in the
story of how we understand African wilderness: former U.S. president
Theodore Roosevelt.

Roosevelt was flush from his conservation successes in the United
States, and had recently returned, laden with animal carcasses, from
his own African safari. He believed that if South Africa followed the
relatively new American model of setting up national parks, it could
prove an example to other countries, and further the global conservation goals to which he felt increasingly committed. So the former
president started advising park proponents in Johannesburg. He suggested they tap into national pride to overcome resistance from other
white South Africans, particularly farmers, who wanted to shoot lions
rather than preserve them. The conservationists eventually heeded this
advice, and named the proposed park after South African president Paul
Kruger. This political move worked like a charm: even the staunchest
lion hunter felt a bit moved by the notion of calling such a place after the
granddaddy of Afrikaner nationalism. Kruger National Park was officially established in 1926.

Nobody involved in creating the park seems to have been all that
worried about one possible glitch in their plans: there were people living
in the so-called nature area. This was not a concern because these
inhabitants were black and therefore had no voice in the matter. When
the white policy makers decided that it was in the best interest of the
land for the area to be human-free, they relocated thousands of black
residents out of the newly formed park, and declared that anyone hunting within the park's boundaries would be labeled a poacher.

Another difficulty for the new Kruger National Park—one of
more interest to the founders—was that there were almost no animals. Because of the hunting throughout the nineteenth century, the
huge numbers of elephants, lions, and buffalo that had once roamed
the lowveld were all but extinct by 1926. Many South Africans scoffed
at the park, calling it the "gameless game reserve." But decades of envi-

ronmental management brought wildlife back, helping create what is now one of southern Africa's main tourist attractions. And although in the postapartheid era new political tensions have moved into the foreground, including concerns about land rights and the well-being of the impoverished blacks who live just outside the park, South Africa's black-led government has repeatedly voiced its commitment to conservation in general, and to Kruger Park—still named for that Afrikaner forebearer—in particular.

(This stance is particularly impressive when one considers the apartheid-era history of the park. Not only were blacks barred from almost all its recreation areas, but the park was also used as an undercover military training ground for the South African Defence Force, which battled Nelson Mandela's African National Congress and other liberation movements. It was also the place where the apartheid government helped train guerrilla forces to destabilize Mozambique.)

Today Kruger is not only chock-full of animals, but it is profitable—a rarity among protected areas, especially in Africa, and one of the reasons Greg Carr believed that Gorongosa could prove a similar economic boon to central Mozambique. More than a million tourists visit Kruger Park every year, and each one of them pays an entrance fee. Thousands of South Africans have jobs in the park, and it is the site of internationally renowned scientific ventures, environmental preservation efforts, global conservation initiatives, and educational programming.

It is also home to a whole lot of elephants. Too many, Kruger Park officials say. So many, in fact, that officials at the park have said that they would very much like to kill them.

I remember reading about the Elephant Problem for the first time as a newbie Africa correspondent, sitting in my pretty garden office in the northern suburbs of Johannesburg. It seemed absurd. To Americans like me, elephants are one of the endangered species that grace the covers of WWF brochures and San Diego Zoo pledge pamphlets. You could "adopt" one for fifty dollars a month and help make sure that its adorable babies, with their too-big ears and big brown eyes, didn't end up orphaned like Babar. How was it possible that they were being described here, essentially, as pests?

I started to look into the topic some more. It turned out that in much of Africa, elephants were indeed endangered. Despite a 1989 world ban on ivory trading, well-armed international smuggling syndicates were still very much in operation across the continent. In South Africa, however, many park officials were saying that their earlier conservation efforts had been *too* successful. Now, the officials said, there were so many elephants roaming around Kruger and other parks that they were destroying the ecosystem. The elephants were eating too much—a large bull will consume more than six hundred pounds of vegetation a day— and knocking over too many trees. Other animals were suffering, the officials said. Something had to be done.

This concept of "too many elephants" was not new. During the apartheid era, the park's management team had dealt with what they saw as elephant overpopulation by regularly culling the animals. "Culling," of course, is a nice way to say "killing." For years, rangers would fly around the park in helicopters, shooting elephants.

This was not a pretty practice. A former game ranger from Kruger told me that although some of his coworkers seemed to get off on rounding up and executing elephants, he hated it. He said it was one of the most distasteful jobs he ever had. He explained that the rangers would first use the park's helicopters to herd a group of elephants into a tight circle. Then they would shoot the animals with darts that held a lethal tranquilizing drug called succinylcholine chloride. The drug paralyzed the elephants, who would fall to their knees gasping for breath. The animals would remain conscious as they became increasingly immobilized and eventually suffocated. If the process was taking too long—more than a couple of minutes—one of the rangers would shoot the struggling elephant in the head.

Between 1966 and 1994, the park killed more than 16,000 elephants this way, an average of some 550 per year. With thousands of elephants in the park, the majority of them—such as G5, who was growing up during this period—avoided the trauma. But the psychological effect on the elephants who did witness the killings was immense.

Increasingly, scientific studies of elephants have shown levels of intelligence and even empathy that rival those of humans. Biologists have reported elephants participating in mourning rituals, with the animals returning again and again to the place where an older herd member has died, caressing her skull with their trunks. They also show clear concern when one member of a herd is shot, especially if it is the leading matriarch. Often elephants make themselves vulnerable to follow-up attacks because they will not leave a fallen grandmother; instead, they will try desperately to lift her back to her feet, crying a harrowing sound all the while. Unlike many other animals, elephants— who are too big to have natural predators—do not seem to notice a hunter reloading.

Behavior changes are evident in young elephants whose mothers are killed. During the apartheid-era culling program, for instance, rangers did not shoot the cute baby elephants, perhaps worried about making the culls too distasteful to the public. Instead, they moved many of the young animals to the small Pilanesberg Game Reserve, north of Johannesburg. Soon, it became clear that these orphaned elephants were traumatized from witnessing the death of their family groups, and from being left to live on their own without the guidance of older relatives.

As they grew up, the Pilanesberg elephants turned deviant. They acted aggressively toward humans and safari vehicles, which was not too surprising. But more creepily, they also started killing and, according to some reports, raping rhinoceroses in the reserve—a highly abnormal behavior pattern. Elephants are herbivores, and relatively peaceful. They rarely kill other animals, or one another, in territory disputes or for any other reason. Scientists at Pilanesberg eventually imported six older elephant males from Kruger Park herds that had not been subjected to culling, and the younger males calmed down. Still, the experience convinced some park officials that the culling program was flawed, inflicting more damage than they had realized.

Around the same time, international animal welfare organizations increased their calls for an end to South Africa's elephant killing. In prior years, the apartheid government had simply ignored these protests; it was, after all, quite used to tuning out demands for justice from the rest of the world. But after the widely watched South African elections of 1994, which marked the official end to the racist regime and installed Nelson Mandela as president, the management policy in Kruger Park changed. In 1995 new park officials stopped the culling. At that point the elephant population of Kruger Park was listed at about 7,500. By the time Greg began his Gorongosa project, that number had increased to an estimated 12,500 elephants.

In the early 2000s, top officials in South Africa's national parks service broached the idea of starting the cull anew. The reaction was furiously contentious. Many global conservation groups decried the proposed policy as cruel and misguided; some called on nature lovers around the world to boycott the 2010 soccer World Cup being held in South Africa. Other organizations, such as the World Wildlife Fund—which has ties to many African park administrations—said that the culling was an unfortunate but necessary way to maintain an ecosystem that, for better or worse, was dependent on its human managers.

The scientific community within southern Africa was angrily divided on the issue as well. The South African government called various conferences for biologists, zoologists, ecologists, and other scientific specialists, but these gatherings often dissolved into racial accusations and name-calling.

A young scientist named Audrey Delsink told me a bit about the acrimony. Audrey was running an elephant contraception experiment at the Makalali Game Reserve, one of several small private game parks that border Kruger National Park. Her work involved a vaccine known as porcine zona pellucida, or PZP, which she and her colleagues shot into female elephants at the reserve. A nonhormonal immuno-contraceptive, PZP works by prompting the female elephants to form antibodies that essentially block the bulls' sperm. Seven years in, the experiment was proving startlingly successful: not only had Audrey's team dramatically slowed the growth rate of their reserve's elephant population, but the vaccine did not appear to cause any behavioral disruptions within the herds. (An earlier experiment using a hormonal contraceptive—basically putting elephants on the Pill—had resulted in all sorts of mayhem.)

I was intrigued by Audrey's experiment, which seemed to lie outside the main factions of the culling debate. So I arranged to spend a few days with her at the reserve. Mostly, we rode around the park in her *bakkie*—the affectionate term here for a small pickup truck—looking for elephants. She knew each of the reserve's seventy-two elephants by sight, and had definite opinions about their personalities. The matriarch named Queenie, for instance, was tough but benevolent; Dracula was "such a bitch." Audrey had been a game ranger before becoming a full-time researcher, and she'd perfected the art of driving while scanning the shrubby, brown landscape for animals. (The ranger job had been romantic, she said, but all that schmoozing with tourists could get old. "Elephants were better," she said.)

Eventually we would find one of the herds and stop. Audrey would spend an hour or so watching the animals, noting down aspects of their behavior: what they were eating, whether their tails were up in nervousness, how they moved their trunks, in what direction they were strolling, whether any of the females were in estrus. The reserve had decided to allow every newly mature elephant cow to have at least one baby, since raising calves is a defining feature of elephant life—all of a herd's females participate—so we would occasionally spot some of the young Makalali elies, all feet and ears and trunks.

As far as she could tell, Audrey said, the vaccinations had simply not affected the dynamics among elephants, sexual or otherwise. It was a finding that I thought must be of interest to Kruger Park officials. Although there were clear differences between vaccinating elephants in Makalali's one hundred or so square miles versus doing the same in the Israel-size Kruger Park, it seemed that if Kruger's top management was considering the expensive and logistically challenging culling operations anyway, they might be excited by this new science.

I mentioned this to Audrey and she laughed.

It won't happen, she said. "Everyone has so much at stake; people don't want to back away from their own positions," she told me. "If you think there are politics in politics, try conservation."

She put the *bakkie* in reverse, to get a better look at what she thought might be the faintest shade of gray moving behind a distant tree.

"It's a bit ridiculous, really," she said as she scanned the horizon through her binoculars. "We're busy contracepting lions and elephants, and we're not asking what the real problem is. There's too many of us. There are too many people."

It was a dramatic statement, but as I watched the orange sun execute its rapid African exit behind the thorn trees, I couldn't help but think that Audrey was on to something. Within the culling debate, which I had been reporting about for months, people argued endlessly about how many elephants the land could really support. They discussed water systems, fire management strategies, and whether boreholes should be pumped full during the dry season to keep animals alive. Park officials reviewed their data and polished their operating procedures; scientists examined animal behavior and drafted new biological impact statements. But nobody discussed Audrey's point. Nobody was talking about the human side of the equation.

Perhaps this was because it didn't seem particularly useful to do so. Nobody was going to promote culling people for the benefit of the ecosystem. But it was hard to deny that if we really wanted to do what was best for the elephants, the animals would not be confined to a fenced park such as Kruger, no matter how large the enclosure. Nor would they be expected to stay in an unfenced area, as at Gorongosa, just because humans had claimed the surrounding land. And they would not be transported hundreds of miles away to make a prettier, calmer herd for tourists.

If elephants were allowed access to their traditional habitats and migration routes, they would not be damaging the land in the way that park managers now found unacceptable. Indeed, park managers wouldn't be managing them at all. The elephants would simply be living on their own, flourishing or dwindling as their environment dictated.

Humans would not have the responsibility for deciding which elephants would have to die and which ones would get to have babies.

Again, perhaps this is not a useful scenario to think about. It is a fanciful vision, far from reality. In southern Africa, the human population has increased far more rapidly than the elephant one. And these humans have scant inclination to share their daily lives, or their living space, with massive, temperamentally peaceful but potentially deadly animals that trample crops, disrupt traffic, and generally present a nuisance. Moreover, because of some humans' inclination to kill other species in unnatural numbers, the conservationists among us feel a need to shelter those animals. To keep modern-day ivory hunters from finishing the job that European hunters started in the 1800s, we say that elephants must be kept in protected, natural areas—which, one could argue, are those patches of southern Africa most controlled by people.

Aside from worrying about population numbers, we don't usually pay attention to what our new world has meant for elephants. In 2005, however, the scientist G. A. Bradshaw took a stab at the issue. In an essay published in the journal *Nature*, she suggested that human-elephant conflicts over the past century—war, culling, and habitat loss, among other ills—have disrupted the social fabric of elephants to the point that the species has become dysfunctional. She and her colleagues pointed to the misbehavior of the orphaned Kruger elephants, the skittishness of herds such as those in Gorongosa, and other examples of increased elephant angst to argue that the species seemed to be exhibiting a collective form of post-traumatic stress disorder. Essentially, they said, we might be witnessing the breakdown of the entire millennia-old elephant culture.

Carlos and the other environmental managers at Gorongosa and Kruger knew the full context of the elephants' plight. They had dedicated much of their professional lives to finding a tenuous, imperfect middle ground between the complete end of the species and the fantasy of unrestricted roaming. But now the elephant named G5 was testing all their theories.

The GPS coordinates came in on Monday, along with angry phone calls from the district administrator in the nearby town of Nhamatanda.

"One of your elephants is here! It's huge—it's just walking around, through the fields!" The administrator seemed both furious and flabbergasted. "The people are very upset. This is entirely unacceptable."

Nhamatanda sits along the main transportation corridor running from Zimbabwe to the port town of Beira. The railway that cut through Nhamatanda was once one of the most important in southern Africa, carrying timber, ivory, and coal from the continent's interior to the Indian Ocean. Although it was destroyed in the civil war—the rebel forces were brutally thorough in their demolition, dismantling train tracks tie by tie—a paved highway has taken its place, and the town has a bustle to it. It is a place where truckers stop to buy beer and Cokes and sex; where farmers take a break on their bikes piled with seventy-pound bags of homemade charcoal; where brightly painted shacks of turquoise blue and sunshine yellow sell everything from plastic sandals to tin pots to rice.

Most of the commerce is along the paved road, but the commotion extends well into a grid of dirt streets and mud-walled, aluminum-topped one-room houses. The town is arranged around a few concrete administrative buildings and an old Portuguese church with a dramatically leaning cross; along the streets are small plots of corn and other crops, often next to stands selling home-cooked meals. Not far beyond the dusty roadways are larger fields and traditional rural Mozambican homesteads, and a district high school with so many students that the teenagers attend to their learning in shifts.

Add to this scene, now, an elephant.

The local police commander also phoned Carlos. "I am going to shoot it," he shouted. "It is a risk to the public safety."

Carlos looked haggard when I saw him that evening at the *boma*, where he was manning multiple cell phones and conferring with other Gorongosa Park staffers. He had already called the provincial police commissioner, the local commander's boss. He explained that the elephant was a gift from the South African government to Gorongosa National

Park, that it was here to help the resident Mozambican elephants, and that everybody from the president on down would be offended if anything happened to the bull. Carlos acknowledged that they had a problem—the elephant was supposed to be in the park, of course, not hanging around towns—but he assured the police commissioner that the entire park staff was working rapidly to rectify the situation.

The commissioner, who was a supporter of the Gorongosa Park project, promised to order his subordinate not to shoot the elephant. But he also warned Carlos that the townspeople were going to get restless. Already, he explained, people were talking about G5 as a killer elephant.

The timing, you see, was not particularly good for G5. Two days earlier a fisherman from a nearby village had been killed late at night as he rode his bicycle along the banks of the Pungue River, taking a shortcut home after an evening drinking with friends. His neighbors had found his mangled corpse the next morning, next to large elephant footprints. They said it looked like a tractor had dragged the body along the sand. Some speculated that the culprit was an elephant with one tusk, one of the matriarchs of Gorongosa who was known to be particularly touchy with people. But others said it was G5. It would be just like the South Africans to send something dangerous into central Mozambique, they said.

Nobody had seen the attack, though. And Carlos said that any of the park's elephants could be guilty. The whole group was regularly crossing the river to find unburned food, he explained. If an elephant got spooked by the sudden, unexpected arrival of a bicycle, it would be a natural instinct for it to take a swipe with its trunk—an unintentionally deadly move if it struck a person.

This logic did little, however, to assuage the fears of people who were hearing rumors about a huge, man-killing beast supposedly heading their way. The police commissioner told Carlos that he could probably control the local police forces for a day or two. But it would be a challenge to keep his subordinates from succumbing to local pressure after that, or to prevent an independent actor from taking the elephant situation into his own hands.

"He understands, he is a very intelligent man," Carlos said about the commissioner, "but there is only so much he can do."

He leaned back in his chair. "The problem is that is not an easy thing to move an elephant."

Sitting next to Carlos, Mateus Mutemba, then the park's director of community development, nodded in agreement. In its way, Mateus's job was as difficult as Carlos's. Multilingual and globally educated, the thirty-four-year-old had been hired not only to run the economic development programs connected with the park, but also to address the human side of any problem involving human-animal relations. This, he was discovering, was an immense task: virtually every conflict or question in the park came down to balancing humans versus animals and other environmental goals. The job had thrown him into all level of politics, from presidential maneuverings to fights between different spiritual leaders to family squabbling over maize plots and burial customs. And although Mateus came from a prominent Mozambican political family, nothing in his upbringing or his international studies could have prepared him for tasks like this: soothing rural officials outraged about a runaway elephant.

Carlos and Mateus could commiserate. And today, talking about various strategies for getting G5 home, they both looked spectacularly tired.

Mateus's cell phone rang; it was the district administrator again. Mateus sighed, stood up, and answered the call. Carlos rubbed his temples as Mateus walked away, talking rapidly in Portuguese.

"We found a truck," Carlos told me. "But it is in Maputo. Hopefully it should get here tomorrow evening. But there could be problems."

The truck he was talking about was a specialized vehicle used to transport game. As Carlos had noted, moving an elephant is no easy task. Usually such a move is arranged far in advance. Veterinarians and rangers will put together a written plan on how to handle the elephant: how to drug him, move him onto the vehicle, wake him up, release him, and so on. They will coordinate with local and national police as well as customs officials. And they will make sure that all the necessary machinery and supplies—highly customized and hugely expensive—are in place.

This can include a lightweight helicopter from which a veterinarian can dart the elephant with tranquilizers; a tractor-trailer bed with enough axle strength to support the elephant's fourteen thousand pounds; a high-powered hydraulic crane capable of lifting the animal; and specially built crates with drainage, food slots, and ventilation to house the animal on its journey.

Just coordinating all this equipment, which is in high demand across southern Africa, can take months. But Carlos didn't have months. He didn't even have weeks.

"We'll have to do something quickly, or that elephant will die," he said.

He had already ordered some of his most skilled rangers to find the bull and form a perimeter around him. At this point, since the truck was still so far away, it wasn't any use containing G5; that might just stress him unnecessarily. Still, the rangers could clear unsuspecting villagers from his path, and keep an eye out for would-be hunters.

The next day, the elephant crossed the main Beira road going southward—still, apparently, heading back to Kruger Park. He had busted through a farmer's fence and was now hanging out at a cattle ranch just south of town. Carlos ordered his rangers to keep him there in the pastures: to let G5 wander around during the cool of the morning for food and water, but to get in front of him if he tried to leave the confines of the ranch.

The truck, meanwhile, was still in Maputo. Customs officials were demanding tens of thousands of dollars to release it, although their reasoning was unclear and seemed to change from one explanation to the next. At one point they claimed that the truck was too large for Mozambican roads. Then they said that the park should have paid more the last time it transported elephants. It seemed clear to park staffers that the truck was being held hostage for a payoff. But Greg had made it a strict policy for his employees to never, ever pay a bribe, even if one might expedite whatever task was at hand. So Carlos telephoned every political contact he knew. It was how things worked in

Mozambique, he said, glowering. And by evening, his contacts had come through, customs officials had relented, and the truck was ready to start northward.

But the driver hadn't gone more than a few miles before he realized that something was wrong. He pulled over to the side of the road and walked around to inspect the massive crane truck. Three tires had been slashed. It was, the park staff agreed, another attempt by officials to get a bribe.

The next afternoon, two animal translocation specialists arrived in Chitengo Camp. Kester Vickery came from South Africa, Barney O'Hara from Botswana. The two had been working together for years—Kester as the owner and manager of a company called Specialist Game Services, Barney as his trusted pilot. Kester had started the company in 1994, at the end of apartheid, when ecotourism was starting to take off in the region. His company offered to manage the complex and dangerous movement of wild animals from one park to another, whether it was forty rhinos that needed to go from South Africa to Botswana's Okavango Delta, or a family of elephants near Kruger being sent to one of the new private game parks elsewhere in the country. By the time he showed up at Gorongosa Park, Kester was known as one of the top animal relocation specialists around. It was his truck that Carlos had located in Maputo.

Kester and Barney took up residence at the *boma*, drinking sodas and beers and plotting their strategy. They had expected that the truck would already be there; now the operation was being delayed again. Kester called the driver, one of his top employees, and found out that the tires had been fixed but that the truck was still near the capital city—a twelve-hour drive away, over roads moonscaped with potholes. Kester told him to drive through the night, and he and Barney agreed that given the amount of trouble it was taking to get even one truck to Gorongosa, they were going to have to move the elephant without all the usual equipment.

They shared Carlos's worry about G5 in the pasture. Even with the rangers forming their perimeter around the big bull, there was no telling what could happen if the animal became agitated. It was risky to try to move an elephant bull without a second truck equipped with wake-up crates, but it would be even riskier to postpone the move for another two weeks.

That afternoon, Carlos drove the wildlife specialists to the cattle ranch. I tagged along, riding in the open bed of the pickup truck as it zoomed toward Nhamatanda. It was getting toward evening when we turned off the paved road, drove through the dirt streets of the town, and came to a field marked by rough-hewn wooden fencing. The main part of the property, the section where G5 had stopped, was on the other side of a streambed. The waterway was dry this time of year, but it still cut deeply into the earth, with a cracked concrete bridge passing over it. Kester got out to inspect the road and started laughing.

"Check this out," he said, jumping on the bridge. The whole structure jiggled.

"Eish, man, there's no way," Barney said.

The crane truck, weighing thousands of pounds by itself, carrying an animal almost as heavy, would never make it across this bridge. Carlos radioed his scouts and got word that there was another possible entrance. We drove to look at that road, which seemed more secure, and then went to find the group of Gorongosa rangers who had set up camp in the cattle ranch. The elephant was a pasture away, under the watch of a couple of scouts; the rest didn't want to get too close, for fear of spooking G5 even more.

Carlos handed out Coca-Colas and Fantas that he had brought from Chitengo Camp and told the rangers that they would perform the operation at daybreak. The sun was setting, turning the landscape dusty pink. The rangers stood in a semicircle as Carlos explained that moving the elephant would be dangerous, but crucially important to the park project—for demonstrating its commitment both to conservation and to locals that the Gorongosa team took human security seriously. It would be difficult, he warned. They would be acting without all the necessary equipment, on an animal that was already stressed. But they needed to act now, he said. And he believed they could succeed.

A number of the rangers nodded solemnly. They had already spent several days in the dusty cattle pasture; they were ready to do this. "We will see you in the morning," Carlos said, turning back toward his pickup truck.

I stumbled out of my room at 4:00 a.m. This was before the generator went on in Chitengo Camp, so the place was eerily dark, the flame trees casting even blacker shadows as they blocked the starlight. I always had the feeling at nighttime here that creatures were watching me, and no doubt they were. There were certainly resident bats and snakes and mongoose that noticed unusual early morning activities, not to mention the nocturnal lions and leopards and hyenas prowling just on the other side of the camp's metal fence.

I went to the *boma* to wait for Vasco, who was going to drive me to the elephant. Carlos and a new team of rangers would ride to the cattle ranch in the park's 4×4s; Barney and Kester would fly their helicopter and meet us there. I stood on the ground-level patio by the fire pit, as far away as possible from the restaurant's thatched roof. Lord knew what lived in it. The park staff had cleaned up Chitengo Camp tremendously since I first came to report here, but it was hard to forget the rats that used to run around the *boma* after the lights dimmed.

Eventually I saw the small white circle of Vasco's flashlight coming from the rondavel where he lived with his wife and daughter. "Are we ready?" he asked, and then looked around. We were the only ones up and about. Carlos was still in his trailer office, putting together last-minute paperwork. There were no rangers to be seen. Vasco sighed. This was the way of things here: the best-laid plans running an hour late.

Eventually the various players gathered, and we started our caravan toward Nhamatanda just as the creeping sun began to turn the landscape gray. By the time we got to the paved road, smoke from cooking fires in thatched huts was already twisting into the pastel sky, and men were already walking along the highway, carrying their machetes to labor in the fields.

We drove to Inchope, the town where the internationally paved EN1 highway intersects the Zimbabwe–Beira corridor road, and veered east. Around us, vendors hawked breakfast rolls while motor scooters and bicycles danced past one another to the sounds of Mozambican hip-hop, which pumped from cassette players attached to makeshift generators. It was still before 6:00 a.m., but people here start the day with the light.

After another hour or so we arrived at the Nhamatanda cattle ranch. The huge transport truck had finally made it from Maputo, and it stood impassively in the strengthening sunshine. Kester and Barney were talking with their driver, who looked dazed from his journey. He had had enough of this country, the driver said; he was ready to go back to South Africa.

Carlos parked his pickup truck and gathered various containers from the truck bed. Opening them, he started to prepare the tranquilizing darts with which he intended to immobilize G5.

Tranquilizing a wild animal is always a delicate operation. With an elephant, it is exceptionally risky. Without having any chance to weigh the patient, the darting veterinarian must estimate the correct dosage of sedative: too much, and you can kill the animal; too little, and the drugs are ineffective, leaving you with an upset and likely rampaging elephant. The vet must also estimate how much force to use in shooting the dart: if the needle does not implant it will not do its job, but if it hits with too much speed it can go right through the elephant's body. And although the animal is large, the vet must hit it in a relatively small target area. He must avoid the heart and lungs, for instance, which will fail if punctured by the dart. He must also ensure that the animal falls in a clearing accessible by the transport truck—it's not possible to move an elephant out of a grove of trees or from thick bush. Carlos seemed deep in thought.

Meanwhile, Kester and Barney began testing the truck's crane. They were worried that the hydraulic lift might have been damaged on the potholed road from Maputo.

More waiting.

I wandered off to talk with some of the local farm workers who were watching the process. They were sitting in a small circle of shade, under one of the few trees near the pasture. They seemed less than enthusiastic about the whole operation, but one said that they were happy the elephant would soon be gone.

"Why isn't the park fenced?" another asked. "We haven't slept, we have been so afraid."

The others chimed in with elephant horror stories. One said G5 had passed through his nephew's yard; the family didn't know until they saw the footprints the next morning. Another said that a friend went to pee in the pasture and found himself staring right at the bull.

The group laughed, but then turned serious again. They had been on work furlough ever since the elephant arrived because their boss, the ranch owner, had ordered that all the cattle be confined to one corral until the park dealt with the situation. They were tired of feeling trapped by this animal.

G5 hadn't attacked anyone, they all acknowledged. And if the elephant was simply trying to get home—confused, in an unfamiliar landscape, but somehow guided back to his home country—well, they could sympathize with that. Somewhat. But mostly they just wanted him gone. The park could move him, or someone could shoot him—it didn't matter. As long as they could stop worrying about getting trampled.

We saw Barney's yellow helicopter lift into the air, and I scurried back to Vasco's truck. I didn't know how long it was going to take Carlos to get a direct shot at G5, but I wanted to be ready to drive to the scene. More waiting. I started to doze off. Suddenly, though, the line of rangers and vehicles seemed to jump: Carlos had radioed that he had successfully shot G5 and needed everyone immediately. We sped down the dirt road and saw the helicopter parked near the transport truck. Vasco and I dashed out of the car and tried to keep up with the park rangers, who were running through the last bit of scrubland to where G5 lay, massive, on his side.

"Keep him wet!" Carlos shouted. Teams of rangers formed a bucket line and began tossing cool water onto the elephant's skin.

As precarious as the darting process is, this part of an elephant relocation is even riskier. The animal is so massive that if he lies on his side for too long, or if he falls forward onto his trunk, he can quickly smother himself. He can also overheat, since usually he cools himself by fanning his body with his huge ears. His trunk is another weak point: if it lies flaccid for too long, it can cut off the elephant's oxygen supply.

Carlos was concerned about this as his team scurried to attach leather straps to G5's ankles and neck. "Watch the trunk! Watch the trunk!" he shouted as he stood by the bull's head, monitoring the animal's breathing.

Some of the rangers grabbed the trunk and held it. The gray skin with wiry dark hairs seemed rough and soft at the same time. I put my hand near the opening and felt G5's warm breath coming out. Occasionally he would let out a half trumpet, the way my Labrador retriever gives a muffled bark when he is dreaming.

The team was working quickly. A dozen rangers tugged on the straps that would be connecting G5 to the hydraulic crane. Others gathered branches and tall grasses to line the metal flatbed of the truck, to make it cooler. Another group fanned G5 with palm fronds.

I stared at the supine animal. I had seen elephants up close in the bush before, but this was different. Lying there, G5 was so huge, so peaceful-seeming, oblivious to the humans scrambling all around him. He also looked vulnerable, the power differential between him and the much smaller people gone all wrong, his forceful bulk immobile, a felled giant.

"Okay. Lift him up!" Kester called out. He jumped onto the truck to grab the controls of the hydraulic lift, shouting back and forth with Carlos.

The crane rose into the air, pulling up the huge feet, then the massive legs, and eventually G5 in his entirety, his body unfolding upside down above the ground. He hung like that—suspended, hogtied—for what seemed like minutes, his thick abdomen below his legs, his ears and trunk dangling down, pulled by gravity toward the dust. It seemed an undignified pose for an elephant elder, but this was the safest way to lift him, the literature on translocations assured us, the best way to manage wildlife.

Kester maneuvered the crane over the truck and gently lowered G5 onto the flatbed. "Look, watch the trunk again!" Carlos yelled.

As G5's side draped onto the metal flatbed, the rangers scurried into action. Again they fanned the animal and worked to position him safely. Others scrambled into the bush, dragging in more branches and leaves to cover the body, a makeshift attempt to shade him from the sun in the absence of a wake-up crate. In a well-planned translocation, the elephant would now be placed into one of these specialized crates and injected with an antidote to the tranquilizer. He would wake up, stand, and step backward into a transport crate attached to another truck. That well-ventilated transport truck would be his ride back to the park. But since Carlos and his team didn't have crates or a second truck, they had to simply strap the immobilized elephant to the flatbed and hope for the best.

We started a new, triumphant caravan back toward Gorongosa Park. Some of the rangers drove first, to clear villagers and traffic out of the way. Then came the flatbed truck with the elephant, Kester standing next to him, monitoring G5's breathing and heartbeat. Vasco and I were behind the truck. The ranch workers shouted their good-byes.

We drove slowly through the back streets of Nhamatanda. The villagers did shocked double takes at the huge monster covered with branches. A woman wrapped in bright purple fabric startled and dropped the basket of maize she was carrying on her head. A group of children, giggling and screaming, tried to run next to the prostrate elephant. The men standing at the beer hut turned and pointed. Others whooped and waved. "They are cheering because they think the elephant is dead," said Vasco, who could understand some Sena.

The district administrator and the local police chief rode with Mateus in another pickup. They both waved at the onlookers, as if in a parade, and exchanged thumbs-up.

We turned onto the paved road and started back toward the park. The sun was ferocious now, shimmering above the black pavement, and I squinted behind my sunglasses. The breeze from the drive barely softened the heat in the open cab of Vasco's truck. We were going much slower than one would usually drive, since Kester was balanced on the back of the flatbed with the elephant.

After about twenty minutes of this slow cruising, the crane truck pulled over to the side of the road. Carlos stopped his pickup next to the flatbed and jumped out to join Kester. They talked for a moment and leaned over G5. Within a minute, Carlos jumped back down onto the highway. He looked grim, his jaw set. "You are watching a funeral," he said as he passed my window.

G5 had died.

The cause of death was unclear. Perhaps it was the stress. Perhaps the tranquilizer dosage was too intense—G5 had lost considerable weight, after all, so it was possible that Carlos's measurements were off. Perhaps it was a combination of the blazing sun and general bad luck. Perhaps it was the spirits. All Kester knew was that at a certain point the animal had stopped breathing.

True to Carlos's word, the convoy took on the feel of a funeral procession. We drove on sluggishly, fatigued by the blinding sunlight, the heat, the dust. All of a sudden the whole operation felt to me like pure hubris and ignorance. It was so sweltering outside, so brutally bright, it seemed outrageous to have hoped that any creature—let alone a stressed-out and heavily drugged elephant—would survive hours of being strapped down onto a dark metal flatbed truck. It seemed a metaphor for everything: the underlying absurdity of our projects; the way we toy with nature and reorganize societies, be they human or animal; the truth underneath the stories we tell.

The body of G5 was unchanged. From my spot in Vasco's passenger seat, the bull looked no different now than he had when he was breathing: the feet sticking out horizontally from his body, the ankles crossed absentmindedly, the useless branches on top of him dangling into the street. Vasco and the other park administrators were quiet.

We did not pick up any speed as we made our way back toward the park, as if there were still some point in treating the recumbent elephant carefully. For three hours we rolled onward, hazard lights blinking, until the wooden sign for Gorongosa Park appeared on the horizon, directing us back into the forest.

Carlos wanted to bury the elephant. The tranquilizing drugs made

G5's body poisonous, and Carlos was worried about other animals, or even villagers, scavenging the meat. So before we reached Chitengo Camp, we turned off the spine-rattling access road and into the bush, inching along one of the overgrown fire lanes in the tall grasses.

When we reached a clearing, Carlos motioned for the truck to stop. This was the place. He had phoned ahead for one of the park's bulldozers to meet us, and now he directed its operator to start digging a grave. Then he told his rangers to remove G5's tusks.

Because of the worldwide ban on ivory trading, no game reserve or individual is allowed to possess new ivory. When Carlos or his rangers find a dead elephant in the park, they are supposed to collect the tusks and ship them to a central stockpile controlled by the government. But there is still a lucrative black market trade, and Carlos worried that if he buried G5 with the tusks intact, people would surely dig up the body and potentially spread poisoned meat into the local bush meat market.

Two rangers—including one named Manuel, who had been an ivory poacher—climbed onto the flatbed truck with their machetes. They moved the branches off the dead elephant and straightened one of G5's ears, which had flopped inside out. They removed the straps that held him secure. A hot wind kicked up dust, and the shrill of midday insects mixed with the beeping of the bulldozer as it backed up, preparing to dig. Manuel carefully sliced the elephant's flesh above the tusks, peeling it outward. Then he lifted his machete high and slammed it downward into the skin. The other ranger mimicked him, and the two began to alternate their chops, the sound of the metal on bone and skin adding to the buzz of the insects and the bulldozer noise and the wind through the grasses. They cut and cut, wiping sweat from their foreheads. Chunks of pink and gray skin flew from the elephant's face. A trickle and then a flow of deep red started down.

It feels very, very hot, I thought.

"It's a shame, hey," said Kester. He was standing next to me under a tree, also trying to avoid the sun. "We usually pick them up and put them into the wake-up crate. Our anesthetic had to last two hours—that's a long time. But we had no choice. The other option was to shoot it. So we did what we could. We knew what the risks were. If you move a hundred elephants, you lose one. But with older elies, the risks are more." He sighed. "Such a lot of effort, and a lot of expense."

He and Barney had offered their services for free; they had asked Carlos and the park to cover only the costs of the transport truck and its mileage. But that was still thousands upon thousands of dollars.

We waited.

"Kester, can you give these guys some tips on where to cut?" Carlos asked. "They're taking a long time, and it's only one tusk."

Kester shrugged.

The bulldozer dug deeper, shoving the dusty gray earth into mounds. The air started to smell like dead animal. G5's face was mangled, a patchwork of skin flaps and blood and tusk. Manuel and his partner looked exhausted.

They decided to use the crane truck. They strapped the tusk to the hydraulic lift, and the machine tugged. But the ivory would not separate. As the crane lifted, G5's mutilated head followed, and then his entire body, wobbling in the air. Even the force of fourteen thousand pounds seemed insufficient to separate the tusk from its fleshy home. Then, suddenly, the head jerked and something gave. The tusk slid out with a sickening, slurping sound, twice as long as it had appeared when G5 was living, and the elephant's body flopped back toward the earth.

The rangers did the same with the other tusk, and this time they let G5 drop all the way into the grave. He was facedown, his round feet still poking out above ground level.

The bulldozer reversed its work, pushing the gray earth over the gray animal. Everything about the task seemed interminable: the dust swirling in the oppressive dry season heat, the rumble of the engine, the incessant beeping as the machine backed up, moved forward, backed up again. Carlos stood at grim attention, his hat off, as the minutes dragged into an hour.

Eventually G5 was buried, and Carlos lined up his rangers, military style. They stood at attention with their old rifles, the way they did in drills back in Chitengo Camp. Many of these men had been soldiers once. Soldiers, poachers, and rangers, I thought, the three professions of Gorongosa.

"You did your best," Carlos barked, walking up and down the line like a general. "You should be proud. The mission was not successful, but you acted with honor."

He called for one of the rangers to fire a shot over the grave of G5. At first the rifle caught; the ranger looked at it quizzically, and I worried that an errant bullet would explode into some innocent bystander. The ranger readjusted the rifle and tried again. The shot rang out over the insects and the grasses. He fired another, then marched backward into the line. The rangers slammed down their rifles in unison and saluted.

Then the line dissipated, and the rangers, the scientists, and the park administrators wandered off in their own directions. Some of the rangers grumbled quietly. The bosses never ordered a gunshot salute at any of *their* funerals, they noted.

One by one, we drove away.

The fate of G4, the other elephant bull, was not much better than that of G5. More than a year later, when I was already back in the United States, I heard from a park staffer that the elephant was still missing—still, apparently, wandering through the privately owned hunting reserves to the north of the national park. The Gorongosa administrators decided not to try to move him, given the expense and failure of their efforts with G5, but just to keep tabs on the bull's whereabouts.

Eventually, however, Carlos received GPS transmissions indicating that something was wrong. The elephant's movements had slowed significantly, and two days later they stopped completely. The next data indicated that the radio collar was in Beira, a hundred miles from the elephant's last known location.

Carlos called the Mozambican Criminal Investigation Police. Together, they used the GPS signal to track down the collar. It was in a house used by a professional Portuguese hunter. When the park and Mozambican officials raided the place, they found six guns, a large amount of ammunition, five elephant tusks (including those of G4), several elephant feet, and various buffalo trophies. The radio collar was

there as well; the hunter apparently had not realized it was still trans-
mitting a signal.

The police arrested the Portuguese hunter and a French national
who had been his client. They were charged with killing a protected
species, hunting during the closed season, illegal possession of firearms, and theft of the radio collar.

The men posted bail and were quickly released. Their only punishment would be a fine.

PART III

THE STORIES WE TELL OURSELVES

10

The Disconnect

One might wonder, given the complications with everything—the people, the animals, the spirits—whether the administrators of the Gorongosa National Park might have paused to rethink their project. Or whether they might at least have had some second thoughts about the sweep of their plans, their hope of creating an ecological utopia. But it seemed they did not. On the contrary, Greg and his team began planning more animal introductions to Gorongosa. They wanted more elephants, more buffalo. They would add hippos, they said, as difficult as it was to transport them, and cheetahs. Ambition and optimism, rebounding after setbacks, learning from mistakes, and thinking big—they are as much a part of our story in Africa as they are part of our American self-help bibliography. (Indeed, "confront the brutal facts but never lose faith" is one of the seven key principles outlined in the best-selling management book *Good to Great*, which Greg had instructed all his staff to read.)

Greg and his top administrators felt great enough about their project, and the potential it held, that they were even considering expanding the geographical scope of their operations. This took me aback. Having spent a year talking to people who lived around the park, I thought the last thing the project needed was more land, more obligations, more tensions with the locals.

One late morning, though, as I sat in the *boma*, trying to get out of the sun, I noticed some of the park administrators standing around a nearby table. I walked over to them. Greg, Carlos, and the man who was in charge of the business operations of the park, a Portuguese-Mozambican named João Viseu, were looking down at a map. The paper's edges curled as if it were trying to protect itself from the heat. João, with some annoyance, grabbed one of the salt shakers (an absurd table item for Chitengo, I had by then realized, since salt clumped so much in the humid air that it wouldn't go through the holes) and placed it firmly on a corner.

Even in the bush, João looked like the smooth-talking businessman he was. He wore pressed khakis, expensive polo shirts, and a shiny gold watch. He was so polished in his pitch about the park, so poetic about his love for Gorongosa and his enthusiasm for working with Greg, that a colleague of mine who had come to shoot some film footage turned to me after João had left and said, "What's up with *that* guy?" Journalists do not like smooth-talking spin. That aversion is part of our story.

João seemed to relish being Greg's right-hand man. And that afternoon, in the thatched-roof shade, he inched closer to Greg to gaze at the map spread out on the table, the representation of possibility. Greg traced a circle in the middle of the page—a circle far larger than the one that would have encompassed Gorongosa.

"This is a fabulous national park," he said.

Carlos nodded, serious but affirming. "That's the movement, the logical movement of animals," the veterinarian agreed.

"And I mean, you could . . ." Greg trailed off, thinking.

João seemed eager to join in. "I'm just talking, thinking on the tourism side, I mean the romance about this . . . All the way to the Zambezi." He glanced at Greg for validation.

Greg looked up, seeming to respond to João and instruct at the same time.

"The Zambezi River," he said. It was a statement. "*Every*body's heard of the Zambezi River."

Each appeared lost in his own thoughts for a moment, and Greg sighed. It was as if he were picturing not just geography, but harmony and restoration. The men were looking at ancient animal migration routes that extended across southeast Africa. Scientists believe that tens of thousands of buffalo and wildebeest, along with quite a few elephants and other animals, once embarked yearly along this journey, grazing their way from Gorongosa toward the coast, through the vast Zambezi Delta to an area now designated as the Marromeu Buffalo Reserve. To be able to protect a large section of that route, to restore a full *system* of how nature once worked, before man started to destroy it . . . They seemed enraptured.

Indeed, there was a growing recognition within conservation circles that although setting up protected areas was still necessary for saving nature, there also needed to be something more. One idea that had acquired popularity proposed something called "rewilding." This was more or less the same approach that Greg Rasmussen was promoting in Zimbabwe with regard to the wild dogs: restoring ecosystems and changing human behavior so that endangered species could flourish outside national parks. The parks by themselves, rewilding advocates say, are too small and isolated to allow for real preservation.

Rewilding plans frequently call for linking protected areas via wildlife corridors. They also often suggest reintroducing animals into the ecosystems that once held them. There are efforts to bring back pine trees, beavers, and wolves to swaths of northern Europe, for example; more dramatically, there are proposals to introduce cheetahs and elephants into protected sections of the American Great Plains. (This latter idea, outlandish though it may seem, is in fact supported by a number of respected conservationists as part of a philosophy called Pleistocene rewilding. Its theory is that such modern analogues of animals now extinct—saber-toothed tigers and woolly mammoths, in this case—will help revive ecosystems by replicating their ancient relatives' ecological roles.)

But what Greg and his advisers were imagining was, in some ways, even bigger, a more complete return to a prior age of wildlife dominance. They were talking about a vast national park that would allow not only for the reintroduction of species in a particular place, but also for the resurrection of a migration pattern that was itself extinct.

"When it comes to the discussion of the limits of the park, we can always argue with those maps [and show] the movement of the animals," Carlos said. "It's clear. That's the real natural movement of animals."

"That's right," Greg answered. "You know, otherwise you have a zoo. A big zoo." He spat out the word. "And this"—he traced the area on the map—"is nature." He pronounced the phrase with emphasis: This. Is. Nature.

There were, however, some 3.8 million Mozambicans living within the Zambezi Delta. I kept thinking about that as I began to realize, with some disbelief, that the men were not engaged in idle daydreaming. The park administrators had discovered that at least some more land might be available to them. Near the borders of Gorongosa National Park were hunting *coutadas*, areas of less intensive preservation handled by independent operators. And the park had learned that, thanks to the intricacies of regulations and contracts and governmental whims, there was a chance it could extend its boundaries and absorb them. And then the possibilities seemed limitless.

Greg used his thumb and forefinger to measure the lines. One finger after another, northeast toward the banks of the Zambezi River, then east toward the Indian Ocean. "Three hundred kilometers," he announced. He looked back over the map. "This is eighty kilometers. Taking into account all the twists and turns, it's probably three hundred kilometers."

The men were quiet for a moment, and then João flashed his gleaming white smile. "You know what, Greg, we need to put on our budget a helicopter," he said. "You know you can't do this by road."

Greg glanced at him sharply. "This road is so good you can drive from here to here in probably three and a half hours."

Greg was a bit touchy about roads. There was a lot of grumbling by staffers who drove into camp that he didn't realize the extent of the infrastructure challenges because he always flew to Chitengo in a helicopter.

João was not going to contradict him. "Yeah."

"You know what," Greg continued, "this is not even half of Kruger. It's not crazy."

"No, no, it's not crazy." The other men nodded.

"It's not crazy. For a country's premier national park . . ."

"Greg, I think it will be easy to sell."

"It's the glory of Mozambique to have a proper park," Greg said.

It was for Mozambique, after all, that he was doing this. For Africa. That's been the Western story all along, of course, from the explorers on forward, through all the colonial mergers and acquisitions, the generations of white men standing around maps.

"This is a once-in-our-lives . . ." Greg trailed off again as the others looked on admiringly. "How exciting. The world's conservation community will get really excited about this."

They turned back to the table.

"We have to grab this little strip here, too," Greg said. "There'll be human-animal conflict all the way up. . . . But this is worth spending, you know, a lifetime. This is worth twenty years. Of making this a reality."

"Absolutely."

"I'll phone and organize for a Thursday meeting," João said crisply.

"We're going to need, um, more budget," Greg said slowly, and then laughed. "More people." The others joined in, chuckling. Then Greg turned serious. "You see, what happens is that a bigger project attracts more money, and sometimes it's actually easier. Because the dream becomes so big that you get million-dollar donors rather than hundred-thousand-dollar donors."

The other men nodded.

"And actually," he continued, "sometimes it's easier to do a big thing, and do it right with a bunch of professionals, than a little thing. You know, for USAID, you go to them and you say, 'Look, we need three or four million dollars a year. . . .' No more 'four hundred thousand.' You know, we're doing a big thing here. And people want to have their name associated with a big thing."

The plans for a bigger Gorongosa National Park were not realized that year. I don't know exactly why they fell through; there was an awful lot of staff turnover at the time, and certain governmental shifts as well, and perhaps some of the park administrators dealing with existing community challenges persuasively argued that stretching themselves further would be, at the moment, a terrible idea. Whatever the reason, within a few months I was hearing only general references to the nearby hunting reserves. Every now and then Greg would mention how beneficial it would be to have a more expansive park protecting a more complete ecosystem, or talk about his desire to allow animals to reclaim their ancient rights to the land. But nothing concrete happened for a long time.

Still, I regularly found myself thinking back to that conversation in the *boma*. I was amazed that at no point did the people involved ever seem to see themselves from the outside. They did not appear to recognize that they were three white men standing over a map, dividing up Africa for their own use.

I have no doubt that this characterization would have made each of them angry, for different reasons. Greg is a philanthropist, pouring his life and wealth into doing good. Carlos and João are Mozambicans themselves. Carlos has worked on behalf of animals his entire life, struggling to make his country better for them. João later had a bad falling-out with the project, but at the time I had no reason to believe he was doing anything other than trying to create the most successful business and conservation venture. And yet it was a stunning scene, the very image of disconnect.

It was also a metaphor, I thought, for much of what was going on in the region. In the reports of the big development organizations, Mozambique was going from good to great. Its government had closely followed the recommendations of the World Bank and the International Monetary Fund, and the country's economy was expanding rapidly, by 7 or 8 percent almost every year. By 2012, Mozambique would be one of the fastest-growing economies in the world, with a currency—the metical—that was the world's best performer against the dollar. There was major construction across the country, and more and more foreign investment. The Live Aid story was working. The end of poverty was nigh.

In villages and shantytowns across the country, though, the people lived a different narrative. By almost all standard-of-living measures, ranging from the percentage of the population living on less than a dollar a day to the average individual's ability to access health care, Mozambique had maintained its same grim standing as one of the world's most underdeveloped countries. From this perspective, the nationwide numbers seemed misleading at best. A significant percentage of Mozambique's GDP through the early 2000s came from a single aluminum processing plant outside Maputo. It was owned by foreign investors, had received significant tax breaks, and employed hundreds of Mozambicans in low-level, low-paying jobs. Meanwhile, most people's lives were getting harder. Their trust in government was evaporating.

In 2008, the same year that Greg, Carlos, and João were tracing out a larger park, the tension between these different stories—the flourishing donors' darling and the struggling country of Disorder—finally became unbearable. Prices of rice, bread, and other essential goods were rising; the drivers of the *chapas*, the minibus taxis that many city residents took to get to their jobs, announced that their fares would go up by some 50 percent. Unrest erupted in Maputo, the capital city. Young men took to the streets, dragging tires and cinderblocks into makeshift barriers and throwing stones at the police, who fired back with rubber bullets and sometimes with lead. News commentators pointed out the inequality on display in the capital, showing footage of the dusty, raw-sewage suburbs not far from the building boom of mansions and shiny glass office towers.

And then the lynchings began.

In a city called Chimoio, a couple of hours from Gorongosa, a string of violent attacks had put the residents on edge. Someone's throat had been slit. Someone's home robbed. Someone's wife assaulted. The people learned to wait by the door at night, tensed for a fight in the darkness. There was electricity in some parts of Chimoio, but it did not extend to the poorer neighborhoods.

Then, early one morning, just before dawn began to fill in the earth's colors, word spread that the bandits who'd terrorized the city had been caught. A crowd gathered, emerging from the tentacles of dirt roads that run between the cinderblock houses, and pushed toward the local police station. They demanded that the police turn over the criminals. In one surging movement they forced their way past the police officers, trampling one of them, and grabbed the five prisoners suspected of the home invasions. Beatings came first. Then someone brought the "necklace"—a tire doused with propane, the execution style imported from South Africa. By the end, all five were dead. At least one was a woman—either a bandit or a witch, people said. They made little distinction between the two.

The next day, when I went to Chimoio to see the scene myself, the city was calm. Women strolled along the lazy boulevards of crumbling concrete and perfectly placed colonial trees. Sun glistened on the whitewash of old mansions. Laundry swayed sensually on lines strung along the chipped balconies of apartment buildings. A young man hustled toward a *chapa* parked in the central traffic circle, where a mural showed freedom fighters with AK-47s taking their country back from the Portuguese. *Viva!* All was back to normal, and two days later they beat to death an outsider—from either Beira or Zimbabwe, or somewhere else altogether, depending on who was telling the story—who had stolen an ear of corn.

I called up some academics who I thought might be able to help explain to me what the heck was going on in peaceful, prosperous Mozambique. Several told me that this sort of vigilante justice is a common response when marginalized people feel disconnected from government systems; one said that he'd been predicting violence in Mozambique for some time now. Others, schooled in a more anthropological approach, identified as particularly pertinent the issue of witchcraft. They explained that they used this term, *witchcraft*, with some hesitation, but could come up with no better English word to describe spiritual beliefs connected to antisocial evildoing. The populace was clearly displeased, these scholars said, that the state justice system refused to consider evidence presented by spiritual mediums that one person or another was collaborating with an evil force. This frustration, combined with the inefficacy of a justice system largely viewed as corrupt, was leading people to take matters into their own hands.

The academics wrote reports. Few read them. And then, in the northern part of the country, peasants began attacking Red Cross workers.

These victims were Mozambicans, "local" employees of the International Red Cross organization, who were paid far less than their expatriate bosses but still far more than the villagers they'd come to help. In some ways these workers were easy targets for the discontent brewing in the countryside. They were outsiders, often from the cities, and their education level and socioeconomic background set them apart. Their work with the Red Cross was another mark of privileged status. It was well known throughout Mozambique that the best jobs were those with organizations founded and funded elsewhere. The pay was higher, and more reliable, than that from any Mozambican employer, including the government. Indeed, local businesses and agencies grumbled that it was near impossible to keep talented workers. Anyone with a legal driver's license would quickly get a job with one of a variety of NGOs operating in country, handling the clean Land Rovers marked with the emblems of the West: Red Cross, World Vision, UNICEF. The elites of the country, thinking strategically, focused their higher education on development work, since that was the sector most likely to be hiring.

The development industry boomed, but the poverty remained. Now, in the northern province of Nampula, a crowd became convinced that Red Cross workers were deliberately spreading cholera in the wells that the various NGOs were always talking about. And so there was another *lynchamento*.

The minsters in Maputo expressed shock and frustration at this violent ignorance. The workers were putting *chlorine* in the wells, they explained, not cholera, the disease that kills hundreds of people in Mozambique every year. (The words sound similar in Portuguese as well: *cloro* and *cólera*, respectively.) The confusion, perhaps compounded by local politics, resulted in the tragic deaths, government officials said with some disgust.

But the peasants of Nampula had a different story. They were quite sure, they said, that the rich of the world—the foreigners, the international aid organizations, the government ministers with their mansions by the Indian Ocean—were trying to kill them. Didn't the evidence point to this conclusion? Didn't the very existence of those nonprofits, with their high salaries, new cars, expense accounts, *depend* on misery? Forget those who waxed poetic about how everyone could be wealthy. It was false; they all knew it. All things are linked and balanced: if one side goes up too far, the other has to go down. That is how the spirits work. A *gamba* improves one's fortunes at the price of another's suffering.

In those distant lands, from Washington to London to Maputo, choices about trade, war, politics, money, lifestyle, consumption, natural resources, and the like all but guaranteed the continued inequity of the world, no matter how many NGO workers the foreigners sent. And this inequity, they recognized, was exacerbated every time those rich outsiders tried to get closer to them—tried to "bring them along" or "raise them up," "move them into the twenty-first century," or simply "help."

Stop snapping and leave us alone, they cried. But it was too late, the peasants recognized. The rich were already killing them.

While I was reporting in Mozambique, and for a long stretch thereafter, I wasted a lot of time trying to figure out what was *true* in Gorongosa. This was foolish, of course, because to try to tease truth out of any complicated, intercultural, multireligious, secular-spiritual, good-and-evil, humanity-and-nature debate—let alone one in a foreign land, conducted primarily in a language that is not one's mother tongue—is the sort of quest that has stumped more than a few famous philosophers and mystics. There is no absolute certainty here that even the best investigative reporter could hope to find. But this didn't stop me from trying, for quite a while, to tally up the evidence.

On one hand, the park seemed to be doing pretty well. There were more animals, although continued problems with some species, such as lions, were confusing conservationists. A number of tree-planting campaigns were under way on the mountain, continuing despite the controversy on the ground. Chitengo Camp was a lot nicer, and more expensive, than when I had first arrived. There were slightly better roads, the airstrip was going to open for tourists, and across the river, in the village of Vinho, there were a new school and health clinic. The park administration was forming collaborations with public health institutes in the United States to set up a home health outreach program. And Greg kept up with the latest in conservation philosophy. Although I saw him in a number of scenes like the one with the map—the powerful outsider influencing the lives of poor Africans who often had very little say—I also heard him speak reflectively and sensitively about his own place in Mozambique.

On the other hand, the more I spoke with people living on the mountain and around the park, the more anger I heard. Many complained that they could not use their natural resources as effectively as before. Meanwhile, poaching continued. The big carnivores were not really coming back to the park. The number of tourists had increased, but the total number of visitors was still minuscule in comparison to the grand—laughable, some said—estimate of a hundred thousand per year that Greg and Vasco had made when I first started reporting on the project. And many people in Gorongosa still believed that the spirits were angry, and that the white foreigners were basically invaders.

Sometimes I wondered if the answer to these clashing stories wasn't just better communication. This idea is not new, of course. "Cultural competency" and "local input" are central to the modern-day Live Aid discourse. We realize that we have been bad at explaining our intentions, at listening to our intended beneficiaries, at recognizing how to avoid gaffes such as landing in a helicopter painted the color of angry spirits. We know we should be better at it. As Greg said that day when he first tried to visit the rainmaker, what if he could just find a way to make people understand that he was *here to help*? Of course he wasn't there to steal their mountain. What did that even mean anyhow?

But in a place like Gorongosa, nailing down facts misses the point. Because even if an action is completely legal, what feels like helping to one person can feel like stealing to another.

Not long after I left Mozambique, I received an e-mail from Greg. "Hi Stephanie," he wrote. "I would like to share with you that today the Council of Ministers voted to add Mt Gorongosa to the Park boundaries."

I sat staring at the computer screen for a while. What Greg was saying was that, after months and months of lobbying, the administrators of Gorongosa Park had convinced the central government—the government that was not the party of most of the people on the mountain—to put the highest elevations of the massif under the direct control of the park. Which essentially (although not officially) meant "under the direct control of Greg." He and his advisers would now basically have the legal authority to regulate how the locals farmed and cut trees, lived and worshipped there. For all practical purposes, control was now his.

What about the people? I asked.

Greg wrote back that it would not be appealing to him from an ethical standpoint to force people to resettle. Others on his team would disagree, he said. But he wanted to *persuade* residents to come off the higher elevations of the mountain.

He was hopeful, he wrote, that there could be a balanced approach.

11

National Geographic

The headquarters of the National Geographic Society is a four-building complex taking up most of a city block in downtown Washington, DC, not far from the White House. It is both grand and "green," combining the sort of pillared marble one might expect in the American capital with roof gardens, low-flush toilets, and extra racks for bike commuters. The complex holds the offices of administrators who help run the society's massive media empire, which, with its print, television, and online presence, reaches an estimated 280 million people a year. There is also a museum, a gift shop, and an auditorium offering a series of culturally diverse events—everything from Brazilian dance troupes to lectures about Mayan ruins. And on one drizzly March evening a few years ago, it hosted the world premiere of a new National Geographic documentary about Gorongosa National Park.

The production of this film had been the source of quite a bit of excitement for many of the park staffers while I was reporting in Gorongosa. I heard about the filmmakers and the big cameras, the way they would train those high-tech lenses on, say, a crocodile egg and film for what seemed like hours. If someone rocked the Land Rover even the tiniest little bit, or let out the slightest of sighs, the shot was ruined. Nature videography is an art, and it takes an awful lot of equipment, time, and people to make an animal look as if it is alone in the wild.

I was interested to see how the film would portray the complicated Gorongosa experiment. The producers had asked me to share some of the footage I'd shot during the failed operation to rescue G5, so I figured the elephant would be part of the film, but I wasn't sure in what context. I knew, though, that whatever story the documentary chose to tell, it would powerfully shape the way the American public saw the Gorongosa project. For although there had already been a number of print pieces about the park, including my own, few institutions influence our perspectives on the rest of the world and its environment quite like National Geographic.

Indeed, you can't talk about the stories we tell of Africa and its wilderness without lingering for a moment here, at the National Geographic Society. The adventurer-explorers, the missionary do-gooders, and the hunter-conservationists may have provided the foundations for our Western narrative of the continent, but it's the professional popularizers, the journalists and documentarians, who have expanded and reinforced it over the decades. And a remarkable number of these storytellers have come out of, or had some connection with, this century-and-a-quarter-old institution.

The National Geographic Society was founded in 1888 by a wealthy Boston lawyer named Gardiner Greene Hubbard. An amateur scientist himself, Hubbard wanted to create an institution that would both deepen and spread the scientific knowledge of geography. Reaching out to some of the top geographers of the day, he invited them to a series of meetings at the Cosmos Club, then an elite Washington men's club off Dupont Circle. There, surrounded by leather and mahogany, these luminaries of science and letters sketched the outlines of the National Geographic Society and what would become its magazine.

This undertaking came at a moment when contact between the West and other parts of the world was rapidly increasing. For half a century the public had been devouring the African tales of adventurers such as Stanley and Livingstone, and gazing at items that explorers had brought back from faraway lands—everything from minerals to wooden sculptures to preserved lion heads. As time went on, these collections took the form of natural history museums, world's fair exhibits, and even human zoos. (Shocking though the notion may seem today, such zoos, with "exotic" people placed in cages or in ersatz "natural habitats," are not very far in the past.) The American Museum of Natural History opened about a decade before Hubbard and his friends gathered at their club, the Smithsonian Institution was in the process of expanding, and the National Zoo would open the following year.

All these collections, historians point out, share the central characteristic of being highly curated. In other words, the collectors did a lot of picking and choosing, deciding which items to take back with them, which ones of those to display, and in what order. This curation process often obliterated context, distorting whatever meaning these objects had had before. (Imagine someone going into your house and taking random items from each room to display later: perhaps a collage of oatmeal boxes and dirty socks framed by flowers from your dining room vase, with a taxidermic version of your cat sitting nearby. Bizarre and not terribly informative, right?) But the audiences of these Victorian-age collections felt that they were getting a genuine insight into faraway places, because the collectors arranged the objects in a way that made sense for their own culture and time.

And if there were any lingering mysteries surrounding these collections, a new group was ready with explanations: professional scientists. During this era of the collection, the sciences, long the purview of the gentleman intellectual, were becoming part of a growing university system. In other words, men were now trained to be scientists, rather than merely dabbling in the activity. And science, people believed, was a tool that could identify and give insight into the strikingly different flora, fauna, and people of darkest Africa.

It could also, some thought, explain *why* those differences existed. A generation after Charles Darwin published his *On the Origin of Species*, the late-Victorian era saw the emergence of various theories that applied the notion of evolution to social and policy matters—what later became known as social Darwinism. The basic gist of this rhetoric was that the poorer, darker, more "primitive" people of the world were simply lagging behind white industrialized society in the world's sure and steady progression toward modernity. This theory handily helped explain away a whole host of inequalities that might otherwise have bothered democracy-loving Americans and Europeans. And it also suggested that progressive science could propel those primitive populations toward enlightenment and understanding. Science was to be not only a tool of measurement and mapping, but also the method of social improvement.

One doesn't have to look too deeply into development literature today to see the staying power of this particular story. In everything from conservation to economic revitalization projects, the West uses the language of scientific analysis and intervention, aiming to improve the lot of those people whose lifestyles are not as "modern" as ours. The language is different—we think only a racist would say that Africans as a category are somehow, inherently, *behind*—but we snap our fingers all the same, hoping to move people along that evolutionary line we call development.

The men at the Cosmos Club in 1888 shared the faithful, almost romantic dedication to this idea of the progressive sciences. United in their desire to spread scientific enlightenment, they outlined a set of values that would guide their new institution and its publication. *National Geographic* magazine, they agreed, would be globally focused and ecologically minded. The founders explicitly vowed to approach the rest of the world with kindness—which to them meant that they would not be controversial. They could try to intrigue readers, to spark interest, curiosity, and even empathy, but they would not try to challenge them, or to make their audience feel uncomfortable or guilty.

This tenet has held through much of the society's existence, to the point that (in an extreme case of "If you can't say something nice . . ."), during the Cold War, the magazine editors decided that it was best to act as though the Soviet Union simply didn't exist. From 1945 to 1959, the *National Geographic* magazine ran no pieces whatsoever about this rather large chunk of the world. Better to not write anything at all, the editors figured, than to wade into the morass.

Over the decades, what had started as a thin professional journal blossomed into one of the most iconic and widely read magazines in American history. The notion of enlightenment without too much challenge was a winner—particularly, scholars say, for an aspiring middle-class America with educated sensibilities. (I'm sure I'm not the only one who found boxes and boxes full of *National Geographic* magazines in her grandparents' basement.) And eventually the society branched out into a new form of storytelling that arguably would become even more powerful in shaping Western understanding of the natural world: the wildlife film.

Today, spoiled for choice by dozens of David Attenborough documentaries and Discovery Channel specials, we find it easy to take wildlife films for granted. But their origins are actually quite recent, dating back just to the middle of the twentieth century. And their visual and storytelling conventions owe much to one pioneer in particular: a German veterinarian named Bernhard Grzimek.

Grzimek first began making waves in conservation circles in 1945, when he convinced Allied occupying forces to help him save the handful of animals still alive in the Frankfurt Zoo. According to biographers, the veterinarian—who was explicit about his opinion that most animals are far nobler and more sympathetic than humans—then took advantage of the postwar chaos to expand the zoo by about a third, closing roads and annexing nearby sites without any government approval. He was soon appointed the zoo's director, and over the next few years he built up both its animal collection and its reputation. By the 1950s the institution had become secure enough that Grzimek felt he could go to Africa on "collecting expeditions," journeys that essentially involved trapping animals in remote locales to bring them back to European zoos.

In 1953, Grzimek traveled to the Congo with his teenage son Michael. The two were on a quest for the okapi, a rare animal related to the giraffe but with a shorter neck and zebra-like stripes on its legs. Its only natural habitat is within the dense rain forests of the Congo River

Basin—not a particularly easy area for travel, even today. On their journey, the Grzimeks drove a battered pickup deep into the Congo, stayed
for days with "child like" Pygmies, and watched with disgust as hunters on safari slaughtered what the Grzimeks regarded as defenseless
creatures.

On their return, Bernhard Grzimek wrote the first of what would
be a slew of best-selling books, *No Room for Wild Animals*. The title
reflects the book's basic premise. Because of factors ranging from population growth to our inherent bloodthirstiness, Grzimek wrote, we are
making our planet into a desert; soon, "all the wild animals on earth
will be compelled to yield to the 'Human Locust.'" The success of the
book—part emotional argument, part scientific treatise, part adventure
travelogue—suggested to the young Michael Grzimek, a budding filmmaker, that they should make a film of the same name. The Grzimeks
poured their savings into the venture, and to their surprise it also
became a resounding commercial and critical international success.

The sort of anthropomorphized footage that we've come to expect
today from nature documentaries—playful music underscoring a scene
of knobby-kneed zebra foals, a melancholy tune accompanying a for-
lorn pelican who's lost her eggs—was a novelty in the 1950s. So viewers
in the United States and Europe who saw the Grzimeks' film got to
know African animals up close for the first time as emotional beings.
This was a big shift. Previous documentaries had portrayed animals as
just moving scenery in a wild landscape, eye-catching but disposable.
Hunters were the main characters. With the Grzimeks, the animals
moved to center stage, and the hunter shifted from a noble adventurer
to a goon.

This was not the universal take on the matter, of course. Safari
hunters have long considered themselves conservationists. In the early
1900s, for instance, a group of hunters in the British colonies, worried
about the dwindling number of animals to shoot, formed the Society
for the Preservation of the Wild Fauna of the Empire. (The British press
dubbed them the Penitent Butchers Club; notably, the group's key rec-
ommendation to preserve wildlife was to ban hunting by Africans.) A
generation later, many old-school hunters were greatly offended by the

new trend of automobile-assisted hunting safaris, which allowed tourists to shoot more animals more quickly. Denys Finch Hatton, the big
game hunter immortalized as Baroness Karen von Blixen's lover in *Out
of Africa*, decried what he called "the orgy of slaughter" on the Serengeti, and urged others in the business to limit the butchery. Today,
many hunters and hunting safari outfits claim to be far more connected
to (and better for) nature than their photographic safari counterparts.

By the 1950s, though, it was the Grzimeks' attitude that was becoming widely accepted. Game reserves, people were beginning to believe,
were not for human sport; they were places for wildlife to rebound from
the evil pressures of man. The Grzimeks had a chance to establish this
position even more firmly in 1958, when they were invited to do an
animal survey of the Serengeti—a sort of fact-finding mission in a long-
simmering conservation controversy.

At the time, the British government and the colonial government of
Tanganyika were trying to figure out where to draw park boundaries
in the Serengeti region, one of the most spectacular ecosystems on
earth. Stretching from the Ngorongoro Crater in present-day Tanzania
into southwestern Kenya, the Serengeti is the site of one of the world's
largest land-based mammal migrations, a mind-blowing annual movement of some two million wildebeest and two hundred thousand zebra.
But the region has also been home for centuries to the Masai people.
And in the 1940s, squeezed out of other areas because of population
growth, a number of these Masai decided to ignore government warn-
ings about restrictions in the region. They began grazing their cattle
on land that they believed was their ancestors' but that the colonial
government believed should be protected.

Given the complexity of the situation, government officials hoped
that the Grzimeks would be able to shed some light on the exact whereabouts of animals in the region, adding scientific authority to the ongoing negotiations about protected area borders. The two Grzimeks
decided to use a light aircraft to survey the wildlife—the first scientists
to do so—and tried to follow the migration, filming all the way. They
were aghast that there might be any compromise in the effort to keep
this magnificent wilderness safe from people, and they lobbied intensely

for the government to ban all humans, including the Masai, from permanent residence in the park.

In early 1959, Michael Grzimek was at the controls of the plane when it collided with a vulture and crashed north of Ngorongoro. He died in the wreckage. His heartbroken father returned to Frankfurt with reels of footage, and soon he produced yet another book and movie with a shared title: *Serengeti Shall Not Die*. Again, the work had a clear message: Africa is in grave peril and can be saved only if we protect its animals from people. The film was a huge success, winning an Oscar for Best Documentary. The debates in Tanganyika and Kenya continued, but in Europe and the United States, public opinion was already clear: the scientifically managed protected area, keeping humans out and animals in, was the only way to save wildlife in beautiful, soulful, natural Africa.

Half a century later, these ideas are still central to the nature documentaries that come out of the National Geographic Society, which—in addition to its flagship publication, various other magazines, educational programs, and a strong Internet presence—now has its own television channels and film production teams.

National Geographic films have been quite popular, and for good reason. They are scientific but also, well, awesome. They've got great music, beautiful scenery, and often some really exciting scenes of predator action. And they remain true to what academics Catherine A. Lutz and Jane L. Collins have described as the "high middlebrow" positioning of National Geographic, which "strategically occupies the spaces between science and pleasure, truth and beauty." In its films as in its magazine, National Geographic has managed to define itself, as Lutz and Collins put it, as "a purveyor of the facts worth knowing about the world."

In other words, National Geographic still functions in a way that would have been largely familiar to those nineteenth-century geographers gathered at the Cosmos Club. Its explorers—the filmmakers and photographers, journalists and scientists—go out into foreign lands and bring back images and stories, which they then reassemble for an American audience. (An audience, as all of us who write for public consumption know, that does not take particularly well to complication, doom and gloom, or suggestions of culpability.) And although the National Geographic Society has certainly evolved since the early 1900s, it's hard to miss the original themes lingering in its work. There is a recurring plot line of scientific progress versus barbarism, often couched in the language of conservationism versus environmental destruction. Places and people are regularly struggling toward something better—often with the help of Western science—and there is always exoticism, beauty, and adventure.

The film about Gorongosa premiering that night at the society headquarters was entitled *Africa's Lost Eden*. This fact, I will admit, made me groan when I first heard it. It's hard to count how many times Africa has been described as an Eden (which, biblically, mind you, is a place of natural bliss spoiled by its own inhabitants). Do an online search for "Eden" and "Africa," and you find not just a slew of plain "Edens," but also quite a number of "Lost" and "Last" Edens, as well as a smattering of "Squandered" Edens and (somewhat redundantly) "Wild" Edens. And alongside this profusion of Edenic references, you'll see an almost equal number of scholarly papers decrying the trend. Restrainedly outraged academics point out in various ways that the description of African nature as an Eden—lost, found, or anything in between—rather obscures the modern-day Africans and their real, twenty-first-century lives. Regarding Africa as an Eden, or a would-be Eden that needs us to repair it, makes the continent into something permanently premodern, blank, lacking a human history as complex as our own.

But Edens work well with five-act plays. Here is how the promotional materials for *Africa's Lost Eden* describe its subject. "It was known as 'the place where Noah left his Ark': 4,000 square kilometers of lush floodplains in central Mozambique, packed with wild animals. But 15 years of civil war took a heavy toll—many species were almost completely wiped out for meat. Today, conservationists battle to restore the park to its former glory, and save it from present-day threats that could destroy it forever." When I first read this description, I sort of wished that I could tell the Gorongosa story like that: a straightforward tale, enlightenment and entertainment without complication.

A Washington crowd in suits and not-quite-flashy work-to-evening wear was already in full room-working mode when I arrived in the lobby of the National Geographic Society's Gilbert H. Grosvenor Auditorium. People mingled and passed around business cards. I spotted some employees of the Carr Foundation and various conservation organizations, as well as Greg and a few others I knew from reporting in Mozambique. A few interns sat at tables covered with paper lists, importantly checking off names before they allowed anyone into the venue. There was even a velvet rope. It was a sold-out event.

Eventually everyone took a seat and the film began. First came the music—tribal-sounding, happy African music. Then the tune turned a bit spookier, and on the screen appeared a heavy yellow sun shimmering in a mysterious red sky partially covered by clouds. There was a shot of one of the waterfalls on the mountain, mist floating over a verdant woodland. Then the floodplain. Then an elephant. Narrator Keith David's deep voice broke in, full of honey and gravitas.

"At the southern end of Africa's Great Rift Valley lies Gorongosa National Park, Mozambique."

He paused.

"It's April, the end of the wet season, and the rivers run deep and wide."

The Gorongosa National Park was a place of amazing wildlife, the narration continued, an ecosystem unrivaled for its diversity. But there was a problem in paradise. It was quiet, empty. The animals had been destroyed by man and war. Now, though, conservationists had a grand plan, a scheme to introduce a new ark full of creatures and restore the park to its former glory. Would they succeed?

The filmmakers had made great use of the helicopter, with panoramic aerial shots of Lake Urema and the floodplain, the impossible blues and greens of the water and sky and trees. The producer had interspersed breathtaking slow-motion shots of pelicans, storks, and fish eagles, their wings flapping angelically, with dramatic close-ups of a blinking crocodile eye. Elephants moved regally through the bush, and lion cubs tussled with one another. The music even made you feel kinship with a mama crocodile guarding her eggs—not a creature I usually find cuddly. It was nature videography at its best.

But as the film went on I began to feel a little uncomfortable. I noticed that none of the local black people spoke. The first scene of Mozambicans came from old war footage: gun-toting, angry Africans in black and white. These spliced-in shots were contrasted with the beautiful, full-color, human-less scenery of today. The movie did mention local people as "one final species" the conservationists were trying to help, and showed images of happy women with babies and men building health clinics, but these people had no more voice or context than the crocodiles and hippos. There was little mention of the mountain, or the power struggle going on there.

The climax of the film was the footage I had shot of G5, with some smooth narration to gloss over the fact that the poor elephant had died in the heat thanks to a whole host of disputes and missteps. Indeed, there was no reference to any kind of mistakes or misjudgments at all. G5's death was presented as the sort of unavoidable heartbreak that demonstrates just how much the park and its staff are up against: it showed the dedicated conservationists doing their all, working brilliantly, and just being unable to overcome—in this single, specific moment—the environmental challenges they were facing, such as the fires set by the locals. Still, there was no doubt, the narrator assured us, that this committed group would be able to rebound from that sort of setback, bringing a recovering park with them. Happy tribal music emphasized the point.

Things didn't get any better after the screening. As promised, there was a panel discussion with Greg, along with the World Wildlife Fund's Judy Oglethorpe (who had pointed me to Gorongosa in the first place), filmmaker James Byrne, and the Mozambican minister of tourism, Fernando Sumbana Jr. *Hardball* host Chris Matthews was the moderator.

Matthews was one of Greg's many friends, and about a year earlier he and his wife, Kathleen, had visited the park on Greg's invitation. Matthews was so impressed by what he saw that when he got back to the States, he shared photos from his trip on his television show. "I just got back from Africa," he told his audience. "This is serious business. It's HIV stuff, and it's saving the wildlife, the number-one treasure of Africa. They have got to save it. They have to. That's what they can sell in years to come."

On *Hardball*, Matthews gave a "real shout-out" to Greg, who is "is working and investing so hard to rebuild the great Gorongosa game park in Mozambique. He's working with the government there of that country to bring back that country's precious resource." Matthews also wanted to "pay tribute" to Ted Reilly, the controversial conservationist in Swaziland whose rangers' shoot-to-kill practices were opposed by Thuli Brilliance Makama, the Goldman Prize winner. Matthews was proud of the get-tough approach to conservation. "I have got to praise King Mswati himself for having the strength and vision to mean it. And he bans poaching, zero tolerance, no bail, no breaks. You kill, you go to jail. We have had too many elephants and rhinos killed in that part of the world."

Now, in front of the National Geographic crowd, Matthews took a similar position of knowing authority. To back it up, he explained to the audience that he had been a Peace Corps volunteer in Swaziland during the 1960s. I wondered if anyone else noted that this is a different country from the one in which Gorongosa is located. Or if anyone else had doubts about whether going to southern Africa as a twenty-something in the 1960s to "develop small business enterprise," as Matthews has described his efforts, gave one the authority to issue judgments on complicated present-day questions about the environment, culture, politics, and economics . . . in what, again, is *a different country*. (And I raise these points with much loving respect for the Peace Corps volunteers of the 1960s—including, coincidentally, my mother- and father-in-law, who happened to overlap with Matthews in Swaziland.)

But the audience seemed generally unfazed. They asked lots of questions, primarily of Greg and James. They were so glad that Greg was doing this work. They were fascinated with James's filmmaking and wanted to know more about how he did it. They wanted to know how things were going now.

As the discussion neared its end, with the wine and cheese reception ready for VIP guests, Matthews spoke sternly to Sumbana. Mozambique was a beautiful country, Matthews told him. He hoped that the Mozambican people would realize what a jewel they had in Gorongosa Park. I squirmed in my seat, and glanced around to check if seeing this African get lectured by yet another white American man was making anyone else uncomfortable. People in Washington have good game faces, though. I couldn't tell what anyone there thought. Moments later, the crowd stood up to give Greg and his project a standing ovation.

And here you might ask, so what? So the National Geographic story of Gorongosa is a National Geographic story. It's not like this is a surprise. But as Matthews and the audience members made clear that night, in one micromoment of awkward cultural obliviousness, the stories we tell do matter. They shape the lectures we give, the projects we support, the decisions we make. They determine who (and what) we deem worthy of being saved—and, as Mount Gorongosa shows, what we think "saving" actually means. To go even further, you could say that our stories shape what we see in the first place. They are our truth.

The Washington power brokers who came to watch *Africa's Last Eden* probably had some preexisting understanding of conservation, of international relations, and perhaps even of southern Africa. And while their ideas might have varied to some extent, they had all been shaped by over a century of narratives about the African continent and our relationship to it. The film, with the particular way it presented Gorongosa, no doubt reinforced and solidified those preexisting narratives. Conservation is good. Africa needs help. Progressive science will save the day.

Sociologists have long recognized the particular importance of storytelling when it comes to Africa and its wildlife. A safari, they say, is a narrative frame through which we often approach the continent as

a whole. And stories from the bush—whether they take the form of
photographs, hunting trophies, documentary films, or dinner party
conversation—are not just a way to introduce a little of that wilderness
into our own lives, but also a crucial part of the adventure itself. It's the
fantastic images we see of sunsets and lions, the tales we hear of crocodiles and baobab trees, that create our desire to acquire those experiences for ourselves. So when we do travel to Africa, we expect a
replication of those stories, with ourselves now as the central characters. We want to see and do and feel what the storytellers saw and did
and felt.

This is why visitors to game reserves in Africa zoom around in Land
Rovers chasing the Big Five and ignore the rest of the complicated,
magnificent ecosystem in the process. Safari guides will tell you that it
doesn't matter if their clients see a herd of baby impala teetering on
newborn legs, or a secretary bird shaking its astonishing plumage, or a
dung beetle performing that essential task of clearing the bush of feces,
rolling animal waste into balls for brooding. (Fun fact about the dung
beetle: it's the only creature known to use light from the galaxy for its
navigational purposes. Its movements are intricately connected to the
Milky Way. But does seeing one help compensate tourists for missing a
rhino? Nope. They want the Big Five.) A number of guides have told me
that unless they check off the lion, rhino, elephant, buffalo, and leopard, safari-goers feel cheated. The other animals, those other stories
nature has to tell, are at best sidebars. Without the preordained narrative, safari tourists get grumpy.

National Geographic, you might say, has helped turn our experiences with the rest of the world into a safari. This may be particularly
true when it comes to nature and conservation, and our troubled efforts
to figure out our own role within (or sometimes, we insist, separate
from) the complex network of all the living creatures on earth. But it is
also true of our relationships with other people. Somehow, despite the
breathtaking variety of the world's cultures, languages, histories, and
norms, and despite our modern-day assurances that we truly care about
"local input," we perpetually emerge from our encounters with other
people with our old comfortable beliefs safely intact.

The safari-going attitude—the essential approach of National Geographic documentaries and Live Aid consciousness raising—may be outward-looking and, in its own way, caring. But it leaves us decidedly unprepared to recognize the realities that other people inhabit. We have become so good at reciting our own particular script that, on some level, we recognize only those actions and plot points that fit within it. We are expert curators, immediately—almost subconsciously—tossing everything else aside.

The problem with this is not only that we become blind to other people's truths. It's also that when the evidence starts to undermine our own beliefs we do everything we can to ignore it.

Not long after the release of *Africa's Lost Eden*, a small but well-respected group of scholars whose work had taken them to Mozambique began arguing that the Gorongosa Park restoration project was backfiring.

One of these academics was Heidi Gengenbach, then an assistant professor of African history at Harvard University. She had worked with the Carr Foundation on a project to study the food security and livelihood coping mechanisms of the people living around the Gorongosa National Park, and I remember Greg suggesting that I might find her research interesting. We exchanged some e-mails but never connected at the park. It was only after I was back in the United States that I heard about what she had found.

Heidi's work was part of a collaborative effort between the Woods Hole Research Center and the Gorongosa National Park, with funding from the National Science Foundation. Other researchers involved in the project were planning to analyze natural resource use around the park and map it with state-of-the-art geographic information systems technology—a decidedly tech-era approach, using all sorts of statistical analyses to probe ecological change. Heidi's task was different. She was supposed to be the "ethnographic data collector," which, in everyday terms, means she was supposed to get her information directly from the local people.

She had already worked extensively in Mozambique and was familiar with conducting interviews there. For this effort, she and a research team, which included Mozambican scholars, planned to travel through the communities around the park and survey residents about how they made ends meet: where and how they farmed, what their strategy was for using fire in agriculture, whether they hunted, how they earned cash, and so on. The researchers would also ask people about their social networks and living arrangements. After they gathered responses to these survey questions, the plan was to go back and conduct what academics call "qualitative interviews," which basically means sitting down with subjects and getting more personal details about their lives. In other words, listening to their stories.

Even before she got to that second phase, though, Heidi realized that she had stumbled onto something troubling. The answers people gave to her team's surveys suggested not only that the Gorongosa restoration project was not helping the Mozambicans living around the park, but that it was actually undermining their health and food security. People were achieving smaller plant yields, they were eating less protein, and they felt less sure of their futures. Moreover, it seemed from the surveys that the park's efforts to spread ecological awareness were provoking a backlash. Faced with what they perceived to be unfair new rules about agricultural practices such as slash-and-burn farming, people living around Gorongosa said they were taking less care to manage their fires. After all, they told researchers, the land wasn't theirs anymore. "The more the park said, 'This is not your land, this is our land,' the more the people said, 'Well, then, we don't need to take care of it,'" Heidi recounted to me.

She went back the next year to do more substantive interviews. The attitudes had not gotten any better. People were out-and-out angry at the park, she said. They were also fearful. She recalls, for instance, that farmers were reluctant to admit to researchers that they kept bees.

This was telling. Beekeeping is a hugely valuable agricultural practice, both for human health and for the greater ecosystem. But in southern Africa, as elsewhere, it typically involves a smoldering fire. Beekeepers use smoke to calm bees and make them less likely to attack, a technique that modern-day science is only starting to explain. We know that smoke inhibits particular alarm pheromones that would otherwise cause bees to become aggressive, and it also triggers a feeding mechanism that basically makes the bees too full to sting. But biologists are still not sure quite why it works so well. We just know that the beekeepers, including the Gorongosa peasant farmers, are on to something.

By the time Heidi's researchers came along, though, many people living around the park believed that it was now illegal to use any kind of fire in agricultural ventures. They also knew that they were not supposed to be practicing any agriculture within the (still contested) park borders. This meant, effectively, that they believed beekeeping itself had been made illegal. So what had once been a regular, ecologically important practice was now performed less frequently, often on the sly and with less care.

The same was true when it came to slash-and-burn activity, Heidi's team found. Many of the local farmers believed they were no longer allowed to use fire-based management techniques on their fields, the common way of returning nutrients and fertility to their land. This was a problem, Heidi explained, because her team's research had discovered that rather than being the blunt tool of an undereducated rural peasantry, agricultural fire use in Gorongosa was in fact stunningly sophisticated. Different plants required different types of burns, at different times of the year. Farmers had complex ways of controlling their blazes and making sure each did its specific job. Now, though, facing what they saw as prohibitions being imposed by outsiders, the farmers had started a campaign of defiance by neglect. Their actions would be characterized as illegal regardless of what sort of care they took, they said, so they looked the other way as their flames danced into the park.

Now, it's important to point out here that park administrators insist they never told anyone that using fire in agriculture was illegal. They say they simply "discouraged" it within the "buffer zone," the area around the park. And they certainly never told any locals that the park was not theirs, the Mozambican people's. To the contrary, Greg and his leadership team regularly explained that they were doing their work *for*

Mozambicans, particularly for those living within the buffer zone. The park was the *Mozambicans'* national treasure, *their* economic engine.

It was clear to researchers, though—both to Heidi's team and to a group from USAID that visited some years later—that few people living around the park absorbed the nuances of "discouraged" versus "illegal." Which isn't particularly surprising, given the context. After all, Gorongosa is an area that for generations has functioned somewhat independent of the larger state. All the trappings of government that we take for granted in our lives—transport infrastructure, health care, public safety—are far more nebulous there, and the rule of law is kind of sketchy as well. Police enforce the law except when, you know, the officer's son is in the hospital, and if only he had a little bit extra to pay for the medicine, perhaps he would be inclined not to notice how fast you were just driving. . . . Meanwhile, park rangers enforce the rules as well, but what they're enforcing are sometimes not really laws at all but park regulations. It all gets rather muddled.

(What's more, foreign suggestions for improvement, such as "recommendations" that a certain road or another be paved, have a dangerous history of their own. During the war, for instance, when Mozambican people were facing a devastating food shortage, the big donor organizations of the West "recommended" that the socialist Frelimo government switch gears and adopt free-market reforms. Only then, the donor groups said, would they offer the desperately needed food aid that would keep Mozambicans from starving.)

In such an environment, those who have power make the rules. And these rules need not be written down, or described in the formal language of legal and not legal. It's like when the neighborhood heavy asks for "a favor." Everyone knows what that means.

Around Gorongosa, Greg and his team—whiter, more moneyed, and with far greater access to the ear of the central government than the local population—appeared to be the heavies, even if they did not intend to be. The park rangers were thus newly empowered as well, which created further tensions in the area. Heidi told me that she had interviewed two men caught by park law enforcement for allegedly poaching cane rats, a typical food item in rural Mozambique. The men told her that the rangers brought them back to one of the remote ranger posts and beat them. "We were catching rats—just rats!" she recalls them saying as they showed her the scars. "They tortured us for rats."

Local officials also told Heidi in 2008 that over the prior five years there had been a "dramatic increase" in alcoholism, prostitution, violent property crime, domestic violence, and HIV infection. This couldn't all be blamed on the park restoration project, of course, but Heidi was of the mind that it certainly hadn't helped. In any case, she believed that the communities surrounding Gorongosa Park had become not wealthier and healthier, as Greg had hoped they would when he began his work in central Mozambique, but hungrier, sicker, and poorer.

In light of this, Heidi and others said, resistance through active neglect was an understandable response. Locals, Heidi wrote later, were "deliberately abandoning traditional fire-control techniques, hunting limits, and monitoring of valuable tree species because, they claim, 'The land has a new owner now, doesn't it?'" It was not exactly the same as the Portuguese leaving the Mozambican sewer systems full of concrete, but there was a similar human quality to it. When we are stripped of something we believe is rightfully ours, we are not inclined to help the new owners.

The more she heard these stories, the more Heidi became worried that this trend would only continue, with devastating consequences both for people and for the rest of the environment. In the National Geographic story of Gorongosa, the peasants around the park were at once the "marginalized people" whom Greg's philanthropy focused on, and also the ones to blame for the ongoing ecological troubles of the land. Yet Heidi's research convinced her that the small farmers of Gorongosa were the true preservationists. The ecology of Gorongosa was still as rich as it was not *despite* these peasants, but *because* of them.

Indeed, the Gorongosans had been managing the land for generations, repeated intrusions by outsiders notwithstanding. They managed it because it was necessary for their livelihoods, but also because it was part of their moral code. The land was linked to the spirits. The rich ecosystem that the park itself was built on existed because of these people, and because of the way of life that the new park administrators were trying to change.

"Local farmers are not bad for biodiversity conservation in Gorongosa Park," Heidi wrote in a public forum not long after the premiere of *Africa's Lost Eden*. "They have long been, and seek to continue to be, its primary guardians." Greg and the "high-handedness" of many of his efforts in the park, she continued, along with his unfamiliarity with the agricultural history of the region, were as much to blame as anything for the ecological destruction that "he and the media so loudly lament."

A handful of other scholars also posted comments criticizing Greg, his project, and the many positive media portrayals of it—including the National Geographic film and a particularly fawning *60 Minutes* segment about Greg's work in Mozambique. Among these scholars was Christy Schuetze, the anthropologist who had lived on Mount Gorongosa and found the reports of deforestation there to be at odds with reality. "This video is an example of irresponsible journalism," she wrote about the *60 Minutes* broadcast, "more like propaganda for the Carr Foundation than a balanced look at the situation in Gorongosa."

I had interviewed Schuetze briefly for my *Smithsonian* piece about the park project, but after that she hadn't returned my phone calls or e-mails. I would see her now and then when I was accompanying park staffers on their outings onto the mountain, and never understood why she always seemed so nervously standoffish. Later, though, I read her dissertation, in which she described living on the mountain and learning Chi-Gorongosi, a local dialect of Sena. She regularly had to insist that even though she was white, and probably looked like a lot of the park staffers, she was not connected with the park. To associate with a group of park staffers—or with the journalist who looked just like them—would have endangered her work.

Now, writing online, Schuetze was unsparing in her assessment. "It is particularly reprehensible that Greg Carr is presented as a savior idolized by an admiring, passive, and impoverished population, when this is far from the reality on the ground," she wrote. "In actuality, there is a large and vociferous group of district residents who are standing up in opposition to different aspects of the Carr Foundation's project."

All this criticism prompted Greg to write in to the forum himself. He had, I thought, an amazing ability to shift the discussion back to where it felt comfortable: to uncontested generalities, pleasant platitudes, and his own role as a helper.

"My background is human rights, not conservation and certainly not ecotourism," he wrote. He went on to explain that he cofounded Harvard's Carr Center for Human Rights Policy because he felt an "urgent need to protect the rights of vulnerable people"—like those who lived in central Mozambique. He agreed that the Mozambicans' agricultural practices were sustainable. He praised Mozambican spiritual beliefs, saying that he preferred them "to those I was taught as a child." He agreed that outside interests caused much of the country's "environmental degradation," and even said he believed that much of the media attention to him and the park was "too positive."

"These are complicated issues," he wrote. "I welcome the best advice anyone can give us."

The online discussion died down. Heidi told me that people just didn't want a public fight with the well-connected multimillionaire. But although he sounded conciliatory and gracious in the public forum, she said, Greg still seemed incensed about the criticism in private.

Heidi found this out firsthand. Shortly after Greg read her posts, he contacted her and offered to fly her to Washington so they could talk about the issues face-to-face. It struck Heidi as an odd invitation, but she was ready to give the philanthropist the benefit of the doubt. She hoped that she might even convince him to readjust his project in a way that would better value the local farmers' perspectives. So she went to meet with him and ended up in what she describes as one of the strangest conversations of her life.

"He was so angry," she told me. "He just kept bombarding me with the reasons for why they didn't need to get [the local] people's opinions." She had a hard time squeezing a word in, she says. Greg seemed far more interested in convincing her to embrace his opinion than he was in expanding the way he thought about his work in Mozambique.

And he seemed to grow increasingly angry as Heidi stuck to her own position. "He just kept saying, 'Do you think it would actually be better if we weren't there?'"

Heidi didn't understand why Greg was getting so worked up about persuading her—a relatively low-level academic with a limited audience—that what he was doing was *right*. "It was bizarre," she recalled. "I'm like, 'You're a multimillionaire running this whole project. Why do you care what I think?'"

But her story didn't seem so bizarre to me. During the time I was reporting in Gorongosa, Greg often seemed mindful of how he'd be seen—in the academic world, in development and humanitarian circles, in history. He may have had the executive's ability to be thick-skinned in matters of personnel management, but he seemed genuinely bothered, even hurt, if people in the realms he valued, such as academia or the arts, doubted the purity of his work. It wouldn't surprise me if he wanted, or on some level even needed, to convince Heidi that she was wrong. She and the other academics, after all, were a threat to his story, the five-act play.

But if he was bothered by these critics, Greg would soon get reassurance from a far more prominent voice: a famous scientist who would become one of the project's most high-profile and influential supporters.

12

The Bioblitz

On July 27, 2011, the celebrated biologist E. O. Wilson—two-time Pulitzer Prize winner, distinguished Harvard professor emeritus, lauded as "the father of biodiversity," and widely regarded as the world's leading expert on ants—landed in a helicopter some 3,600 feet up the slopes of Mount Gorongosa. This location, just beneath the lower elevations of the montane rain forest, had been agreed upon by the scientist, park staffers, and a number of mountain residents, who had been prepped for the day's activity by a young park employee named Tonga Torcida. About thirty children were waiting in the grass, along with quite a few parents and several park rangers.

It's unlikely that any of the locals recognized the famous scientist. But they listened attentively as he explained, through Tonga's translation, that they were about to embark together on something very special. Right there on the mountain, the American said, they were going to conduct Mozambique's very first bioblitz.

This may not have meant much to the mountain residents, who were isolated by language and culture even from the inhabitants of their own country's capital. The term would have been instantly familiar to

Western conservationists, though. Over the past two decades, the bioblitz has become a popular tool for both science and public relations. It is, essentially, crowd-sourced biology, with professional scientists and laypeople working together to try to find as many species as possible within a certain area in a given amount of time. The scientists identify the finds, and the data are recorded in a variety of ways—including, these days, in the online "Encyclopedia of Life," a project supported by the MacArthur Foundation that has the breathtaking goal of combining on one website all known data about every living species.

Wilson has been one of the main proponents of the bioblitz. In 1998, newly retired from nearly half a century of teaching at Harvard, he helped organize the first popular one. It was held around Walden Pond, in Concord, Massachusetts, the place where Henry David Thoreau once set up camp. Since then, the concept has taken off—first locally, with every school system in Massachusetts "engaged in bioblitz," as Wilson put it to an Audubon Society interviewer, and then across the United States. By the mid-2000s, there had been bioblitzes in at least eighteen other countries, many of them organized by Wilson himself.

These gatherings often felt like ecological revival meetings, with teachers and students, parents and neighbors, serious scientists and people totally new to fieldwork joining together for one intense, joyful period of biological investigation. The enthusiasm that laypeople brought to the gatherings was hugely hopeful for longtime naturalists such as Wilson. Not only did bioblitzes help with conservation, since hundreds of bug spotters and bird counters could catalog the populations of any microecosystem far more quickly than one or two professional biologists, but they also connected people with the world around them. For a child to go out into an urban park, for instance, and start looking, really looking, into the dirt and leaves and grass, finding creatures she never knew were there, and then to see her own discoveries added to the communal portrait of an environment—it was the sort of thing that changed people. The participants said as much.

This was a natural narrative for Wilson. The central story of the scientist's career has been the link between humans and the other creatures who make up our world. In his 1984 book *Biophilia*, he argues that our connection to (and love of) nature is not socially fabricated but rather inherent, instinctual, written into our genes. "We are human in good part because of the particular way we affiliate with other organisms," he writes. "They are the matrix in which the human mind originated and is permanently rooted, and they offer the challenge and freedom innately sought. To the extent that each person can feel like a naturalist, the old excitement of the untrammeled world will be regained."

It made sense, then, that when E. O. Wilson and Greg Carr began talking about the Gorongosa National Park, and the challenge of getting local people invested in saving its ecosystem, they soon came up with the idea of holding a bioblitz on Mount Gorongosa.

Greg invited the scientist to visit the park, and the two men quickly became friends. This did not surprise me. Wilson seemed the sort of figure to whom the philanthropist gravitated. A generation older than Greg, he was a renowned intellectual, both an extraordinary scientist and a wonderfully creative thinker. (Being an expert on ants may sound trivial, but as anyone who has read Wilson's work knows, the complexities of the ant world can be downright fascinating.) He also brought a sort of spirituality to his work, regularly pushing scientific discovery into a moral and humanistic realm. His exhortations about the ethical role of humans on the planet had religious overtones to them. I suspected that this might appeal to Greg. While Greg told interviewers he was no longer an active church member, he acknowledged that his Mormon upbringing had left him with a sense that there was something bigger than our own lives and needs. This touched upon human rights, one of Greg's passions, but also implied an even greater moral code of goodness—one that would, indeed, include lions, trees, and ants. Wilson's scientific secular humanism, with its conservationist bent, was, it seemed to me, a perspective that Greg shared.

Wilson was also, like Greg, a transplant to the insular academic world of Boston, and in some ways a bit of an outsider. By the turn of the twenty-first century, his work had become controversial among a number of academics. Many of his peers disagreed vehemently with some of his intellectual positions, particularly those involving the question of whether Darwin's theories of evolution and natural selection applied to the individual or the group. In 2012, the prominent evolutionary biologist Richard Dawkins sparked quite a spat in the rarefied air of academic science by saying that Wilson had written "pages of erroneous and downright perverse misunderstandings of evolutionary theory." Yet even before the controversies, Wilson suggested to interviewers that he had always felt somewhat apart. "A southern boy who came north to earn a living" is how the Alabama-born Wilson described himself—and perhaps the Idaho-born Greg, who seemed increasingly exasperated by Cambridge, Massachusetts, could relate. (Although he leaned politically to the left himself, Greg told me at one point that he was having trouble understanding the apparent eagerness of other privileged American liberals to claim victimhood of one type or another. I could sympathize. It is kind of hard to sit in an impoverished Mozambican village one day, hearing about yet another child who has died of malaria, and then to fly to Boston the next, where the passionate topic of the day in academia is whether political signage may be chalked on campus sidewalks.) Overall, Wilson projected the sort of earnest passion and wonder at the world that struck me as fitting well with Greg's.

For Wilson, there was no relativism when it came to discussing nature or the importance of preserving it. Indeed, in his prolific writings and numerous public appearances, he regularly seemed appalled by the increasingly popular position among younger conservationists that the very concepts of "wilderness" and "nature" needed a rehab. These neoenvironmentalists took the position that nature—rather than something found in its best form away from humans, within national parks or in other places of low human impact—should be considered through a more neutral lens: simply as an evolving mixture of species, existing with as much value in interstate median strips as within the Amazon jungle. After all, they argued, archaeological evidence shows that "pristine" wilderness areas, including Gorongosa, have actually been the site of thousands of years of human activity. People have always been a part of the so-called natural world, they pointed out, so trying to preserve nature as something separate from humans is both misguided and impossible.

It was a position that seemed to annoy Wilson greatly. "Where do you plant the white flag that you're carrying?" he snapped during an Aspen Institute panel with writer Emma Marris, whose book *Rambunctious Garden* challenges the traditional conservationist ideal of saving pristine wilderness. In Wilson's view, drawing borders around regions of spectacular biodiversity is still not just the best approach, but the only worthwhile one. And faced with threats from every direction, including from his fellow conservationists, it was more important than ever.

This may have been one of the reasons Wilson found himself enraptured by the Gorongosa Park restoration project. Much of his work has centered on the biology of islands—both actual islands surrounded by water, and places that might as well be enclosed by water as far as animal and plant life are concerned. A mountaintop is one example of this sort of "island"; so, one might argue, is a protected area such the Gorongosa National Park, where the ecosystem is isolated by the human behavior around it. In many ways, these islands are the earth's bone marrow of biodiversity. They have a disproportionately high number of species, which helps create the sort of global genetic diversity that biologists agree is essential for the health of our planet.

While these islands have an unusually rich collection of plants and animals, though, they are also particularly prone to *losing* species. Wilson has worked to explain why. In his widely accepted theory of island biogeography, he details how biodiversity depends on a balance of sorts between new species immigrating onto the island and existing species there going extinct. Some level of extinction is normal. But the smaller the "island," Wilson notes, the faster its species go extinct, and the more likely it is to essentially go into an ecological tailspin of biodiversity reduction. This was one of the reasons Greg and his scientists lobbied so hard for the Mozambican government to give them control of the top of Mount Gorongosa. They worried that the expanse of trees and wildlife there would become so small that it would enter this tailspin, bringing the park along with it.

Wilson's first visit to the park came about a year after the central Mozambican government put the top of the mountain under the park's control. It was his first trip to sub-Saharan Africa. As he later described it, he was quickly taken with Gorongosa, and with Greg. He delighted in the views from the helicopter (the first one, he wrote, in which he had ridden) and in the biodiversity of the park. He was thrilled by the potential of discovering previously unidentified species within its borders. And he was humbled, he wrote, to be working alongside Greg, who impressed him tremendously with his devotion to nature and his generosity of money and spirit. Wilson agreed with the philanthropist that Mount Gorongosa was particularly fascinating.

The bioblitz there was going to be only two hours long, shorter than most, for logistical reasons ranging from the helicopter's schedule to the fact that Wilson was going to be the only scientist identifying species. "Everyone can join," he told the gathered children and parents through Tonga's translation. "We will find all the kinds of animals we can, living in this particular place, and here and now on the eastern side of Mount Gorongosa. The game is this: how many kinds of insects and other kinds of animals can we find in two hours in this spot on the mountain? We are going to have a combination of science, social gathering, and treasure hunt."

"Why is a bioblitz important?" he continued. "Because what we are doing today is real science! Scientists and everybody need to know what the different kinds are in order to study and understand life here, and take care of the environment."

The children took plastic bags from the park staff and gleefully dove into the grasses and forest, collecting beetles and flies, ants and spiders. Wilson peered at each specimen brought to him, attempting to come up with an identification. Six species of grasshoppers, one species of cricket, some bark lice, three species of ants, one of crane fly.

"The children, about four to twelve years old, proved remarkably gifted hunters," Wilson noted. Far more so, he pointed out, than their peers in the United States, who were more likely to live indoors, away from nature. By the end of two hours, the crowd had found sixty different species, belonging to thirty-nine families in thirteen orders.

Park administrators were thrilled. Here, in many ways, was Greg's original vision: the brightest scientific minds of the West joining forces with Mozambicans to honor an ecologically spectacular patch of Africa. This sort of endeavor, park administrators believed, could usher a new generation of Mozambicans along the path of environmental understanding and scientific inspiration, with all the conservation and economic possibilities that this would hold. It was exciting and hopeful, especially when combined with the rest of Greg's project.

"Here," Wilson wrote, "in one of the remotest parts of Africa, a great environmental tragedy has been averted just in time."

But again there is another way to tell this story, and I wondered as I read the breathless press releases if any of the conservationists had stopped to think of the scene differently. A white man, who had never been to the country before (let alone the specific region), being deemed the person with the most authority to talk about creatures that had long existed in this African environment. A little uncomfortable, no?

Now, to be fair, the basic premise of a bioblitz is that this sort of expert scientific identification opens people's eyes to the sheer diversity of life generally overlooked in one patch of earth. As Wilson said, you need to know the different kinds of life in order to take care of them. But some scholars suggested to me that the eyes most needing to be opened were not those of the people who live on the mountain. The Gorongosans likely knew their ecosystem far better than the outsiders, these scholars said. Even if the mountain residents didn't know the Latin names of all those insects, they knew the creatures themselves far more intimately than would a new Western arrival.

After all, as Heidi Gengenbach and others argued, the people who lived on the mountain were the keepers of biodiversity, not the ignorant underminers of it. The ones who most needed education of how the ecosystem—including the human part of it—really worked were those outsiders who now purported to know what was best for the mountain.

How one sees the story of the bioblitz, I realized, depends a lot on what one thinks about science. For Westerners, science is objective. It is so objective, indeed, that we believe you can be ignorant of a particular place, its culture and its history, and still be the most expert person around, as long as you are schooled in a particular scientific field. In other words, we do not believe that biology itself changes just because one is sitting in Gorongosa rather than in Concord, Massachusetts. Biology is biology. It is omnipresent. We view science the way we describe our gods.

But although science presents itself as unassailable truth, equations solved and theories proven, in fact it regularly turns out to be wrong. Think about everything from bloodletting, which doctors swore by for some two thousand years (mistake!), to the new understanding of the malleability of genetics (a dramatic change from what I learned in high school), to the recent astronomical theories about dark energy, which give us a totally new way of understanding the universe. Think about this last one for a moment: some observations made less than twenty years ago have radically changed how we conceive of *the universe*. It's hard even to try to wrap one's mind around that.

There are many big shifts like this in scientific truth. But there are also other, subtler ways in which science can be unreliable. We know, for instance, that scientists are suggestible. If a pharmaceutical company pays researchers to test a particular drug, those researchers—performing what in their minds is objective science—will disproportionately find the drug in question to be safe. This is not because of corruption, scholars say. These researchers are trying to do exactly the same science that they do in other studies. But the human subconscious affects the results. Human perceptions and hidden understandings are intimately and inexorably connected with what we believe to be true.

It's not a huge jump to suggest that the same might happen with scientific research funded and supported by a national park. The issue is not that conservation scientists are making up their findings. It's not even that they're performing bad science. It's that any scientists will have an unconsciously subjective way of seeing the world and their own results, and working with and for a national park will tend to tug them in a certain direction. Science, in this context, becomes part of one specific, curated story.

Indeed, science is one of our most powerful curating tools as we go through the world. For even if we admit that science is malleable, even if we recognize that scientific truth changes, most of us in the West nonetheless still simply do not believe what our science of the moment cannot explain. We do not believe in the spirits, for instance, because they are impossible—or perhaps only indescribable—in our logic system. We certainly do not believe that spirits can be angry, or that, as many Gorongosans tell us, social and environmental problems are not the scientific products of various inputs but rather the visible manifestation of spiritual displeasure.

In the glow of the bioblitz, at that moment on Mount Gorongosa, the declaration of Western science was clear and optimistic. It was a story of life understood, ecosystems preserved, and, as Wilson said, tragedy averted just in time.

But in the other story, the spiritual disorder was just about to get worse. For it was around the same time that the old Renamo leader Afonso Dhlakama reappeared on the mountain.

The people who lived there knew this was an ominous sign. For years, Dhlakama had resided in the northern part of the country, surrounded by a small group of fighters that described itself as the "presidential guard." Although the 1992 peace accord had turned the Renamo rebel group into an opposition political party, the Frelimo government had agreed to let Dhlakama keep his few soldiers. Why not? A handful of fighters posed little threat to national security. And, for the most part, the Renamo leadership was making itself irrelevant. Every now and then Dhlakama would release a threatening statement, but most people just rolled their eyes. The country was not only tired of fighting; it was prospering. Meanwhile, Renamo, even as a political party, was weak. In 2012 it held only 51 seats out of 250 in parliament, and it was losing more and more support every year. Dhlakama, people figured, was just upset that he wasn't able to cash in on the country's rapid economic growth. He was stuck in the bush, hanging out with his ragtag fighters, watching his old Frelimo enemies become some of the wealthiest men

in southern Africa. His threats were just a way to get some more attention, most commentators assumed.

But now he, along with about seven hundred fighters, had returned
to Renamo's old Casa Banana headquarters on the slopes of Mount
Gorongosa. Casa Banana was in the traditional district of a *régulo*
named Sandjungira, which was also the district where Samatenje, the
rainmaker, had his shrine. Dhlakama announced that he was going to
begin military training again. Only force, he said, would convince the
ruling Mozambican government that it should distribute more of
the money pouring in from all those donors who considered the country their darling.

Renamo's parliamentary head, Maria Angelina Enoque, warned the
country that there were troubles ahead. "Despite the silencing of the
guns, we are not at peace," she said. The tensions and rhetoric swelled
along with the wet season's rivers. The fighters were ready to destroy
Mozambique if that's what it took, the Renamo faithful said. They were
ready to fight to defend themselves. If you don't take us seriously, just
you wait.

To those who lived on the mountain, it did not look like tragedy had
been averted just in time. It looked like tragedy was on its way.

The reports coming out of the Gorongosa region over the next year or
two were bizarre in their disparity. The stories continued to break down
into the same two themes. One was the joy and optimism of the bioblitz,
the logic of the conservationists. The other was the narrative of violence
and disorder. It was as if two sets of actors on the same stage, long frustrated by having to navigate around one another's performances, were
getting out of control. They were shouting now.

Back in the United States, I was receiving regular updates from
the Gorongosa Park public relations team. There was news—exciting
news!—about a new vendor taking over the management of Chitengo
Camp. No longer would the park administrators try to manage this
tourist center, which had already been getting increasingly fancy and
expensive. They would instead turn over Chitengo to the international

Visabeira Group, which would open a Girassol hotel, charge higher prices, and bring a more professional (and corporate) tourism experience. The park also announced that a new luxury safari operator would provide lantern-lit romance deep in the bush, as well as walking safaris for those who wanted to pay to see nature up close. There were notices about travel awards and conferences. And in 2013, the park was thrilled to announce the release of a film about the budding relationship between Tonga Torcida and his new mentor, E. O. Wilson.

The film, called *The Guide*, was produced by the Academy Award–winning director Jessica Yu. (Yu had been a friend and regular collaborator of Greg's ever since he commissioned her some years earlier to do a modern-style documentary film using themes from Euripides.) The movie was beautiful, in scenery and narrative, and would eventually be packaged with E. O. Wilson's book on Gorongosa, which came out shortly afterward.

That arrangement struck me as somewhat questionable, the sort of mushiness that makes it hard to know where storytelling ends and propaganda begins. In this case, however, I also knew Tonga, and a good bit about his story. And there was no denying it: his tale was inspiring.

Tonga grew up on the mountain in a family of farmers. He attracted Greg's attention as a fifteen-year-old, when he noticed the philanthropist's helicopter landing not far from his family's land and approached to practice the English he was learning in school. "Good morning, sir. How are you?" he remembers saying. Greg was taken aback, impressed. He asked Tonga to guide him to one of the nearby waterfalls. Their connection blossomed from there.

Tonga explained to Greg that he attended school in Gorongosa Town, boarding with a friend of his father's, since it was too far to walk from his family's plot on the mountain. He did domestic chores and other work for rent and studied as much as he could. He was enthusiastic when he heard about Greg's plan for Gorongosa. Greg told him that one day Tonga could be a guide in the new Gorongosa National Park.

Eventually Tonga did get a full-time job in the park, and when E. O.

Wilson arrived for his visit it was Tonga who got the nod to be the scientist's assistant. Before that, Tonga's main professional goal was to become a tour guide, the only career that seemed at all realistic—and quite ambitious, really—for the son of rural peasants. But as the film shows it, the young man's relationship with Wilson opened up a broader world, and Tonga admitted that his real dream now was to become a biologist. "After meeting and working with Professor Wilson," he says, "I fell into passion the same way that someone falls asleep: gradually and suddenly, from one moment to another." Greg and Wilson encouraged him, and the next year Tonga received a scholarship to attend a wildlife college in Tanzania. His story, Wilson wrote, was a "spearhead for his people and Mozambique's natural environment."

Now, I could approach this cynically, and focus on the somewhat suspect overtones of a young African saved by his exposure to an older white man—along with the implication that there is something wrong with the rural African world and that one should desire to go beyond it. I could claim it to be a return to the Cosmos Club geographers' faith in the progressive forces of Western science, and a (very successful) iteration of Live Aid–style snapping, an African saved from poverty. But I won't do that. Because here's the thing: I actually tear up every time I think about *The Guide*, just from the sheer beauty and hope of it all. Tonga was one of my favorite people at the park, gentle and gracious and funny. I love that he's had the chance to educate himself and follow a passion in a way that most American kids simply take for granted. And although I don't know the scientist personally, I'm glad for E. O. Wilson that he got to meet Tonga. His life must be better for it.

Yet here's the other thing: *The Guide* also shows how stories can be both true and misleading at the same time. Storytellers in the West know that highlighting one personal story is a lot more effective in our culture than speaking in generalities. Think about all those political speeches, for instance, where the candidate talks about meeting so-and-so from Ohio who works three jobs and still can't afford health care. In my journalism classes, I tell college students that they need to find "characters" to illustrate a story's point: it doesn't matter how many great statistics you have, the way to get readers to *care* is to find one or two moving personal examples.

This isn't wrong. It's just effective storytelling. But as I also tell my students, we have a responsibility, when we are purporting to explain the way things are, to put these individual stories into honest context. If there is only one Ohio resident out there working three jobs and unable to afford health care, then we as journalists need to make that clear. We should not let readers think that her story is representative. But what often happens—in my field as much as any other, unfortunately—is that we become so impressed by the single example that we don't look at the big picture. We assume, and allow our readers to assume, that our one character's experience is in some way typical of most.

Other disciplines don't necessarily have the same obligation as journalism does to present context. A book or documentary film may intentionally focus on a character who is unusual, or a relationship that is extraordinary. We all adore tales of kings and queens and up-by-their-bootstraps millionaires, of solo adventurers going off into Antarctica (or Africa, for that matter), of quirky geniuses and superheroes. These stories are beautiful and enriching parts of our culture, and I certainly wouldn't want to change them. The issue, I'd argue, comes when the latter type of storytelling, the exception-to-the-rule tale that's told for the sake of a good story, blends with the former, the representative story that attempts on some level to show how something *is*. When, for instance, the National Geographic view of southern Africa becomes our understanding of it. Or when *The Guide* is taken as a definitive take on Gorongosa and how it is changing lives.

The Guide and Tonga's relationship with Wilson are true, but they are also beautiful anomalies. There are, as I've said, more than 150,000 people living in the "buffer zone" around the Gorongosa National Park. The vast, vast majority of them have not scored jobs, education, or relationships with powerful figures of the West, and many of them, if you believe the academics, may have actually seen their living situations deteriorate. But *The Guide* fits with our other stories of Africa and of ourselves. It makes us feel hopeful and proud. And it lets us ignore the other story, the Disorder, that by the early 2010s was starting to rage ever more intensely in the forests and banana fields of the great Gorongosa ecosystem.

While American audiences were watching the peaceful, heartwarming tale of Wilson and Tonga, government forces were moving into the Gorongosa area with the goal of isolating the old rebels at their Casa Banana base. Mozambican army patrols, men with olive-green uniforms and machine guns draped over their chests, set up roadblocks around the mountain. They were not going to let Renamo fighters in or out, they said, because they did not want this violence to spread. The peasants eyed the soldiers warily. There is a saying in Mozambique: when elephants fight, the grass gets trampled.

The Renamo leadership responded angrily, accusing the government of plotting to assassinate Dhlakama and other leaders. Then government forces stormed a different Renamo stronghold, a few hours south of the park. Government spokespeople explained that this raid was to disrupt a group plotting violent attacks on Mozambican citizens. Renamo fighters, who said the raid was unprovoked, responded by attacking the local police department. Five people died.

The roads became dangerous.

Someone, or some ones, dug a trench in the internationally rebuilt EN1. Motorists had to slow down to drive around it, which made them perfect targets for ambushers. This strategy was used with cruel efficiency during the civil war. For years, only the desperate or crazy drove alone on the highways in Mozambique. Those who couldn't avoid traveling would go in convoys, hoping that strength in numbers would bring them safely past the twisted wrecks of other vehicles.

Sure enough, soon there were more bullets. Machine guns fired not just into army vehicles but into buses. Attacks left women bleeding by the side of the road and soldiers, poor like all of them, dead. Then even more victims. The government recommended that civilians travel only in convoy or with a military escort.

The international response was, at first, stunned, a collective rubbing of the eyes to make sure the press reports and security dispatches were real. It was as if nobody could believe this was happening. It was impossible. Mozambique was no longer a conflict zone. It was the peaceful neighbor, the donors' darling, the exemplar of southern Africa leaving behind its war-torn past and entering a new era of prosperity and development. But then came more attacks, and slowly the regional leaders began to make phone calls, to conference on the matter. The intergovernmental Southern African Development Community, through high-ranking officials, shared its concern with Mozambican representatives and offered mediation services.

The Renamo vanguard explained that it did not want a return to war either, but that it had no choice. There was no other way to get the Frelimo government to take seriously its demands for more representation in government and in the army. Meanwhile, in coffee shops and boardrooms, people wondered: Why was this starting again? How could it have happened? Who was really in control there, on the slopes of Mount Gorongosa, the heart of it all?

On the mountain, the peasants, too, expressed their stress and fear about what was going on. But they also told researchers that it was not unexpected. They knew they were living in disorder, that the spirits were unhappy. The Mozambican government had supported and encouraged the park project. To many on the mountain, that fact only confirmed what they'd suspected: the state was corrupt and interested in taking more control. The *mhondoro* ancestor spirits had demonstrated—through all those catastrophes that the conservationists chalked up to chance—that resistance was the natural, spirit-approved course of action.

In June 2013, as government forces gathered around the territory of Sadjungira, park administrators decided to postpone any new bookings for Chitengo Camp. They said it was a temporary measure, just in case there was a full-scale raid on Casa Banana. On travel forums, they insisted that the situation would soon resolve itself; just call before heading out, to confirm that accommodation would be available.

I was not there. But I got in touch with an Al Jazeera reporter who was covering the unrest, and she told me that the region was tense. Locals said Renamo soldiers were hiding within the park itself.

The same month, *National Geographic* magazine published an article by E. O. Wilson. Titled "The Rebirth of Gorongosa," it was a glowing account of the scientist's experience in the park. He wrote about the region's stunning biodiversity, its troubled past, and how much the locals were benefiting from Greg Carr's project. It was the same old five-act play, presented for the *National Geographic* audience. Wilson also told his story of the bioblitz, the cross-cultural sharing of biophilic joy and adventure. The park, he wrote, "fulfilled all the yearnings for adventure and discovery I have felt since my boyhood, when I was the age of my helpers on Mount Gorongosa and was venturing into the forests of Alabama and Florida with a net, spade, and collecting jars."

In the article, Wilson acknowledged that the Gorongosa ecosystem was confronting a new threat. But in his story, this threat did not come from the government soldiers who were increasingly crowding around the protected area, or from the rebels who had sequestered themselves on the slopes of the mountain. It did not have to do with the regional concern that Mozambique was spiraling out of control, or with the various moments of disconnect between the managers of the park and the people who lived around it. (Later, Wilson would write that Greg "has, so far as I have seen and heard, gained the complete respect of the people of Gorongosa.") Instead, the danger was clearly stated in the *National Geographic* article's subhead: "Biologist E. O. Wilson Takes a Close Look at a Famed Park in Mozambique. Recovering from Civil War, It Faces a New Challenge: Settlers Are Deforesting Its Sacred Mountain."

In other words, in this setting of our adventure and discovery, this place of blissful nature, the problem is the people who happen to live there. Or, to put it more bluntly, the problem with Africa is the Africans.

Soon the peasants from the mountain began to arrive in Gorongosa Town. Some stayed up on the slopes, by their fields of sorghum and cassava, but many did not want to risk death again. They remembered what had happened to those who tried to stay during the war. There were many, like Tatu's brother, shot by soldiers, or, like Tomás's brother, killed by land mines. Nearly everyone I interviewed had some close relation killed in the war. When elephants fight, the grass gets trampled. So now many left their plots of land and their homesteads and came into town to stay with relatives or friends, to wait and worry, as civilian traffic along the still mostly smooth highway thinned out, replaced by the periodic rumble of a military vehicle.

Renamo declared an end to the peace deal, that 1992 accord brokered by the United Nations, which once seemed to have stopped one of Africa's harrowing wars for good. The opinion writers and analysts decried the move. Why? they asked. What would anyone, really, have to gain by a return to war and destabilization? Business groups threw up their hands in frustration. Tourist numbers dropped precipitously. And on the mountain, the center of resistance, there was movement, the maneuvering of men in fatigues carrying AK-47s.

The place where the road curves over the Pungue River bridge—a spot that had always cheered me because it meant there were only two miles left to the park's entrance—became a danger zone. I heard reports that Renamo had started to ransack the park's tree nurseries on the mountain. The park, some said, was a symbol in this new conflict, representing government and outside control, even though Greg and other park officials insisted that they were simply neutral, friends with everyone. The international press began to speak of "the conflict-hit Gorongosa district."

There was no mention of any of this from the park's PR department. The park website still invited travelers to journey into "the heart of the wild," to "experience real Africa on your wild Mozambican safari through Gorongosa's wilderness." It seemed to me that the words now took on a different meaning than the park staff intended. Not that most potential tourists would have known. There was very little press in the United States about the growing Mozambican conflict. This is not particularly surprising: there are few American foreign correspondents left in Africa, and little space in American daily newspapers for international news in general, let alone dispatches from this particular region. Compared to crises such as those in Syria or South Sudan, Myanmar or Iraq, the Mozambique situation was minor. Besides, as one of my editors pointed out to me, who could even find Mozambique on a map?

There were more deaths, though the exact number was unknown. It was far from the hundreds of thousands killed in the civil war, but it was pushing up into the hundreds, according to some estimates. Frelimo organized marches throughout the country, with people carrying banners that cried, "No to War!" The government launched a coordinated attack on the mountain base of Casa Banana. More Renamo attacks and more retaliations followed.

Meanwhile, I received notice from the park that the E. O. Wilson Biodiversity Laboratory had opened, to many accolades, outside Chitengo Camp. The purpose of the lab, according to the park, was both to conduct long-term ecological research and to train a new generation of Mozambican scientists. They could not depend only on expertise coming from outside the country, they said. The future of African biodiversity, "and thus the very survival and well-being of the continent's population, rests in the hands of a new generation of local conservationists, scientists, experts and educators," park officials wrote on the website. "No amount of external influence and prowess will ever match the effectiveness of personal engagement and dedication of Mozambican stakeholders." To achieve this personal engagement and dedication, the lab promised a lecture series on topics such as invertebrate conservation and pollination biology. There would be workshops for locals that would combine those lectures with live field research, and an opportunity for Mozambican students and researchers to "participate in scientific projects conducted by visiting international scientists." They could even "develop their own projects under guidance."

Wilson was thrilled and humbled by the lab's dedication, and by the potential for this expansion of science into Mozambique. "Gorongosa, I will say it now, is ecologically the most diverse park in the world," he declared.

The warring parties in Mozambique signed a fragile peace accord in September 2014. Those who studied the country were nervous, though.

Some of the scholars I'd spoken to about the return to violence in Gorongosa told me that they were saddened but not surprised when renewed conflict broke out, and they did not expect things to quiet down completely. The tensions in that region—over the park project, over development, over the evil spirits—were so great that something was bound to explode. All of Mozambique, really, was a tinderbox, some academics told me.

As if proving them right, I soon read about a rash of kidnappings in Maputo, both of wealthy locals and of foreigners. There were suggestions that perhaps the police or other government officials were involved. The crime rate across the country was increasing. And sure enough, within another year or two, the violence erupted again. The newsletters I read about Mozambique carried updates on "the war." The British government released a travel advisory warning tourists about heightened tensions and violence in the central provinces, including around Gorongosa National Park.

The word from the park, though, was that everything was great. They were still open for tourists. They had embarked on new scientific ventures. Their human development programs were going strong. And they were still, according to news reports, considering the idea of expanding the park yet further, creating the sort of wildlife corridors that Wilson and other biologists said were essential for conservation.

Wilson published his book about Gorongosa, *A Window on Eternity*, in the spring of 2014, some months before the ill-fated peace agreement. He dedicated it to "Gregory C. Carr, world citizen, who conceived and brought to reality the rebirth of Gorongosa National Park."

13

A Multitude of Voices

Toward the end of my time living in southern Africa, in the latter part of 2008, I went to visit the Moholoholo Wildlife Rehabilitation Centre in South Africa, not far outside the borders of Kruger National Park. There I met up with the organization's founder, a sun-leathered white South African named Brian Jones. Brian, I'd gathered, was a different breed of environmentalist, a sort of Dr. Dolittle meets macho ranger meets bush preacher. I knew from talking to sources that he rankled traditional conservationists, but also that he had a growing local and international following. Everyone, from local poachers to foreign veterinary students, saw him as someone who truly loved nature.

Brian's rehabilitation center felt like something between a zoo and a fairy tale. A series of enclosures, which Brian built ad hoc as he got funding, held a motley assortment of animals, from hawks and honey badgers to zebras and lions. Meanwhile, creatures that Brian and his staff deemed sufficiently safe roamed freely around the complex. Marabou storks teetered and preened; round-bellied warthogs grazed under the thick-trunked flame trees. All the animals were recovering from some version of suffering. They had been poisoned or shot, snared or broken in some other way before they arrived at Moholoholo.

I sat with Brian in his chaotic office, which seemed very dark after the bright sunshine outside. "They just call me," Brian said, explaining how he got his animals. "It's word of mouth."

He picked up a phone, which had been ringing nonstop. "A wild dog, eh? What's that? His leg? Shame, man, but those buggers. . . . We'll be on it, hear?"

He hung up and looked back at me. "On Sunday they called me for a leopard. A few weeks back they called me for a rhino that had been abandoned by mommy. I got a buzzard two days ago, with one leg."

Brian has no formal veterinary training, no degrees in biology, no years at wildlife college. After fourth grade, he told me, he fled formal schooling for the bush, which he knew was all the teacher he needed. He nursed his first animal back to health when he was fifteen, repairing the crushed wing of a sparrow. People told him to just let it die, but he knew that wasn't right. Since then, he has taught himself the ins and outs of veterinary medicine and pharmaceuticals. He has practiced surgery on birds on his wife's kitchen table. ("She's a good one," he told me, smiling. "Married forty years, hey. Met on a blind date on Wednesday, proposed on Friday. I know my birds.") When he was in the South African National Parks service, he "fostered" baby rhinos whose mothers had been poached for their horns, letting the creatures into the sparse little cottage where he lived and feeding them out of a bottle. By the time I met him, he had veterinary students from around the world coming to train with him.

He took me on a tour of his facilities. He had stories for every animal. Each had been hovering at the edge of death when someone called Brian and told him that there was another one and they were thinking of just shooting it, but maybe he could come and fetch it instead? And he would always go and get it, bringing it back here to try his damnedest to nurse it back to health, because . . .

Because all creatures are God's creatures, he said. And he was a man of God, living in God's perfect creation.

Sure, he told me, it would be great if he could get the animals back to the point where they could return to the wild. That was popular these days in conservation theory—reintroduction. Most of the time, though, he knew that was never going to happen. The maimed lion and the limping cheetah were just going to die if they'd gone back. That bird without wing strength would starve to death. Most conservationists would have declared these animals lost causes. They'd have said it was appropriate to let nature take its course. But he would give them sanctuary, he decided. To him, helping injured creatures seemed perfectly natural in its own right.

When I asked people in conservation about Brian's work, they were skeptical. He was more like an SPCA member than a real conservationist, they said. He did feel-good animal welfare work, but probably made little difference in the big picture of ecology and biodiversity. Conservationists particularly did not approve when he helped animals who were suffering from natural causes, as opposed to man-made wounds. Conservation dogma says that man should not interfere in life-or-death matters in the bush. In other words, we should protect nature but then let it be, respecting it in all its brutality. As for the injuries caused by people—well, there were lots of more substantial programs for fixing human-animal conflict than what Brian was doing there in his strange Noah's ark of trauma. The big conservation organizations were setting up task forces and collaborative networks, sharing thoughts on "human-wildlife coexistence methods" throughout the world.

"It's such bullshit," Brian said when I brought this up.

He peered at me, lines of the sun and lowveld heat etched across his face under the khaki hat. He had been a paratrooper for South Africa, trained in the apartheid-era mandatory military service that taught all white men how to kill. He had shot animals he could not save; he knew how to place a bullet that would work instantly.

The protected areas that everyone talks about these days—they are Band-Aids, he said. A way to hide the real problem of humans and the way we have taken over the land, grabbing more than our share. The so-called experts who called his work *unnatural*—what's natural about anything we do with the world? The conservation projects are no more natural than the splint on the cheetah's hind leg.

"We've come like a cancerous growth and disturbed their habitat," he said. "You talk about renewal projects, about bringing parks back. These parks—the tsetse fly kept the whiteys out. Now we've made them rich white havens."

In other words, the parks were once just areas where it wasn't possible for European settlers to graze their cows. The white people didn't want the land, so they didn't feel the need to control it. Now that's changed. And we're making up our own stories about it to ignore the truth, he said.

At the very least, he suggested, we could recognize our weakness and listen to nature. Nature would tell us that if we really wanted to save the environment, we'd need to change the entire way we live, the way we consume resources and manage economies. We'd have to stop oozing onto other creatures' lands and wrecking them. And we should stop blaming the damage on the blacks, he said, as if we didn't mess it all up first. At the very least, we could recognize all this, stop with our so-called great plans, and spend our energies trying to work in line with the creation. We could *repent*.

"I believe the Almighty put it together," he said. "We had the freedom to live by the law of nature, but we had the freedom to make a choice. We've made the wrong choice. We've already lost."

"But then why, Brian?" I asked him, looking around. "Why all this, if you believe there's no use, that we've lost?" Why are you here, I wondered, bandaging your birds, crying over your injured lions, defending the predator, scavenger, and prey?

He looked at me. "They say even if you're the last guy alive, if you have bullets on you, you get up and fight." He paused. "But come now, let me show you . . ."

He wanted to introduce me to a leopard. She had been poisoned and was so sick that she had been refusing to eat. They thought she was going to die. But for some reason, just before I arrived, she'd begun trying to save herself.

"My leopard is eating now," Brian said softly. "I'm so happy about that. It's funny how animals make you excited and make you cry."

We walked along, and then he said quietly, "We can tell ourselves another story. But we've lost, Stephanie. We've lost."

I have often wondered if Brian is right. Perhaps we are all just doomed, and our scurrying around trying to help Gorongosa—or trying to save any beautiful bit of biodiversity, the human species included—is just a distraction from that grim reality. Maybe *all* the stories are silly. Death and extinction are the true act 5, for every person and, ultimately, every species on the planet.

To take the gloom even further, there is a lot of evidence that we, humans, are pushing the world toward this ultimate curtain call faster than ever. A growing number of scientists say that we have created a whole new geologic epoch, the Anthropocene: human behavior has so altered the planet that the changes are written in the earth itself. This is not presented as a good thing. Talk to people who study topics such as climate change, pollution, and biodiversity loss—or water conservation, or food history, or population growth—and it's quite clear that the Anthropocene does not seem to be headed in a particularly good direction for us.

All this, frankly, is a miserable intellectual place to land. When I've wound up here myself, I have lost a good number of days feeling downright nihilistic. At the same time, I am quite sure this is not where Brian lives. He might believe that "we've lost," as he says, but he still feels some compelling desire to make the here and now as good as possible. And for him, that means negotiating in the purest, most beneficial way his relationship with other life in the world. My guess is that many of us would like to do this, too.

The question, then, is how. Brian has one answer; Greg is working toward another. E. O. Wilson has recently suggested that we set aside half the land on the planet for wilderness preservation—an audacious position that strikes me as both awe-inspiring and terrifying, depending on whether you consider what might become of the people currently inhabiting that land. The Mozambicans living on Mount Gorongosa and in the park's buffer zone have their own answers. We just generally do not hear them.

That's why I found Brian so compelling: he was steadfast and determined in his work, but he also seemed rather clear-sighted about the fact that his good was not everyone's good. In negotiating his own path through the multitude of the world's creatures, he recognized that there were many different perspectives. He was explicit about his own frame of reference, about his God and God's rules; he recognized that these rules were not universally accepted, although they guided him. And he seemed consciously to tread as lightly as possible on the beliefs of others.

Whether his program was "working," in any macro analysis of global conservation issues, was not as important to him as whether his personal work was effective. The lion with the mangled leg did not die—and this, Brian knew, was good. The vulture who'd been poisoned was still alive. His work was small. But man is small, upon the mountain.

Around the time I was finishing this book, the American public went into collective mourning—and engaged in a remarkable amount of collective outrage—about a Zimbabwean lion named Cecil.

Cecil lived in Hwange National Park, about 150 miles from the famous Victoria Falls. I had visited Hwange a few times during my stint in Africa, always somewhat nervously and on the sly, since at the time American journalists were not allowed to work in Zimbabwe and had been jailed for doing so. The park was beautiful but depressing. Unlike Gorongosa, Hwange did not have enough water to support its animals all year round, so the park managers, in better days, had built a series of boreholes with fresh water for the dry season. But years of political turmoil in Zimbabwe under the rule of President Robert Mugabe had left the park without sufficient tourists or resources. This meant that many of the man-made water sources had gone dry. There simply weren't enough funds to keep them going, park officials said.

Animals were dying in droves, particularly elephants. Dozens of elephants had died in the dry season before my visit. Their skulls and bones littered the streambeds, as if the creatures had made one last desperate attempt to quench their thirst. It was creepy and depressing, to say the least. And it got worse. In 2013, poachers used cyanide to poison one of the park's main salt pans. Animals regularly use salt pans to get needed minerals; if you watch at one of them, you might catch an elephant actually licking the ground. So the poisoning was effective, and devastating. More than a hundred elephants were killed; some sources put the death toll as high as three hundred. Most of their tusks were removed and sold.

All this got some attention in the international press. But it was nothing compared to the story of Cecil.

Cecil was a well-known lion in Hwange. He had a telltale dark mane and was considered to be fairly calm around tourists. "Friendly" is how the foreign press came to describe him, an improbable adjective for those who actually live around lions and know that they are not at all cuddly. Starting in 2008, Cecil was one of the lions collared and tracked by the Wildlife Conservation Research Unit in the Department of Zoology at Oxford University. (It was these foreign conservationists, by the way, who named him Cecil—a questionable choice perhaps, since it's a reference to Cecil Rhodes, the British imperialist diamond magnate who founded Rhodesia, the white minority–ruled precursor to Zimbabwe.)

In July 2015, Cecil's GPS collar alerted researchers that he had left Hwange Park, which is unfenced, and gone into a nearby hunting concession. Later, the researchers and Zimbabwean wildlife officials would say that a hunting outfit had "baited" Cecil out of the protected area, luring him with an animal carcass on the back of a pickup truck. I had heard about this sort of baiting when I was in Hwange. It was not all that uncommon, to the dismay of conservationists. But according to my contacts, many of the people responsible were connected to Mugabe's regime, so everyone knew that nothing could be done.

In Cecil's case, the trick was fatally effective. Once he was out of the protected area, he was shot (poorly, it seems) with a hunter's crossbow. For forty hours the wounded lion stumbled through the hunting reserve, trying to escape, until the hunting party found him again and shot him dead. As is the custom in hunting safaris, the head and skin were removed from Cecil's body, to be stuffed and mounted as a trophy.

Had it been some other lion, the kill would almost certainly have gone unnoticed. Big game hunting is still relatively commonplace in southern Africa. In some areas, including the concessions around Hwange Park, it is actually official conservation policy. Indeed, Zimbabwe is probably the world leader in using hunting as part of nature protection. Decades earlier, wildlife officials in Zimbabwe introduced a groundbreaking new conservation initiative called the Communal Areas Management Programme for Indigenous Resources, or CAMPFIRE. The basic premise of CAMPFIRE was that wildlife, in its various forms, is a renewable natural resource with a monetary value. So instead of having outside conservationists come in and tell people how to manage their land, local communities should decide how to leverage it for the best possible return. The theory was that this policy would end up protecting nature, because locals would share in its financial benefits.

Sometimes nature's value was in, say, logging. Other times it was in eco resorts. Quite often, though, it was in hunting, specifically in a particular type of big game hunting. It worked like this: a local group, working with regional officials, would decide on a limited number of lions, rhinos, elephants, and other animals that could be shot on their land. Then they would sell the privilege—fifty thousand dollars for a lion, for instance—to wealthy foreigners. The number of animals killed was relatively low, but the income was high. So was the incentive to keep the overall area as "wild" as possible, since that's what the foreign hunters wanted. According to Zimbabwean statistics, between 1989 and 2001 the CAMPFIRE program brought in some twenty million dollars to local communities, the vast majority of which came from this sort of hunting.

The United States and other free-market donors loved this approach. USAID gave huge amounts of support to CAMPFIRE-style conservation programs. The results have been mixed: some reports from Botswana, another country to adopt community conservation programs, show that wildlife preservation has actually decreased in areas where locals were given control over their natural resource use, and in Zimbabwe there's a question as to how the money has been dispersed (especially since Mugabe's political allies have grabbed the land around Hwange and other parks). Despite these shortcomings, though, the United States and other donors still generally support the approach of monetizing nature. All of which is to say that lions are shot, skinned, and decapitated quite regularly in southern Africa, with the full backing of the U.S. government and many mainstream conservation groups.

But none of this context made it into the news reports in July 2015, when Johnny Rodrigues, head of a group called the Zimbabwe Conservation Task Force, announced that an American dentist named Walter Palmer had murdered their beloved Cecil. The American press and public went crazy. Reporters talked about how Palmer had "bribed" safari guides fifty thousand dollars to be allowed to shoot Cecil; celebrities and Fox News hosts called for swift justice; footage of regal Cecil dominated prime-time newscasts. The fearful news lingo of the day—*beheaded, terrorized*—quickly made its way into the story. The Twitterati got nasty, calling for Palmer to be skinned and beheaded himself. Palmer's protests that he thought he was on a legal hunt fell flat.

The Zimbabwean government reacted to the nonstop international press by putting a hunting ban on the areas around Hwange. They arrested the safari operator and landowner responsible for guiding Palmer and luring Cecil out of the park. And they demanded Palmer be extradited to face charges.

I watched the whole saga with some amazement. Like Brian at his wildlife rehabilitation center, we in the West really do care about nature and animals. We want good to triumph over evil. We are outraged by injustice—particularly when, as in *The Guide*, it is presented as a straightforward tale, with just one or two characters, that we can easily insert into our own frames of reference.

But boy are we confused. Because here's the thing: Cecil the Lion was, indeed, killed. But Cecil the Tragedy, what we were really reacting to, is a created story, a narrative crafted with particular goals in mind. I don't know what political chess move Johnny Rodrigues had in mind when he decided to publicize the story of Cecil's killing. It's worth noting, however, that although Rodrigues is the official Zimbabwean source quoted in most of the news stories that appeared in the United States, his Zimbabwe Conservation Task Force is not a government entity. On the contrary, it has tussled quite regularly with government officials and the national parks department.

I spent a good bit of time with Johnny in Zimbabwe. He was an amazing character, tough and gruff, facing down intimidation from the Zimbabwean government with teeth-clenched defiance. He'd established his organization explicitly to counteract what he saw as governmental mismanagement and corruption. It would not surprise me if his efforts to spread the story of Cecil had something to do with his trying to fight the cronyism he saw undermining the Hwange protected area. Whatever his motives, it's pretty clear they had more to do with political maneuvering than with the fate of one animal—who, at thirteen years old, was already approaching the upper end of the known life span for lions in the wild.

In the West, our obsession with Cecil eventually petered out, leaving the somewhat murky sense that justice would be done. But ten days after the Zimbabwean government instituted the hunting ban around Hwange, it dropped it and quickly released the safari operator and landowner on very little bail. (A Zimbabwean court would later throw out the charges against both Palmer and the safari operator.) The high-end hunting safaris swung back into operation. The debates about payment for ecosystem "services" continued.

The stories we tell may be their own truths. But they are not *the* truth.

That is what I eventually realized in Africa. Stories are true in that they come from somewhere, they grow, they take form, they shape lives and realities. But if you start craving *truth* in the larger sense, you need to step back and pay attention more broadly to the entire accumulation of stories—the varied voices overlapping in a chorus, each one offering something on its own but fully meaningful only when heard with the others as a single whole.

This notion is somewhat at odds with the prevailing culture in the

United States. Here, journalists, like everyone else—politicians and voters, celebrities and NGO staffers—live in a world of definitive answers and snappy proclamations. We often see nuance as an impediment to a great story, not the story itself. To admit otherwise in our society is to risk being labeled wishy-washy, unmoored, even immoral. Our public discourse is about drowning out opposing voices, not accommodating them. We rarely stop to contemplate that we are always just adding another sound to the mix, our own expression of how we exist.

But becoming aware of the entire polyphonic reverberation—stepping back to that less comfortable, more complicated spot where we start to recognize the multitude of voices in one space, all separate but influencing one another, in dissonance or harmony—is both a principled and a pragmatic act. For when we finally admit that our own story is just one voice among many, we may open a path toward interacting far more effectively with the rest of the world.

I say "may" here, because it is quite possible that some parts of the world do not want us to interact with them at all. If we want to improve our global track record, we are going to need to accept this. We must reconsider our well-intentioned efforts to convince others that, as Greg Carr said on Mount Gorongosa, we are here to help. And we also need to stop assuming that the people who say "thanks but no thanks" just don't understand or aren't representative.

Think, for a moment, about an analogy. A philanthropist from Singapore reads with horror some statistics about the American education system. He talks to some new friends he's made in the U.S. government—a bunch of Democrats, let's say—and takes up their invitation to tour the country's red states and look for a school system to take over. Eventually he picks Texas, or perhaps Alabama—somewhere that's been particularly troublesome for the Dems. The Democratic administration signs an executive order handing over the keys to the state's schools, and says that the Asian philanthropist can make the schools teach whatever he wants, in whatever style he desires. He can essentially write his own rules. The local population is furious, but to no avail. This is the best thing for them, the politicians in Washington say. After all, look at those standardized test scores—getting worse every year. The Singaporean press comes and writes glowing reports about how their philanthropist will repair the education system for poor Americans.

It couldn't happen, right? If anything of the sort were tried, there would be mass protests and congressional hearings. And imagine the uproar once people realized that the Singaporean's foundation was collecting all the taxes earmarked for the state's education budget, to distribute however the philanthropist saw fit.

Yet this is what we do all the time. It is the approach we take to the rest of the world, especially Africa. And when we are doing it, we believe it is not only reasonable but noble. It is justified by our Western history of cultural dominance and by our benevolent finger snapping. In the case of conservation projects, it also draws on those same old tropes of unspoiled nature and exotic African wilderness. It is time for us to step back and recognize these stories for what they are, and realize how they must appear to those we tell, "We're here to help."

I am *not* arguing here that we shouldn't be involved with the rest of the world at all, or that we shouldn't care for the nonhuman aspects of our planet, the animals and plants and air and water. I am saying that recognizing, and starting to understand, the alternative stories that people and places hold would allow us to approach the world from a much humbler perspective—and a far more effective one.

In Gorongosa, for instance, the Western conservationists and the local population actually had quite a bit in common. Most important, they shared a deep love and appreciation for the land and all the species it supported. I wonder what would have happened if the whole project had started differently: if at some point, well before committing to work there, Greg Carr (or whichever philanthropist or group was involved) had started to learn the stories of central Mozambique, and had interacted with the people who lived there, not only to figure out *how* to help, but also *whether* to help. Maybe the answer is that it still would have been really complicated. Look no farther than a neighborhood association meeting in the United States for a reminder that even people living on the same block can have widely different opinions (and can get really acrimonious about them). Still, with a different approach—one that starts well before the decision to help—we may be able to raise the odds of success.

In 2013, USAID commissioned an external review of the Gorongosa National Park restoration project. It had given millions of dollars to Gorongosa since 2006, and it was interested in the project's effectiveness. A South African assessment firm called Khulisa Management Services reviewed documents, interviewed park officials, and conducted 265 household interviews in the Gorongosa region to figure out whether the project had achieved some twenty-two "expected results."

In their summary, the Khulisa consultants gave a lukewarm response. There were clearly some positive aspects to the project, they wrote, such as an experienced management team, a significant number of Mozambicans employed, collaborations with international universities, and "good media exposure." Negative factors included "frequent changes of expatriate senior staff as their contracts end" and "limited road network and poor quality of existing roads." Some other negatives, the consultants wrote, were beyond the park's control; among these were "the political-military situation around Mount Gorongosa" and "the high number of impoverished people living in and around the park, many of whom participate in poaching, illegal logging/mining, and slash and burn agriculture." (In other words, the very problems the project had been created to address were now considered by these USAID consultants to be "beyond the control" of the project.) Overall, the assessors wrote, the Gorongosa National Park had "met" or "partially met" twenty of the twenty-two expected results.

This might sound, at first glance, as if the project were doing just fine. But think about that phrase, "partially met." This is a standard category for our interventions in Africa, one employed regularly by the big donor organizations and conservation groups. It means things haven't gone as well as hoped, but they're not god-awful terrible. In this world, that somehow goes in the positive category.

This doesn't work for most things in our lives. I wouldn't do very well if I *partially met* my mortgage payments or my article deadlines.

I would not be thrilled if my husband *partially met* his wedding vows, or my kids *partially met* their homework assignments. Because, really, "partially met" means that you didn't do it.

Even the "met" category gets kind of squishy. Take the details of the consultants' report about environmental progress in Gorongosa. They found that the overall animal numbers had increased, but the population of lions and other large predators had not. The species that had done the best between 2007 and 2012 were impala and waterbuck. The number of hippos had dropped. Poaching was still rampant, and the park's rangers still lacked effective radio communication. The park was unable to recruit and train additional rangers because the Renamo force on Mount Gorongosa objected. Bringing all that information together, the report concluded that the goal of rehabilitating "the Gorongosa ecosystem, including the wildlife," had been "met."

The "partially met" goals included increasing access to education for local students: the park was building houses for teachers in Vinho, but there had been no investment in schools or teachers in any of the fourteen other communities surrounding the park. The same label was applied to boosting the economy in the region. Forty-two percent of the people surveyed said there had been an increase in employment opportunities since the park project began, but most of the respondents also said that they had not experienced any increase in their own income.

"Partially met" is a powerful category because it so neatly excuses any holes in our story. Rather than acknowledging a failure—or, even more important, acknowledging that our underlying story is not working—we can focus just on those bits and pieces that did work.

All in all, the review of Gorongosa put it in a category shared by the vast majority of Western interventions in Africa. Not bad enough to be called a fiasco; not scandalous enough to join the ranks of Li Quan's tiger breeding project or James Ulysses Blanchard's failed Mozambican eco resort. And certainly the Gorongosa restoration effort has given rise to some beautiful individual stories. But when it comes to the hope of sweeping change that had inspired the project in the first place, it has clearly not yet succeeded.

That "yet," of course, is key. Much could still happen at Gorongosa. That is also part of its story. The same is true of our world overall, where we might yet find a way to save what biodiversity and clean air we have left. But if we want any real improvement, any real chance to avert the doom that seems to await us, then we need to start listening to all the voices, the full range of stories, rather than just the "partially met" fragments of our own play.

Afterword

After four years of reporting from southern Africa, I returned to the United States in 2009. After that, I followed what was happening in Gorongosa from afar. Indeed, it was this distance that put the disparate narratives of the park into such stark relief for me and compelled me to write this book. I realized that the strange mixture of news I was getting about Gorongosa—the cheerful press releases and flattering media coverage interspersed with reports of violence and suffering—showed not only the complexity of this one patch of earth, but also the way that narratives shape how we perceive reality in general. Stories, as I have said, are powerful.

And, as I would find out, powerful people will fight to control them.

In late 2016, just as this book was going to press, I received a series of messages from Greg Carr. He had not read the book—nobody had yet, outside of my publisher. But he had seen a brief description of it online and he was upset. I hadn't been to the park recently enough, he said. He argued, essentially, that if I visited the park now, or interviewed the current set of park officials, then I would fully believe in the original, oft-repeated story of the Gorongosa restoration project: that it was a venture for and by the Mozambicans, doing great deeds for humans and nature. When it came to the people who lived in the area, he wrote, "we are the best friends they have."

I replied that the book was looking at long-standing narratives, not the latest news, and that I explicitly declined to judge any one claim to be the singular truth. But since I was writing about stories, I thought I could try to update his version of what had happened in Gorongosa, if he wanted. I asked him to clarify a couple of points—including the admission in one of his on-the-record e-mails that he knew, relatively early on in the project, that suspected poachers were being tortured by park staff. (I had been told about the torture by the scholar Heidi Gengenbach and others, but it was startling to hear this from the human rights philanthropist himself. Greg said that torture no longer happens in the park and that he removed the wardens responsible as soon as he was able; those wardens, in turn, have disparaged Greg's management and disputed his version of events. All of which shows, at very least, that there are some stories of Gorongosa that do not make it into the breathless news reports.)

More important for the book, though, I asked Greg what he saw as the greatest accomplishments of the Gorongosa restoration project. He did not answer this directly. Instead, he replied with more than a dozen e-mails, by turns friendly and aggressive, upbeat and indignant, saying that criticism of the park was fundamentally misguided. He warned me that I was risking my professional reputation by publishing a book that cast doubt on his work in Mozambique or on the Gorongosa project overall. "I am writing to you as a friend with a warning and not a threat," he said. He was quite sure, he told me, that a group of well-connected academics would write scathing reviews of my book (which none of them had yet seen) when it came out.

As it turned out, I didn't have to wait for the publication date. Within days, without anyone having read the book, what seemed to be a coordinated campaign against it began to unfold. A noted lawyer whose literary agency represents E. O. Wilson, among others, sent formal protests to my publisher, claiming that my book was not only inaccurate and unbalanced but posed a catastrophic threat to African conservation and

Western aid to the continent. Mateus Mutemba—the Mozambican in charge of community relations during the saga of G5, who became the park's warden in 2011—wrote demanding an interview, declaring that it was deeply offensive to treat the Gorongosa restoration effort as a Western initiative rather than a Mozambican one. If I did not include his current perspective on Gorongosa, he said, "my understanding will be that you are treating me like the colonial masters treated us."

Nearly two dozen academics, USAID representatives, and others in the NGO world joined Mateus on the e-mail chain, offering daily criticisms of me mixed with accolades for the Gorongosa project. Even E. O. Wilson himself chimed in. "Ms. Hanes' approach, I am prepared to testify, is bad journalism, with potential serious harm to the park and people there and elsewhere," he wrote. "Gorongosa National Park is one of Mozambique's most important assets. As a fellow author, I hope that Ms. Hanes will do a better job of research, and write a more competent account."

At first, all of this felt, frankly, astonishing. Wilson and the others—including Alex Dickie, the head of the USAID mission in Mozambique; Princeton professor Rob Pringle; and the filmmaker Jessica Yu—were all denouncing a book that none of them had laid eyes on. People in the publishing field told me that they had never seen anything like this preemptive mass attack.

But as I started to explore the connections among these outraged e-mailers, I found that many if not all of them were financially or organizationally tied to Greg. The E. O. Wilson Biodiversity Foundation, for instance, has Greg on its board of directors as its treasurer and receives funding from the Carr Foundation. (Wilson's foundation has also stated in financial papers that the publicity surrounding the E. O. Wilson Biodiversity Laboratory in Gorongosa Park plays a key part in its domestic fund-raising efforts.) Likewise, Greg has commissioned Yu to make films, and the Carr Foundation has helped fund the department at Princeton where Pringle works and is intricately connected with USAID's efforts to show results from its "public-private partnership" initiative in Mozambique.

In other words, it's possible that everyone writing in sincerely believed that the Gorongosa project is unimpeachable and that any book questioning it can be condemned unread. But each of them also had a motivation to fight on Greg's behalf.

I chewed over their voluminous e-mails for a while. I knew that Greg's initial vision for Gorongosa and Mozambique—the country as a peaceful middle-class society, bolstered by a new harmony with nature, with a self-sustaining Gorongosa National Park as inspiration and model— had not, in fact, been realized since my time in the park. On the contrary, the fighting between Renamo and Frelimo was still unraveling central Mozambique. Politically motivated kidnappings and murders were on the rise. Near Gorongosa itself, villagers had allegedly discovered a mass grave with over a hundred corpses. Tourism numbers were plummeting. In 2016, according to Agence France-Presse, Gorongosa had less than a thousand registered visitors.

I also knew that, although Gorongosa National Park is officially under Mozambican control, the overwhelming bulk of its funding comes from outside of Mozambique, from the Carr Foundation and other donors such as USAID. There have been dozens of glowing recent press reports praising the Gorongosa restoration project that cast Greg as the project's primary instigator and champion. I have not heard of similar outrage levied against the authors of those pieces.

At the same time, I fully believed that Greg, Mateus, and their team of conservationists, scientists, and development officials—both Mozambican and foreign—were working diligently and creatively to try to help the people and wildlife of Gorongosa. That is what I had seen when I spent a year traveling back and forth between Johannesburg and the Gorongosa region, and what I'd always assumed continued. I had read the press releases and independent reports; I knew the park officials were piloting new initiatives, learning from their mistakes, reaching more people, implementing more health programs and educational efforts. I believed, as I always have, that they have saved lives. For this, and for having dedicated themselves to trying to help, they have always had my deep respect.

But none of this changed my ultimate point, the story of many stories. It didn't abolish the disconnect between the way locals experience their life and the way donors experience their giving. It didn't do away with the different dramas being acted out simultaneously on the same soil, sharing the same stage but with different protagonists and plot lines. That clash of narratives has been going on for centuries. Whatever progress had been made in Gorongosa in the past few years wasn't going to overturn it.

Still, I wrote back to Greg, Mateus, and everyone else on the e-mail chain, which was now approaching book length in itself. I offered to talk with anyone who thought I had missed something. I requested any information that could help tell the story of Gorongosa's great success. Most of Greg's associates ignored me and just continued dispatching their messages to my publisher. One offered a conversation and talked to me on the phone. Greg and Mateus, for their part, sent me a slew of statistics.

There were ninety-three schools in the park's buffer zone, Greg wrote. In the first nine months of 2016, park-supported mobile health brigades had provided malaria treatment for about a thousand children, distributed twenty-three hundred bed nets and nearly eight thousand condoms, and offered a range of other services, such as vaccines, deworming, prenatal consultations, and traditional birth attendants. They had started a slew of new initiatives—coffee growing on the mountain, beekeeping instruction through the new science lab, an advanced ecology program for Mozambican college students across the country. The park had five hundred permanent employees, most of whom came from neighboring communities, plus up to a hundred seasonal workers. And it was giving 20 percent of its revenues directly to communities within the park and the buffer zone.

All of these statistics sounded positive. But, again, none of them changed the overall argument of the book. And, what's more, many of the numbers were not exactly what they seem.

Take the project's school-building efforts, for instance. "I believe you were here when we were building our first school in Vinho?" Greg wrote to me. "There are 93 schools in our buffer zone. We have continued building schools and we are finishing another this month." When

I looked for details, though, it turned out that of those ninety-three schools the park itself had built only four. Elsewhere, it has provided structural improvements to existing buildings, as well as bathrooms, which are widely considered important for keeping girls in school. Laudable, of course, but not quite what the initial statement artfully suggests by slipping that "93 schools" statistic into a discussion of the park's own construction work.

Likewise, passing out condoms is fine, but there is always doubt about what happens once they're distributed. (A 2009 report from the Mozambican health ministry, for instance, found that 68 percent of men living in rural districts across the country knew a source of condoms, but less than 7 percent of rural men who'd had sex within the past twelve months had actually used one.) The same goes for the park handing out bed nets. While they are clearly helping address the serious health problem of malaria, it's unknown how many of them are actually being used for their intended purpose—and how many have been, say, repurposed as fishing nets, as often happens in Africa.

Some of the other numbers I was given raise their own questions. Greg wrote to me, for instance, that "we are the only rural area in Mozambique to have had zero maternal deaths at childbirth last year." This would be an impressive accomplishment—but in a region where childbirth often happens at home, not in hospitals or health clinics, it is also a very difficult statistic to confirm. When I pressed Mateus on this, asking how they knew that the claim was true, he only reiterated that within the "neighborhoods" the park health programs served there had been no maternal deaths. He did not offer further details.

Overall, many of the claims offered as proof of the success of the Gorongosa initiative are about inputs, not outcomes. There are more students coming to the park for environmental education, more employees hired, more agricultural programs started. But results-based evaluations are few and far between. There are almost no full-scale, independent recent reviews of the park that actually survey its residents to figure out how these efforts are perceived. The reports that do exist tend to be forward looking, adopting the present continuous—not "we have helped," but "we are helping"—so common in development lingo.

Even the park's health program, a joint project with USAID and Mount Sinai Hospital in New York, which on paper is one of the more successful efforts, is described by its officials in terms of its goals rather than accomplishments. "Children who reside in the buffer zone around Gorongosa National Park are faced with severe health problems, including HIV/AIDS, malaria, and pneumonia," said Sigrid Hahn, associate director of Mount Sinai's Global Health Center, at a 2016 United Nations event. "Malnutrition is widespread, and is the underlying cause for up to half of childhood deaths in the area. Our team has worked with the community to identify their major health and environmental concerns, and we look forward to continuing to partner with community members to facilitate their involvement in solutions to these issues."

One gets a similar impression from a 2016 USAID-funded analysis of "sustainable income-generating opportunities" in conservation areas in Mozambique. "Some key, longer-term opportunities for livelihoods may likely be linked to the struggling tourism industry" around Gorongosa, the report says. "If the sector manages to grow, investment in the region could benefit the buffer zone populations as well." However, as the report notes, there are many obstacles in the way of that vision, ranging from the security situation (which it terms "a potentially insurmountable barrier") to poor roads and lack of education. And "additional income may not deter poaching at all," the report adds, in part because "none of the proposed livelihoods could ever financially match the high payoff of poaching."

Notably, this evaluation comes from a source quite friendly to the Gorongosa project overall. The head of the USAID mission in Mozambique was one of my first critics on e-mail. But even for organizations that firmly back him, Greg's win-win scenario—in which Gorongosa's beauty brings in tourists, and the tourism income encourages locals to preserve the park's beauty—is to this day largely just a distant dream.

All this, again, is in keeping with the usual tone that I've seen over the years in the Western coverage of Gorongosa. The emphasis is perpetually on hopeful promises, on the notion that, if things seem to be going badly right now, one should just look to the bright potential future. "We have been asked to play a special role after the peace agreement is signed," Greg wrote to me in late 2016, as fighting between Frelimo and Renamo continued with no clear end in sight. "We'll create more farms, health clinics and schools, especially in the areas most affected by the conflict." It is a lovely vision. But one should also acknowledge that it is the same vision—prosperity is just around the corner—that the park restoration project has been pitching to the Gorongosans, and Western donors, for almost a decade.

After about a month of e-mails from Greg and his supporters, Greg finally gave a direct answer to my question about what he believed to be the project's greatest accomplishment in Gorongosa. It was, he wrote, something that was going to happen in a few months, or maybe a bit later. The president of Mozambique, Filipe Nyusi, was going to declare Gorongosa a "peace park." The peace park label is usually applied to protected areas that straddle national borders; Nelson Mandela lauded them as vehicles for ending division and hostility. In the case of Gorongosa, Greg explained, the park could become a key player in resolving Mozambique's growing internal conflict, a place that both sides could trust and that one day could play an instrumental role in healing the country.

It is a savvy piece of storytelling. (The e-mails from Greg and Mateus made a point of mentioning Mandela repeatedly, even though the former president of South Africa in fact had nothing to do with the Gorongosa project.) But this vision of Gorongosa as an emblem of peace is also another future-focused hope, a dream and a mission impossible to evaluate in the present day.

I care deeply about the Gorongosa National Park and the people living in and around it. That's why I wrote this book. The glossy, adulatory coverage that the project has largely received, from E. O. Wilson's beautiful coffee-table volume to the National Geographic film, may be great for promoting the park and securing donor money. But it doesn't tell us what is truly happening there, or in other places around the developing world. It doesn't help us understand why our best intentions and diligent efforts fall short of creating the ecologically sound, peaceful, prosperous places we long to see.

We live in a time of shouting. And so, although I was taken aback at first by the reaction to this book from people who had not read it, I soon recognized that it was just a microcosm of what is happening in our larger society. We deny the right of other stories to exist. We find them threatening and offensive. We want to build a powerful alliance to destroy or at least discredit them. But this doesn't move us toward any solutions. For real change, we need to grapple with others' viewpoints, however uncomfortable they may be.

SOURCES AND SUGGESTIONS FOR FURTHER READING

White Man's Game is based on a combination of my own firsthand observations, interviews with more than a hundred people, and thousands of pages of documents—including reports by academics, nongovernmental organizations, and bilateral donors, as well as books written by historians and by other journalists. Most of the stories set in southern Africa stem from my own on-the-ground reporting between 2005 and 2009; I have indicated within the text when I rely on secondary sources. All words in quotation marks were either recorded directly by me at the moment of the conversation or are reported verbatim elsewhere. Passages not in quotes were reconstructed from my own recollections or recounted by other people.

There is a wealth of material for readers interested in any of the many stories I touch upon in *White Man's Game*. Although by no means an exhaustive list, here are some sources for those seeking more information.

1: THE TROUBLE WITH PAINTED DOGS

For more information about African wild dogs, check out the somewhat dense but highly informative website of the Wild Dog Advisory Group South Africa at http://wagsa.org.za. That site has a full bibliography of literature about *Lycaon pictus* and about managed metapopulations in general.

For a nuanced history of the Madikwe Reserve, try the article "Partnerships in Conservation: The State, Private Sector and the Community at Madikwe Game Reserve, North-West Province, South Africa" by scholars Hector Magome, David Grossman, Saliem Fakir, and Yolande Stowell, available at http://pubs.iied.org/pdfs/7802IIED.pdf. That piece is part of a larger project, the International Institute for Environment and Development's "Evaluating Eden" series (http://pubs.iied.org/search/?s=EDEN), which also features a number of other articles that touch upon the themes of this book.

2: SWIMMING WITH SHARKS

A quick online search will reveal a slew of shark cage diving operators offering their services in South Africa. It will also turn up many articles about the long-standing debate over the ethics of shark cage diving. For a full exploration of the animal itself, try Michael Scholl's book *South Africa's Great White Shark* (Cape Town: Struik Publishers, 2006), cowritten with Thomas Peschak.

The early explorers all produced their own writings, which are still worth reading today. Many are available in the public domain. Although it is more than half a century old, I found Margery Perham and J. Simmons's *African Discovery: An Anthology of Exploration* (London: Faber and Faber, 1942) a useful compilation of writings by James Bruce, Mungo Park, and others.

There is a substantial body of history and analysis focusing on all of these seventeenth-, eighteenth-, and nineteenth-century explorers, particularly David Livingstone and Henry Morton Stanley. For a modern history and analysis, Jonathan S. Adams and Thomas O. McShane's *The Myth of Wild Africa: Conservation Without Illusion* (New York: W. W. Norton, 1992) is wonderfully insightful. Teddy Roosevelt's *African Game Trails: An Account of the Wanderings of an American Hunter-Naturalist* (New York: C. Scribner's Sons, 1910) reveals much about the mind-set of the conservationist-hunters of the early twentieth century. So does Roosevelt's speech to the National Geographic Society upon his return, printed in the January 1911 issue of the *National Geographic* magazine under the title "Wild Man and Wild Beast in Africa" (https://books.google.com/books?id=nRoRAQAAIAAJ&pg=PA1).

3: SNAPPING FOR AFRICA

Readers interested in delving further into the puzzle of international aid will find many volumes written about international development and the global aid industry, with a substantial percentage of those works focused specifically on how aid has helped or hindered Africa. Some important reads in this category include, for a positive spin, *The End of Poverty: Economic Possibilities for Our Time* by Jeffrey Sachs (New York: Penguin Press, 2005), and, for a more critical approach, *The White Man's Burden: Why the West's Efforts to Aid the Rest Have Done So Much Ill and So Little Good* by William Easterly (Oxford: Oxford University Press, 2006) and *The Crisis Caravan: What's Wrong with Humanitarian Aid?* by Linda Polman (New York: Metropolitan Books, 2010).

There have been a number of articles about the nuances of the well-known Ethiopian famine of the 1980s. Robert Keating's "Live Aid: The Terrible Truth," published in *Spin* magazine in 1986, is a good primer; it is reprinted, with a 2015 introduction, at http://www.spin.com/featured/live-aid-the-terrible-truth-ethiopia-bob-geldof-feature. For more on the effect of Live Aid on Western perceptions of the developing world, check out the Voluntary Service Overseas report on "The Live Aid Legacy" at http://www.eldis.org/vfile/upload/1/document/0708/doc1830.pdf.

4: THE ECO BARONS

I began my reporting of Li Quan and Stuart Bray's "Save China's Tigers" project while I was a foreign correspondent based in Johannesburg. My 2006 article about them for the *Christian Science Monitor* is available at http://www.csmonitor.com/2006/0823/p15s01-lign.html; subsequent news updates are easily findable online.

Naomi Klein is one of many writers who has criticized Big Green; her 2013 article "Time for Big Green to Go Fossil Free" in the *Nation* (https://www.thenation.com/article/time-big-green-go-fossil-free/) looks at some big conservation groups' reluctance to divest from fossil fuels. Another starter piece, for those interested in the Nature Conservancy's relationship with the oil company BP—particularly in light of the 2010 *Deepwater Horizon* explosion and oil spill in the Gulf of Mexico—is Joe Stephens's *Washington Post* article "Nature Conservancy Faces Potential Backlash from Ties

with BP," published on May 24, 2010 (http://www.washingtonpost.com/wp
-dyn/content/article/2010/05/23/AR2010052302164.html).

For those interested in alternative approaches to the traditional conservation groups, Mike Norton Griffiths's work on economics and conservation
is worth a read. He has a compilation of articles on his website, http://www
.mng5.com.

There are many reports on Jim Blanchard's efforts to turn a swath of
Mozambique into an eco-investment paradise. Rosemary Elizabeth Galli's
book *Peoples' Spaces and State Spaces: Land and Governance in Mozambique* (Lanham, MD: Lexington Books, 2003) details what she found on the
ground in the wake of that project.

5: THE FIVE-ACT PLAY

My account of Greg Carr's involvement with Gorongosa National Park is
based on dozens of interviews I conducted with him and others. My 2007
article for *Smithsonian* magazine, "Greg Carr's Big Gamble" (http://www
.smithsonianmag.com/people-places/greg-carrs-big-gamble-153081070/
?all), was the first substantial piece about the Gorongosa restoration effort in
the U.S. media. Since then, a voluminous body of reportage has been devoted
to the park and Greg's work there. A 2009 article by Philip Gourevitch in the
New Yorker, "The Monkey and the Fish" (http://www.newyorker.com
/magazine/2009/12/21/the-monkey-and-the-fish), delved into the nuances of
the project more than most other pieces written about it.

The Gorongosa National Park's website, http://www.gorongosa.org, has
more information about the programs and philosophy of park administrators
today, as well as links to tourism packages. Ken Tinley's 1977 dissertation
with the University of Pretoria, "Framework of the Gorongosa Ecosystem"
(http://www.gorongosa.org/sites/default/files/research/056-tinley_-
_gorongosa_1977_0.pdf), gives a detailed and comprehensive look at the ecosystem of the park.

6: OF BUFFALO AND POACHERS

There are a number of scholarly articles about the epidemiology of tuberculosis in African buffalo. For starters, try the 2001 article "The Epidemiology

of Tuberculosis in Free-Ranging African Buffalo (*Syncerus caffer*) in the Kruger National Park, South Africa" by V. de Vos, R. G. Bengis, N. P. J. Kriek, A. Michel, D. F. Keet, J. P. Raath, and H. F. K. A. Huchzermeyer in the *Onderstepoort Journal of Veterinary Research* (http://www.repository.up.ac.za /bitstream/handle/2263/18491/18devos2001.pdf). For more information about TB-free buffalo breeding, check out the 2012 article in the journal *Sustainability* entitled "An Overview of Disease-Free Buffalo Breeding Projects with Reference to the Different Systems Used in South Africa" by Liesel Laubscher and Louwrens Hoffman (http://www.mdpi.com/2071-1050/4/11/3124/pdf), as well as Markus Hofmeyr's 2006 presentation on Kruger's disease-free buffalo project to the North American Veterinary Conference, which was reprinted by the International Veterinary Information Service (http://www .ivis.org/proceedings/navc/2006/SAE/654.pdf).

As with international aid to Africa, there is a voluminous body of writing about poaching—often with contradictory messages. The United Nations Office on Drugs and Crimes produces a yearly "World Wildlife Crime Report," which details trafficking in protected species (https://www .unodc.org/unodc/en/data-and-analysis/wildlife.html), and all of the large conservation organizations have sections on their websites dedicated to the topic. For a more academic approach, *Black Poachers, White Hunters: A Social History of Hunting in Colonial Kenya* by Edward Steinhart (Athens: Ohio University Press, 2006) is worth reading.

On the militarization of antipoaching efforts, try "The War on African Poaching: Is Militarization Fated to Fail?" by Adam Welz in the *Yale Environment 360* magazine (http://e360.yale.edu/feature/the_war_on_african _poaching_is_militarization_fated_to_fail/2679/), along with a number of other popular press reports. There is substantial scholarship on this topic as well, including the *Conservation & Society* journal article "Conservation Meets Militarisation in Kruger National Park: Historical Encounters and Complex Legacies" by Elizabeth Lunstrum (http://conservationandsociety .org/article.asp?issn=0972-4923;year=2015;volume=13;issue=4;spage =356;epage=369;aulast=Lunstrum).

The *nhacajambe*, the instrument played by Tomás Jeremias, is also known by a variety of other names in different provinces of Mozambique, including *shizambi*, *shivelan*, and *nhacazeze*. Volume 3 of the Smithsonian Folkways Recordings "Music from Mozambique" series (http://www.folkways.si.edu

/music-from-mozambique-vol-3/world/album/smithsonian) offers several *nhacajambe* tracks and some information about the instrument and features a photo of a *nhacajambe* player on the cover.

7: THE DISORDER *and*

8: BEWARE THE MOUNTAIN

For alternative perspectives on the Gorongosa region and its history, it is well worth reading Carolien Jacobs's 2010 article "Navigating Through a Landscape of Powers or Getting Lost on Mount Gorongosa" in the *Journal of Legal Pluralism* (http://commission-on-legal-pluralism.com/volumes/61/jacobs-art .pdf), as well as Christy Schuetze's 2010 PhD thesis " 'The World Is Upside Down': Women's Participation in Religious Movements in Mozambique" (http://repository.upenn.edu/edissertations/101/). Victor Igreja has written extensively about the role of spirits in Mozambique, including his 2008 article in the *Journal of the Royal Anthropological Institute*, "*Gamba* Spirits, Gender Relations, and Healing in Post–Civil War Gorongosa, Mozambique," cowritten with Béatrice Dias-Lambranca and Annemiek Richters (http://www .gorongosa.org/sites/default/files/research/062-igreja.pdf).

For more on Mozambican history, try Malyn Newitt's *A History of Mozambique* (Bloomington: Indiana University Press, 1995) as well as the many works of Allen and Barbara Isaacman. William Finnegan's *A Complicated War: The Harrowing of Mozambique* (Berkeley: University of California Press, 1992) gives a chilling overview of the conflict of the 1970s and '80s.

9: ELEPHANT ON THE RUN

The debate about culling still rages in South Africa, even as the continent as a whole faces a dramatic increase in elephant poaching. For an overview, read the 2009 article by Paul Dickson and William M. Adams, "Science and Uncertainty in South Africa's Elephant Culling Debate," in the journal *Environment and Planning C: Government and Policy* (http://journals.sagepub .com/doi/pdf/10.1068/c0792j). Meanwhile, some news reports suggest that Audrey Delsink's contraceptive approach may be gaining in popularity. Delsink, for her part, is now the executive director of the Humane Society International, Africa.

Carlos Lopes Pereira left the Gorongosa National Park in 2012 and is now the head of law enforcement and antipoaching for Mozambique's national administration of conservation areas. He has been instrumental in pushing for new laws in Mozambique that dramatically increase the penalty for poaching. In 2014, the country passed a law that criminalized wildlife poaching and gave judges the authority to impose prison sentences for the offense; previously, poaching had been categorized as a simple transgression that carried only a fine. Information on the new law is available at http://www.fao.org/faolex/results /details/en/?details=LEX-FAOC134834, and an English translation of the legislation is at http://www.speed-program.com/wp-content/uploads/2014/06/Lei -de-Conserva%C3%A7%C3%A3o-16-2014-English-Free-Translation.pdf.

10: THE DISCONNECT

For more information on the concept of rewilding, read Caroline Fraser's book *Rewilding the World: Dispatches from the Conservation Revolution* (New York: Metropolitan Books, 2009).

For more on the economic disconnect within Mozambique, journalist and social scientist Joseph Hanlon's many books and papers are invaluable. Alfandega Manjoro's 2013 dissertation, "Alleviating Poverty through Local Resources and Local Initiatives: A Case Study of Gorongosa Communities in Mozambique" (http://repositorio.ucm.ac.mz/bitstream/123456789/61/1 /tese-de-doutoramento-AM.pdf), examines why poverty and food insecurity persisted in Gorongosa despite Mozambique's strong economic growth.

As this book was going to press, Gorongosa National Park officials announced that they were indeed going to attempt to expand the park's boundaries by absorbing one of the adjacent *coutadas*. They had signed an agreement with the managers of Coutada 12—Portugal's Entreposto Group, the successor to the Mozambique Company—to survey the area and analyze its tourism potential. The final decision on incorporating the game reserve into the park was projected to be a year away. A December 2016 article by the Mozambique News Agency about the announcement is available at http://allafrica.com/stories/201612040236.html.

11: NATIONAL GEOGRAPHIC

For a comprehensive academic exploration of the impact of the National Geographic Society, see *Reading National Geographic* by Catherine A. Lutz and Jane L. Collins (Chicago: University of Chicago Press, 1993). For other perspectives on the conservation movement, I found invaluable both Mark Dowie's *Conservation Refugees: The Hundred-Year Conflict Between Global Conservation and Native Peoples* (Cambridge, MA: MIT Press, 2009) and Roderick Frazier Nash's classic *Wilderness and the American Mind* (New Haven: Yale University Press, 1967).

The April–June 2015 issue of the *Conservation & Society* journal features several articles dedicated to Gorongosa National Park and the different ways academics see the restoration project there. It is available online at http://www .conservationandsociety.org/showBackIssue.asp?issn=0972-4923;year =2015;volume=13;issue=2;month=April-June.

The online discussion among scholars following the premiere of *Africa's Lost Eden* took place on H-Luso-Africa, a public mailing list of the Lusophone African Studies Organization. The archive of that discussion—including messages from Christy Schuetze and Heidi Gengenbach describing what they saw during their own field research in and around Gorongosa, and Greg Carr's response—is available at http://www.h-net.org/logsearch/?phrase =Gorongosa&type=phrase&smonth=02&syear=2010&emonth=02&eyear =2010&order=DPB.

12: THE BIOBLITZ

Many groups now organize bioblitz activities, including National Geographic, the U.S. National Park Service, and a number of universities and nature centers. All have details on their websites.

E. O. Wilson's work is fascinating; he won the Pulitzer Prize for *On Human Nature* (Cambridge, MA: Harvard University Press, 1978) and again for *The Ants*, cowritten with Bert Hölldobler (Cambridge, MA: Belknap Press, 1990). My description of his Gorongosa bioblitz draws on his June 2013 article for *National Geographic*, "The Rebirth of Gorongosa" (http://ngm .nationalgeographic.com/2013/06/gorongosa-park/wilson-text), and on his subsequent book, *A Window on Eternity: A Biologist's Walk Through Gorongosa National Park* (New York: Simon and Schuster, 2014).

Emma Marris's *Rambunctious Garden: Saving Nature in a Post-Wild World* (New York: Bloomsbury, 2011) is a wonderful exploration of our concept of nature and who defines it.

The war news from central Mozambique changes by the day. Although U.S.

reporting on the conflict is thin, Al Jazeera has covered the clashes in the Gorongosa region and has many updates on its website, as does the BBC.

13: A MULTITUDE OF VOICES

As of early 2017, Brian Jones still runs the Moholoholo Wildlife Rehabilitation Centre. For more information on his work go to http://www.moholoholo.co.za.

The external review of the Gorongosa National Park restoration project that USAID commissioned in 2013 is included in the report "Performance Evaluation of Three Biodiversity and Ecotourism Activities in Mozambique," available at http://pdf.usaid.gov/pdf_docs/pa00jkm6.pdf.

AFTERWORD

The Agence France-Presse article describing the continuing difficulties in Gorongosa was published on August 26, 2016, under the title "Conflict and Drought Threaten Mozambique's Gorongosa Park" (https://phys.org/news/2016-08-conflict-drought-threaten-mozambique-gorongosa.html).

The "Conservation Alternative Livelihood Analysis" report on "Sustainable Income-Generating Opportunities in Mozambique's Lubombo Conservancy Area and Gorongosa Park," produced for USAID in 2016 by economic development organization ACDI/VOCA, is available at http://www.acdivoca.org/2016/04/leo-report-no-26-conservation-alternative-livelihood-analysis-cala/.

ACKNOWLEDGMENTS

My work on *White Man's Game* spanned more than a decade and multiple phases of my life. There were many, many people during that time whose support, conversation, and questioning were invaluable to me and to this project. It is impossible to thank everyone, but to those who have deepened and challenged my reporting, writing, and understanding of these beautiful stories: thank you.

I would like to give special acknowledgment in these pages to the team at Metropolitan Books, and particularly to my extraordinary editor, Grigory Tovbis. I am beyond thankful for his diligence, patience, and confidence; for his sharpness with words and ideas; and for his kindness when he knew I could do better. This is his book, too. I am also immensely grateful to my agent, David Patterson, an early believer and steadfast supporter, without whom this book would not exist.

I would have never traveled to central Mozambique—and may not have been a journalist at all—if it were not for Jon Sawyer. From my first newspaper internship to my work with the Pulitzer Center on Crisis Reporting, he has offered years of professional guidance and friendship. I am endlessly indebted to him and to many others at the Pulitzer Center, including Nathalie Applewhite, Kem Sawyer, Ann Peters, and particularly video journalist Steve

Sapienza, who agreed to help me report in Gorongosa and listened patiently over the years as I obsessed over these stories.

I will forever be thankful to Margaret Engel and others at the Alicia Patterson Foundation, who gave me the financial resources to spend a year reporting on the stories in and around the Gorongosa National Park. Thank you also to Clara Germani, one of the most skilled editors in journalism, for her guidance during my time as a foreign correspondent and afterward, and to the many fine journalists and mentors at the *Christian Science Monitor*, including (but certainly not limited to) Marshall Ingwerson, Scott Armstrong, and Melanie Stetson Freeman. Thank you for your confidence, support, and patience when I said yet again I couldn't take a story because I was working on "the book."

I relied on the expertise, patience, and trust of dozens upon dozens of individuals to write this book. Numerous scholars of southeast African culture and history laid the groundwork for my understanding of what I saw in the Gorongosa region of Mozambique, and elsewhere. I am humbled by and more grateful than I can say to the many residents of the Gorongosa who welcomed me into their homes and shared their stories. And I will be forever thankful to the staff and administrators of the Gorongosa National Park for their patience, openness, and trust.

Over the years, many of my sources became friends. To them, thank you for your time and conversations, your help and your humor, and for coming to my rescue in the face of everything from flat tires to reporting crises to malaria. I recognize that many of you will not like what I have written in this book, and I wish that I could have told a more upbeat tale. But in this age of "gotcha" journalism and confrontation for its own sake, I hope that I have honored your stories by attempting to write mine with the most thoughtfulness, care, and kindness possible.

There are so many friends and colleagues who have offered keen advice at various points along this journey. To the brilliant photographer Jeff Barbee, thank you for traveling around Africa with me, for caring so much about environmental reporting, and for agreeing to keep returning with me to Chitengo Camp. Thank you to Tony Barbieri, Jaimie Baron, Julie Bykowicz, Ruthellen Josselson, Annie Linskey, Abe McLaughin, Jen McLaughlin, Jina Moore, Robert Ruby, Craig Timberg, Ruey Timberg, Karen Tompros, Mark Travis, and many, many others, for sharing during this long project your wisdom about reporting, writing, stories, and truth.

I wrote many pages in the homes of Nancy and David Sadick and of Bob and Lois Sebastian, all of whom handed down to me a deep appreciation of stories. Bob Sebastian, who crossed over during my work on this book, taught me to honor the wisdom of farmers everywhere. Thank you. Jeffrey and Rose Hanes, Barbara Sadick and Ken Goldman, and Modena and Gary Wilson have been hearing about these stories for years and have offered the sort of support, advice, and encouragement that I can only hope to show my own children someday. Thank you also, Gary, for sharing your own story-telling expertise, and for agreeing that debates about voice, pacing, and per-spective should last until the early hours of the morning.

Thank you, Nick Wilson and Julie Huang, for offering so graciously both intellectual and logistical support during my reporting, and for inspir-ing me with the depth of thought that helps reveal stories so often hidden from view.

Thank you, Ania Sobeiszek, for gracing us with the sort of care that allowed me to write this book.

I have read many author acknowledgments where the writer thanks her family profusely while also apologizing for the stress and complete upheaval that her book writing has caused. I never quite understood those senti-ments until now. At the risk of sounding cliché, to my dear, beloved little family: thank you, thank you, and I'm sorry. To Madeline and Lydia, who put up with their mama's writing schedule and closed office door: Thank you for your joy and interruptions, your sticky fingers on my notebooks and your crayon drawings taped next to my computer, your hugs and kisses, and for the new, clear-sighted perspective you have given me on the world. I love you more than you can know, and I apologize for not taking your advice and making this a picture book.

To Christopher: Without you this book would not have been possible, for too many reasons to list here. There are no words that can hold my gratitude. I can only promise you that one day, really, we will have a vacation uninter-rupted by my writing. And that maybe the next book will be easier. I love you.

INDEX

ABOUT THE AUTHOR

STEPHANIE HANES is a regular correspondent for *The Christian Science Monitor*. Her work has appeared in *The Washington Post*, *The Boston Globe*, the *San Francisco Chronicle*, *The Baltimore Sun*, *Smithsonian*, and *USA Today*, among other publications, as well as on *PBS NewsHour*. *White Man's Game* is her first book. She lives in Massachusetts.